*Family Ties*

# Family Ties

Enduring Relations
between Parents and
Their Grown Children

*John R. Logan*
*Glenna D. Spitze*

TEMPLE UNIVERSITY PRESS · PHILADELPHIA

Temple University Press, Philadelphia 19122
Copyright © 1996 by Temple University
All rights reserved
Published 1996
Printed in the United States of America

⊚ The paper used in this publication meets the requirements of the American National Standard for
Information Sciences—Permanence of Paper for Printed Library Materials, ANSI Z39.48-1984

Text design by Gary Gore

Library of Congress Cataloging-in-Publication Data

Logan, John R., 1946–
    Family ties : enduring relations between parents and their grown
children / John R. Logan, Glenna D. Spitze.
       p.    cm.
    Includes bibliographical references and index.
    ISBN 1-56639-471-6 (cloth : alk. paper)
    1. Parent and adult child.   2. Intergenerational relations.
I. Spitze, Glenna D.  II. Title.
HQ755.86.L64   1996
306.874—dc20
                                                  96-13008

*To our parents and children*

# Contents

# Tables and Figures

# Acknowledgments

We have been working together on this project for over ten years and can hardly believe it is finally over. As coauthors of the book, our names are listed alphabetically. We have learned much from each other and gratefully acknowledge each other's contributions. This project was initiated through our involvement with Sheldon Tobin, of the School of Social Welfare at the University at Albany. Shelly was developing a program project grant proposal, and he recruited us to work on that proposal along with several other faculty. We became fascinated by the questions it raised for us in relation to our respective interests in urban sociology and in gender and families. Though that grant never came through, it was the catalyst for our collaboration, and we thank Shelly for making it happen.

We are deeply indebted to the National Institute on Aging for support of this project through Grants AG06831–01 and AG08644–01, and to our program officer Katrina Johnston, whose enthusiastic support we continue to enjoy. This book is based on a major revision of material (and reanalysis of all data) from a number of previously published journal articles. We wish to acknowledge the publishers of these journals and our coauthors for the following articles:

Glenna Spitze and John Logan. 1990. "Sons, Daughters, and Intergenerational Social Support." *Journal of Marriage and the Family* 52 (May): 420–30.

Glenna Spitze and John Logan. 1990. "More Evidence on Women (and Men) in the Middle." *Research on Aging* 12 (June): 182–98.

Glenna Spitze and John Logan. 1991. "Employment and Filial Relations: Is There a Conflict?" *Sociological Forum* 6 (December): 681–98.

Glenna Spitze and John Logan. 1991. "Sibling Structure and Intergenerational Relations." *Journal of Marriage and the Family* 53 (November): 871–84.

Russell Ward, John Logan, and Glenna Spitze. 1992. "The Influence of Parent and Child Needs on Coresidence in Middle and Later Life." *Journal of Marriage and the Family* 54( February): 209–21.

Glenna Spitze and John Logan. 1992. "Helping as a Component of

Parent-Adult Child Relations." *Research on Aging* 14 (September): 291–312.

John Logan, Russell Ward, and Glenna Spitze. 1992. "As Old as You Feel: Age Identity in Middle and Later Life." *Social Forces* 71: 451–67.

John Logan and Glenna Spitze. 1994. "Informal Support and the Use of Formal Services by Older Americans." *The Journals of Gerontology: Social Sciences* 49 (January): S25–S34.

Glenna Spitze, John Logan, Genevieve Joseph, and Eunju Lee. 1994. "Middle-Generation Roles and the Well-Being of Men and Women." *The Journals of Gerontology: Social Sciences* 49 (May): S107–16.

Glenna Spitze, John Logan, Glenn Deane, and Suzanne Zerger. 1994. "Adult Children's Divorce and Intergenerational Relationships." *Journal of Marriage and the Family* 56 (May): 279–93.

John Logan and Glenna Spitze. 1994. "Family Neighbors." *American Journal of Sociology* 100 (September): 453–76.

John Logan and Glenna Spitze. 1995. "Self-Interest and Altruism in Intergenerational Relations." *Demography* 32 (August): 353–64.

Because Russ Ward was centrally involved in two of the four articles that were substantially revised to form chapters 1 and 2, we acknowledge his contribution through a coauthorship of those chapters. Russ gave us helpful comments on other chapters as well as most of the articles we have published from this project. Russ is the ideal colleague in every way, and we have enjoyed working with him on this and other projects for many years.

We wish to thank several current and former students who worked on this project at different points from the proposal stage to final data analyses: Ted Houghton, Genevieve Joseph, Eunju Lee, Sonia Miner, Chris Nemeth, Gaye Reinhold, Beth Roberts, Joyce Robinson, Gene Shackman, and Suzanne Zerger. We also thank Lynn Horowitz, administrative assistant during the initial years of the project, for her help with many aspects of research and administration, and Kathy Vaccariello for administrative help in the later years. We enjoyed working with Hank Steadman and Nan Brady of Policy Research Associates, who organized and supervised the Albany survey, and Claudia Hartmark, who did an early round of pretest interviewing. Seymour Sudman provided helpful advice on survey sampling. The University at Albany and particularly our colleagues in the Department of Sociology provided a warm and collegial environment for our research.

Several people made helpful comments on parts or all of the manuscript and the original articles from which we worked, and we are grateful for their help: Richard Alba, Donald Hernandez, Joan Huber, Susan Sherman, Scott South, Katherine Trent, and anonymous journal and book manuscript reviewers. We are thankful for the support of our spouses during the course of this project. In the spirit of our topic, we dedicate this book to our parents and children.

# Preface
## Aging Parents, Changing Families

*Commentaries on the future of the family are nearly uniform in their concern*
*over the effects of long-term demographic trends: diminished family size,*
*changing women's roles, rising incidence of divorce, survival of more parents*
*to old age. We reject forecasts of the decline of supportive relationships between*
*the generations based on these trends.*

■ The election of Bill Clinton to the presidency in 1992 was a symbol of generational change, capping a series of changes in American life associated with that bulge in the population that we have called baby boomers. Clinton, born in 1946, is in the first wave of this generation, whose needs and aspirations and crises have indelibly marked public life from the beginning. This is the Dr. Spock generation, youngsters of the 1950s whose parents were introduced to new ideas about child rearing. It is the generation of Vietnam War veterans and peace marchers, witnesses of the civil rights movement and uprisings in cities and on campuses in the 1960s, people who started families in the 1970s and have since coped with unprecedented levels of women's employment, divorce, and single parenthood.

The boomers are now the middle generation, experiencing simultaneously the aging of parents and the maturation of children. We are of this very generation, and the family issues discussed in this book are close to our own experiences. Now well into our forties, between the two of our families, we have children ranging from high-school age to college graduates who are busy establishing independent lives. We have experienced divorce, remarriage, and stepfamily relations in both our own generation and our parents' generation. Our parents are living, retired, and they range in age up to eighty years old. They are in varying states of health, but all still live in their own homes.

As our generation has grown up, it has brought new issues into public discussion, particularly about families. The family is suspect: generations live further apart; divorce is common and some people never marry at all; adults have fewer children or none. Its traditional pillars, mothers and daughters, have taken on new roles. Today we hear espe-

xix

cially about "women in the middle"—people who have to juggle being a mother, a daughter, a wife, and a worker—and we wonder whether they can manage after all. And who will take care of today's elderly if their children are already overextended?

## Crisis of the Modern Nuclear Family?

These trends and issues are at the heart of commentaries about the demise of what scholars call the modern nuclear family. Divorce and single parenthood, declining rates of marriage and fertility, women's employment and the two-earner family, the pressures on gender roles that had once seemed well entrenched—all these forces have been interpreted as threats to the integrity of the family and its ability to nurture family members through their life course.

A well-known pessimistic appraisal was offered by Christopher Lasch in his assessment of the family in *Haven in a Heartless World*. "The divorce rate continues to climb, generational conflict intensifies, and enlightened opinion condemns the family as a repressive anachronism. Do these developments signify merely the 'strain' of the family's 'adaptation' to changing social conditions, or do they portend a weakening of the social fabric, a drastic disorganization of all our institutions? Does the family still provide a haven in a heartless world? Or do the very storms out of which the need for such a haven arises threaten to engulf the family as well?" (1977, p. xiii).

Another recent statement of profound concern was made by David Popenoe in the 1993 *Journal of Marriage and the Family* (see also Popenoe 1988). Using a somewhat unusual definition (a family must include at least one "dependent" member), he argues that the family is "declining," citing a decrease in the cultural value of familism, the decreased centrality in and control over people's lives of families, and the decline of families as a "demographic reality." Demographic evidence includes changes in fertility, family structure, divorce, women's employment, and time spent in nonfamily living. He believes that "the family has been declining since the beginning of recorded history . . . but that recent family decline is unlike historical family change" (p. 527).

Popenoe's caveats notwithstanding, historical perspective offers grounds for caution about depictions of the family in crisis. As Janet Hunt and Larry Hunt (1987) point out, the demise of the family has been "a recurrent theme in Western culture." Generally such discussions are based on implicit or explicit notions of a rosier past, termed by Stephanie Coontz (1992) as "the way we never were." For example: Bernard Farber (1987, p. 433) notes, "The family is no longer, as it was in previous generations, a haven, a private domain, protected from intrusion by political and economic conflicts of civil society." Coontz argues that "the actual complexity of our history . . . gets buried under the weight of an idealized image" (1992, p. 1). And Linda Gordon (1988, p. 3) suggests that "these fears have tended to escalate in periods of social stress."

While such worries may in the past have been expressed mainly by conservative commentators who wanted to go back in time, the majority of family researchers asked to comment on the state of the family recently in a *Journal of Family Issues* special issue expressed more "concern" than "sanguinity" (Glenn 1987). This may be because things have actually gotten worse, and it may be because family researchers have decided it is possible to express concern about the well-being of children without calling for a return to a past that many feel was far from rosy. For example, Norval Glenn (1993) suggests that we try to find ways to make marriages more stable without eroding women's gains, and others express concern about children's well-being, in some cases without suggesting that their mothers leave their jobs or that their unhappily married parents stay together for the sake of the children.

### Crisis of the Older Family?

The special issue of the family journal mentioned above was interesting not only because so many people expressed "concern" rather than optimism, but also because so many focused on younger families and the well-being of children. Of seventeen articles, only three mentioned older family members or extended family ties. Gary Lee (1987) wonders about the consequences of intergenerational family support for morale of the elderly, John Edwards (1987) speaks very generally about the larger family context, and Robert Weiss (1987, p. 467) harks to a less selfish past: "The middle-aged have always been responsible for the old, but increasingly this is seen as a burden." Thus, "the family" most often evokes images of early periods in the life course.

Some family sociologists have recently paid more attention to the family in midlife. Larry Bumpass (1990) portrays adult intergenerational relationships as a major source of social support, but also expresses concern that the increased employment of daughters and high level of marital instability will undermine these linkages. Recent gerontological and popular literature has expressed some parallel concerns about the consequences of demographic trends on the future welfare of the elderly. When Alice Day (1985) asked in her article titled "Who Cares? Demographic Trends Challenge Family Care for the Elderly," the trends in question were increasing women's employment, declining and postponed fertility, and increasing life expectancy (see also Treas 1977). Others have focused on how divorces among the younger generation will affect their ability to care for the older, and how divorce among the older generation, whether recent or in the distant past, will affect their later life contact with adult children (e.g., Smyer and Hofland 1982). More recently, Dwyer and Coward (1992) introduced their edited book on gender and family care by raising the question of how four demographic trends will affect future elder care: declining family size, increased female labor force participation, divorce rates, and longer life expectancies.

Along with the concern for the future care of the elderly, a concern has been expressed about the well-being of the middle generation of women. These concerns are diverse: one is that women will be squeezed by many demands at once, including employment, child care, caring for husbands, and caring for elderly parents (Brody 1981). Another is that divorced women, although freed from the demands of their husbands, will have less time and resources to help older parents because they must work for pay and because their incomes have decreased. There is also a worry that, due to increasing life expectancy, by the time older parents need help their daughters will be facing challenges of aging themselves (Day 1985).

One statistic, seemingly based on demographic data, was particularly alarming: a *New York Times* article on May 14, 1989, quoted a recent Older Women's League publication: "America's mothers are finding more than ever that the empty nest left by grown children is quickly refilled by frail parents or other aging relatives in need of care, according to a private study. . . . On average, women today spend seventeen years of their lives caring for children and eighteen years assisting aged parents." This was reported in the October 1989 issue of *Ms. Magazine* and again in the November 1989 issue of *Ladies Home Journal*. By July 1990 it had made its way onto the cover of *Newsweek:* "The Daughter Track: The Average American Woman Spends 17 Years Raising Children and 18 Years Helping Aging Parents."

We will discuss the effect of these demographic trends throughout this book. Our point here is that there is a remarkable similarity in the kinds of concerns being raised about the well-being of children, middle-aged women, and older parents. In all three cases, people are nervous about how changing rates of women's employment, part of a revolution in gender relations, will affect the well-being of all these groups. People are worried about the dislocations caused by increases in divorce, which has replaced the historical role of widowhood in disrupting families. People are concerned about declining fertility, what it means about how much we want to care for the smaller numbers of children we are still having, and how those children in smaller families will cope when their parents are old. Clearly the big families of past eras evoke a more reassuring image.

This book focuses on the family ties of people after childhood, in the long period of life when "children" have matured and for the most part set up their own independent households. We have little to say in this book about the well-being of children, except where contacts between the older and middle generations involve child care or other contact or help that may benefit the child generation. However, we think it is useful to point out the parallel nature of these concerns. These discussions stem from similar kinds of worries: on the one hand, fears by conservatives that the future will be worse than the past due to unwelcome demographic and social change, and on the other hand, concerns of persons of any political persuasion about the well-being of persons who are not capable of taking care of themselves. And we think it possible that both sets of worries will turn out to have been at least somewhat exaggerated. For several decades researchers looked very hard for negative effects of mothers' employment on children, without any success (see reviews in Spitze 1988; Menaghan and Parcel 1991). More recently, research on divorce's effects on children has produced inconclusive results (e.g. Amato 1993). Our own research on older families, as well as work by others to be discussed as we go along, finds a similar lack of consistent evidence for negative results of demographic change.

## The Effects of Family Change on the Older Family

*Family Ties* is a study of how Americans deal with family in adulthood. We look closely at people who are now middle-aged and older (the respondents in our research were all aged forty and above). We explore their social networks: with whom do they live, what kinds of people are they in touch with, whom do they support, and from whom do they receive help? What is the role of family, and what part is played by contacts outside of the family—by neighbors, for example, or particularly for the elderly, by public programs? We also consider how people interpret and respond to their situations. How do people experience the transition from thinking of themselves as young, to middle-aged, to old? Are there generational conflicts in expectations of support, within the family or in the public arena? For the "middle generation," what are the effects of multiplication of roles?

Our conclusions are decidedly upbeat in the following senses. First, we find that families continue to be at the center of people's lives and that people link their family roles smoothly with other commitments. Second, we find that growing older is not generally associated with loss of autonomy, and that the dependency sometimes attributed to older people should better be understood as interdependence between the generations. Our results do not confirm worries about the continuing viability of families in people's daily lives, and they reject images of aging (from middle age to elderly) as self-centered dependency.

To be more precise, we believe that families have retained their role as the central core of social support through midlife and old age, despite speculation to the contrary. This has been possible for the following reasons, which it is our purpose to establish in this book.

First, although it is true that the frail elderly often rely on their spouse and adult children for help, such dependence makes up only a small part of the aging experience. Most people of retirement age, for most of their senior years, are quite capable of managing daily routines on their own. Therefore it would be misleading to base our image of this generation on the reality of health problems that typically appear near the end of life. The older generation on the whole is autonomous, and in fact provides more assistance to adult children than vice versa.

Second, we find evidence that the bonds between generations are strong, founded on mutual caring rather than on generational self-interest. It was popular in the days of the Gray Panthers to anticipate a time when the older generation would develop a highly politicized age consciousness and mobilize in its own interest, and it is clear that the aging lobby today has become very effective in government. Nevertheless, the value system to which the majority of older Americans subscribe is more indelibly marked by concern for the younger generation. The values of mutual caring are the key to understanding how ties between parents and adult children can remain stronger than most other social ties throughout the life course.

Third, parents do not rely exclusively on daughters for contact and help. Intergenerational bonds are sustained by the activities of both men and women in their roles as mothers and fathers, as daughters and sons. There are to be sure differences in the kinds of activities that men and women carry out, and our research bears only tangentially on the special emotional investment in families that is commonly attributed to women or intensive caregiving near the end of life. But time and again throughout this book we will examine the evidence regarding gender differences in various aspects of relationships between parents and adult children, and repeatedly we will show that differences are small, mixed, or in an unexpected direction. The participation of both men and women in maintaining family ties is another key to their durability.

We also consider several ways in which demographic trends may disrupt or limit intergenerational relations. The literature has focused particularly on negative effects of employment or divorce on adult children's, especially daughters', relations with parents. We find no such effects. And turning to the broader question of how adult children combine their various work and nuclear family roles with dealing with their own parents, we detect no cause for concern. Typical relations with aging parents are well within the range of children's ability to manage them without suffering stress. Even in the extreme cases of caregiving for dependent elderly parents (just as may be true in other forms of caregiving, as to a handicapped spouse, child, or sibling) we believe that the full picture includes both anxiety and fulfillment. In this respect perhaps the research literature has put forward an unrealistic image of caregivers as victims, when the reality is more diverse.

Finally, we will show that family ties remain at the core of other sorts of social relations. Much intergenerational support is based on the neighborhood—indeed, families are at the center of neighboring as a social form—belying theories of the withering away of the traditional community/kinship nexus. And public services for the noninstitutionalized older population, despite their expansion over the last several decades, are used by relatively few seniors, and even then principally only in the absence of intimate family members.

## Contradictions between Theory and Research

We would have been surprised at these conclusions when we began working together in 1985. At that time we viewed the older population in quite a different light, and we were sympathetic to concerns about the breakdown of family ties. Recently we reviewed a research proposal that we submitted to the National Institute on Aging in 1987, at a time when we had already been working for about two years with a national data file on older persons. Its text is a faithful reflection of our expectations at that time. "In recent years," we wrote, "formal support systems have taken over a number of functions traditionally performed by families for dependent members, both children and the elderly." We argued at length for the hypothesis that employment and divorce of women in the adult child generation could further disrupt the performance of those functions:

> Demands for assistance are likely to lead to conficting pressures, as middle-aged women ("women in the middle") are caught between needs of parents with increasing life expectan-

cies and children who remain dependent for increasing amounts of time or become so intermittently during marital disruptions.

These demands become even more acute when we consider patterns of middle-aged women's employment. . . . [But] it is unclear how currently middle-aged adults, particularly women, deal with these conflicting demands: whether they decrease paid work to provide more parental care, increase work and use the money to purchase services for parents and children, or increasingly share time-intensive labor with spouses.

Divorce among the adult child generation could also affect availability of aid. Divorced women might be expected to have less time or money to give, due in part to increased labor force participation.

As researchers with a "show me" attitude about social theory, we recognized that "the literature . . . is mostly speculative, with few empirical studies." We also foresaw potential pitfalls in the base of evidence. "Researchers typically focus on only one side of the support network, formal or informal," we pointed out, "and study only persons who have already reached old age. . . . our study of receipt of assistance will be paralleled by research on assistance giving, calling attention to the reciprocal character of social support." But in fact we expected our research mostly to add a little complexity to the literature without challenging any essential assumptions.

And our assumptions found a receptive audience in the peer review panel. In fact, in the first peer review (like most sociologists, we were not clever enough to gain funding the first time around), we were challenged to fit the research design more closely to what was by then "well known" in the literature. "By design, half of the middle-aged respondents will be men," said the critique of our proposal. "But since it is well known that women provide more support than men, and since one key issue is the increasing strain on employed women, why interview middle-aged men?"

Where had we (and our peers) gone wrong in our thinking? We believe that the main pitfall is in the focus on elderly as dependents. It is a convenience in demographic analyses to label persons over age sixty-five as dependent. Demographers calculate dependency ratios, based on the proportion of the total population under age fifteen or above age sixty-four. Samuel Preston's widely discussed 1984 Population Association of America (PAA) presidential address was entitled "Children and the Elderly: Divergent Paths for America's Dependents." Again, because demographic analysis requires clearcut definitions and age cutoffs, Jane Menken's 1985 PAA address projected the person-years spent by U.S. women with children under age eighteen or living parents above the age of sixty-five and labelled this "years of responsibility to dependents." These calculations (which showed approximately seventeen person-years with children and eighteen with living older parents) are probably the source of the data over-interpreted in the Older Women's League report and widely cited in the popular press. It is hardly necessary to note that, although they may receive Medicare and Social Security benefits, not all parents aged sixty-five and over are the responsibility of their children in any sense of the word.

This ambiguous use of the term "dependent" is associated with a parallel ambiguity in the concept of "caregiving." Several researchers before us over the past twenty years had noted that intergenerational help flows both ways and is given more commonly by parents to adult children for most of the life course (e.g., Troll et al. 1979; Bengtson et al. 1990). Yet most research on helping relations has been conducted on help from adult children to frail elderly parents. Caregiving has been used to mean many different things, from caring for a helpless elderly person twenty-four hours a day to helping with errands once a week, and is often used without any definition at all. This ambiguity reflects and reinforces the emphasis on stress and negative consequences (see discussions in Abel 1990b; Barer and Johnson 1990; Matthews 1988).

This book attempts to contribute, along with other recent work (e.g., Eggebeen and Hogan 1990; Cooney and Uhlenberg 1992; Rossi and Rossi 1990), to a more balanced picture of these relations. It examines relations between parents and their adult children using a survey that we organized in 1988. It is based on a probability sample of 1,200 residents in the metropolitan area surrounding Albany, New York, where both of us live and work. This region possesses many population and economic characteristics of moderate-sized metropolitan areas in the Northeast and North Central United States. These include a declining manufacturing base, relative decline and recent partial rejuvenation of central city neighborhoods, and substantial suburbanization encompassing several industrial satellite towns. Among the area's suburbs are older and recently growing neighborhoods, dormitory suburbs and employment centers, and affluent and poor communities. Outlying areas are largely rural. This region represents a common situation in the United States. But of course no single area can fairly portray the diversity of the country. We caution the reader to be alert to ways in which the Albany region may be unique or in which the particular way that we sampled the population or measured key variables might have biased our findings. To limit mistakes of this type, we also provide a thorough review of the research literature and findings of other studies on the topics that we cover. Where results can be directly compared, our findings are generally consistent with those of other researchers.

One advantage of an original survey is that the investigator can probe more deeply into questions that are not included in general purpose surveys. The Albany survey is unusual, for example, in the identification of family members, including all living parents and children, with key data on each of them and on the respondent's relationship with each one. Further details about the survey and questionnaire are provided in Appendix A. The most important detail, compared to many other studies, is that it includes a random sample of respondents. Too many conclusions have been drawn on the basis of very special populations, such as frail elders or widows or family caregivers, or on the basis of nonrandom samples. A limitation of our sample is its age coverage: respondents were all forty and above in 1988–89. This age group includes only the leading edge of the postwar baby boom cohort. We originally chose this range because of our focus on intergenerational relationships involving the middle and older generations. It includes most people who have adult children and most people whose parents are near or beyond retirement age. On many of the questions that we will deal with, it would be preferable to include people in their twenties and thirties. For example, very few of our respondents have young children. Where possible we will refer to research on this younger generation. But mostly our discussion of behaviors of people under forty (the bulk of the baby boom generation at the time of our survey) will be limited to what was reported about them by their parents.

Our respondents are mostly not frail or dependent on others for help in completing routine activities. Few adult children, either among our respondents or among the children on whom they reported, are "caregivers" in any strict sense of the term. They may have been at some time in the past, or they may be for some period in the future, but they are not today. As a result, the error in our work will be the opposite of that found in most past research: by studying the population as a whole, we may minimize the very real issues faced by some parents and their children in specific situations.

There is a dilemma here. There is no reason in principle why researchers could not describe both the typical character of intergenerational ties and the special problems that arise for some people or at some points of the life cycle. In practice the situation is not so simple. Emphasis on the frail elderly and on the pressures experienced by their children as caregivers is part of a public policy debate in which much needed assistance for some Americans hangs in the balance (Abel 1991). Yet the focus on aging as a policy issue has tended to direct the attention of researchers away from examining normal everyday relations between healthy parents and their adult children (Aldous 1987). It may have distorted what we thought we knew about families, and it may also have negatively affected the public's image both of the elderly and of family ties (Matthews 1988). Our purpose is to correct some common misconceptions that have affected both the academic community and the public at large, with the hope that in the long run this approach will contribute to formulating effective public policy toward families.

*Family Ties*

# 1
# Generational Boundaries
*With Russell A. Ward*

*Social scientists often think of the life cycle in terms of an active and autonomous middle group that supports the dependent young and older generations. We support an alternative view, in which generational labels are fluid and in which the generations are characterized not by age consciousness and self-interest but by intergenerational solidarity.*

■ *Family Ties* is mainly about intergenerational relationships within families. In most of this book, when we speak of generations, we refer to one's place in a kinship lineage, which may extend from being a dependent child to being a grandparent or great-grandparent. The parents that we study range in age from about forty to nearly one hundred; their grown children range from twenty-one (by our definition) to seventy-six! The relationship of parent to adult child thus cuts a wide swath through most people's lives, from a time when they are fairly young to a time when they are rather old.

Still, the "parent generation" is older than the "adult child generation." The relationships that people have within families may intersect in some ways with the broader relationships that exist between generations defined as age cohorts or age groups (see Bengtson and Harootyan 1994, pp. 10–12, for a discussion of these dimensions of generation). In fact, the literature on families in midlife and beyond is often imbued with a particular notion of generations in this latter sense. It is common today to think of the life cycle in terms of a long period of independence—the years of young adulthood, middle age, and the earliest portion of retirement age—bracketed by the dependencies of childhood and old age. The parent generation in many studies is characterized by its needs and demands for assistance, which may conflict in some way with the needs of younger generations. The older generation is often represented as self-conscious of its interests and determined to see that they are met.

In this chapter, therefore, we look into the relationships between gen-

1

erations as younger and older age cohorts. We ask how people perceive their own age and at what point one might distinguish between a supportive middle generation and a dependent older one. We consider particularly whether the generations adopt a self-interested view of public policy questions or family obligations. Again, our emphasis in this chapter is on generations defined by age or by perceptions of age.

## Images of Dependency

The notion of generations in conflict is the image projected in Samuel Preston's presidential address that we cited in the Preface (1984). Preston's address is remembered for his conclusion that the needs of the elderly are being relatively well served, to the detriment of children. Their needs conflict, he argues, and the elderly are better served because they are better able to mobilize support in their own self-interest. But of course this conclusion rests on the premise of dependency (on a family structure that can no longer support either generation, on a state that seems not to be able to support both of them) that both groups evince.

The same conception is at the heart of another widely cited image, that of the woman in the middle made prominent by the writings of Elaine Brody (1981). The woman in the middle is the mother of dependent children who must also care for her aging parents, all the while coping with normal demands (marriage, work) of midlife. She symbolizes the "family" whose ability to shoulder these responsibilities is in question in Preston's analysis. And in Brody's view, also, her capacity to bear up under competing demands is uncertain.

Fundamental demographic trends are said to be at work to disrupt the family network, and we will examine evidence for such conclusions in later chapters. Preston emphasizes the family instability represented by rising rates of out of wedlock births and divorce. He doubts the capacity of single mothers, or of mothers or fathers who raise children after divorce, to support their children. Others question their ability to care for aging parents. Some analysts point out the changing composition of families. Higher life expectancy may mean that older parents are dependent for a longer period. Which generation, parent or adult child, is more dependent on the other? That is the key question addressed in Chapter 2. Delayed childbearing and smaller families are said to mean that there are fewer children to support aging parents (and most crucially, a daughter is less likely to be available for this task). How do family size and composition affect intergenerational contact and assistance (Chapter 3)? Regardless of their marital status, women are now more likely to be regular participants in the labor force, placing another claim on their time and energy. Have divorce and gains in women's employment come at the cost of the older parent generation (Chapter 4)? Does the managing of adult children's responsibilities toward parents, simultaneously with roles of worker, spouse, and parent, exert too great a burden on the middle generation (Chapter 5)? Have family ties receded from the core of people's support networks (Chapter 6)?

Our view is that the common thread among these concerns—a conception of the life cycle with the middle generation literally caught in the middle—is fundamentally wrong. Who, in terms of their age, are the middle and older generations? We will show here that it is not until the age of eighty or above that a majority of people think of themselves as old or elderly, and even then there is no unanimity. To what extent is an older generational identity associated with life changes that could be interpreted as a loss of autonomy and increasing dependency? Our analysis demonstrates that those who feel older are in poorer health and they are less likely to have a spouse with whom to share daily routines. Yet an older generational identity is not associated with retirement from work, and aging is actually experienced as a period of greater sense of well-being and life satisfaction. Finally, to what extent do older people—defined objectively by chronological age or subjectively by age identity—develop a collective sense of self-interest in opposition to younger generations? We will show that, to the contrary, the relationships between generations are marked by apparent altruism and concern with meeting the other generation's needs.

## Age Identification

"You're only as old as you feel." This cultural adage captures an understanding of age as more than simple chronology; rather, age is a construct having social content and personal meaning. Among people of the same chronological age, there is likely to be great variety in the age category in which they place themselves. At age fifty-five, for example, some may consider themselves "young," others as "old," and perhaps the majority as "middle-aged." "To me," said Bernard Baruch, "old age is always fifteen years older than I am."

To study seriously the image of older people as fundamentally dependent on the middle generation, we would have to be able to define a boundary between the two. If everybody followed Bernard Baruch's view, such a boundary would be a moving target. How do Americans in fact perceive the aging process?

Despite its limitation to people in their forties and older, our sample includes a wider array of ages than have most previous studies of age identification (but see Rossi and Rossi 1990, p. 78). These have generally focused only on later life; we will also look at midlife and the transition into middle age. Inclusion of many persons in midlife years is a distinct advantage. It allows a particularly careful look at the transition from middle-aged to old, and includes many people who are likely still to think of themselves as young.

Our analysis focuses on responses to a series of questions about people's age identification. Respondents were asked, "Do you describe yourself as young, middle-aged, old, or what?" The name of the category provided by the respondent was recorded and coded into the following categories: young, middle-aged, old, elderly, aged, young-old, and other. In this study, "old" includes the categories of old, elderly, and aged. Although single-item indicators of age identity have been commonly used, George et al. (1980) have raised some issues about their appropriateness, including social desirability patterns related to negative stereotypes about aging and the rank ordering of categories (e.g., "old" versus "elderly"). Some have used semantic differential scales of adjectives describing "middle-aged" and "old age" (e.g., Burke and Tully 1977), but single-item measures tend to correlate with similar factors, including age and health (George et al. 1980; Mutran and George 1982).

A follow-up question asked, for whatever category the respondent mentioned, "What ages would you include in this category?" Both the lower and upper boundaries were recorded. The respondent was then presented with a preset list of age categories and age boundaries: young (to age 30), early middle age (31–50), later middle age (51–64), and older age (65 and over), and asked, "At what age is a person most respected? Least respected?" and "At what age does a person have the most influence? Least influence?"

## Who Is "Old"?

Although none of our respondents is under forty, a surprising minority describe themselves as "young" (21 percent overall). The modal category is "middle-aged" (61 percent), with most of the remaining persons (15 percent) in the category of "old" or "aged." These designations are most meaningful in relation to people's actual ages, so we begin with a simple cross-tabulation of people's responses to the age identity question by their chronological age. Appendix C, table C.1.1 provides the full tabulation for men and women separately. Because gender differences are negligible, we combine men and women in figure 1.1, which depicts the strong relationship between age and age identification. For

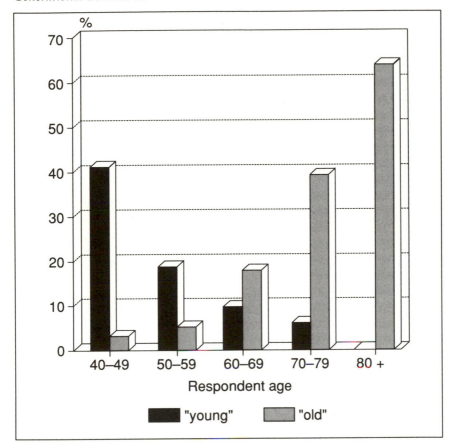

**FIGURE 1.1** Age Identification: Young and Old

simplicity, the figure contrasts the two extremes, those who consider themselves "young" and those who consider themselves "old."

A substantial portion of persons in their forties describe themselves as young (just above 40 percent). This percentage is much lower at age fifty and above, but even in the seventy to seventy-nine age group there are some who identify as young (4 percent of men, and 8 percent of women).

"Middle age" (reported in Appendix C, table C.1.1) comprises a large share of the population at every age over forty. A majority of both men and women in their forties, fifties, and sixties consider themselves middle-aged, with the peak of 75–80 percent in the fifty to fifty-nine age group. In their seventies, more than 40 percent of both men and women still use the middle-aged category. Above age eighty, the proportion remains above 20 percent.

It is unusual for persons in their forties and fifties to describe themselves as old (2–5 percent). In the age group of sixty to sixty-nine, about
one person in four is old or "young-old." But old is not the predominant
category until age eighty, and even then there remains variation in age
identities. Thus, people's self-identified age category corresponds only
very roughly to their chronological age. All of the age categories extend
to people over a wide range of actual ages.

We have further information about age definitions from our questions about what ages each respondent would consider to fall into his
or her own age category. On average, those who described themselves
as "young" gave an upper boundary of 52.4 years for that category, with
a modal category of 50 (remember, of course, that these people are all
forty and older). The range of "middle age" indicated by those who
consider themselves middle-aged is from a mean lower boundary of 44.7
to a mean upper boundary of 62.4 years (modal boundaries are 40 and
60). The mean lower limit of "old" is 64.0 years (modal category is 65).
(Because there are relatively few persons described as "young-old," and
because it is unclear whether these persons might better be combined
with the middle-aged or the old category, we are not able to consider
these cases here or in subsequent analyses.)

These results seem to conform to a conventional view of generational
definition. As seen by our respondents (who may differ in their perceptions from persons under the age of forty), a forty-year-old is probably
young. At age fifty, one is likely to be middle-aged, although some people extend the period of "youth" well into the fifties. There is more
consensus that the transition to being old occurs in the sixties.

But even these figures apparently reflect people's classification of
*others*. People are more flexible in applying the labels to *themselves*. This
can be seen in the strong association between people's actual age and
the age range that they attribute to their age category. This association
is depicted in figure 1.2. One line in this figure maps the average age of
the upper boundary of "young" for those respondents who described
themselves as young. The average of this upper boundary for persons
aged forty to forty-four is about forty-six years old, which implies that
these persons perceived themselves as being very close to middle age.
For persons aged forty-five to forty-nine, the average upper boundary is
about fifty-three—again, just a few years older than these persons' current age. The same is true of the upper boundary of middle age, which
is about fifty-six for people aged forty-five to forty-nine but over seventy
for people aged seventy to seventy-four. This finding may suggest that
people tend to alter their definitions as they age to conform to their own
sense that they are still young, or still middle-aged. A similar finding

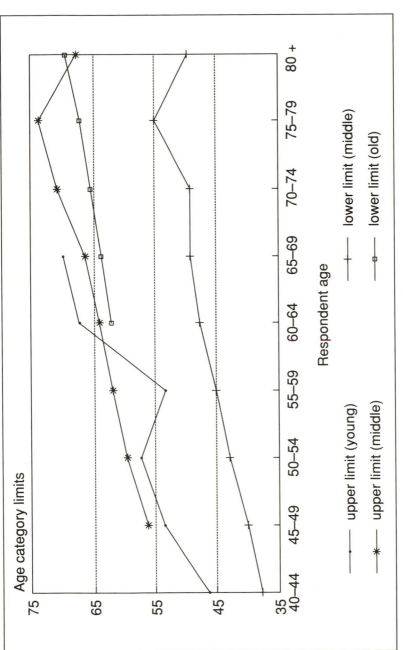

**FIGURE 1.2** Mean Upper and Lower Limits of Age Categories by Respondent Age

was reported by Seccombe and Ishii-Kuntz (1991, p. 531), who argue that cohorts "extend the aging boundary as they themselves approached it." Note that the same phenomenon applies to the lower limits of categories: older people assign a higher lower limit to the age category of both middle-aged and old. We suspect that people change these definitions from year to year as they themselves age.

## Determinants of Generational Identity

How should we interpret these variations in the ways in which people perceive their age? What factors determine these self-perceptions? Age identity, of course, is not divorced from chronological age. But age has social meaning as well, so that age-related self-perceptions reflect images and meanings of age categories in the surrounding culture and more individualized messages received through interactions with others (Karp 1988).

Older age and poorer health have been found to be consistent predictors of older age identities (Bultena and Powers 1978; George et al. 1980; Mutran and George 1982; Ward 1977; Ward et al. 1988). David Karp (1988) cites bodily reminders in midlife—a "slowing down" rather than more serious health problems associated with old age—indicating that although one is not yet old, one is also no longer young. Gordon Bultena and Edward Powers (1978) also indicate the significance of reference group comparisons, as older people who feel worse off than their age peers have older age identities. These patterns indicate that "feeling" old is a product of "being" old and of poor health. Thus, perhaps reflecting cultural stereotypes and stigma associated with old age, self-perception as old is apparently linked with a sense of loss.

Besides health we also investigate the implications of roles, or changes in roles. Perhaps there is some combination of age and social roles that could provide a firm basis for defining generations. The combinations of roles played by individuals, and the age-grading of those roles, are likely to influence self-perceptions of age and changes in age identity (see George 1990). Walter Gove et al. (1989) have described age as a master status that affects the roles occupied by individuals and the ways they are perceived by others.

Adult development in general is tied less to chronological age than to the timing of events in work and family spheres. Roles and role changes in work and family shape the rhythm of the life course and can be expected to influence age-related self-perceptions. More specifically, different roles and role transitions are associated with different stages in the life course, and therefore with related shifts in age identity. Entrance into young adulthood, for example, involves completion of education, early stages in work careers, and establishment of independent households and families (getting married and having children) (Marini 1984). This movement into young adulthood is characterized by a number of role-related events that represent signposts or rites of passage, such as graduations, weddings, and the birth of a child.

Shifts in age identity from "young" to "middle-aged," in turn, may be associated with progressive stages in work careers or with the increasing age of children. For example, parents of young children may be kept young by their involvement in school groups and concerns, whereas parents following the empty nest have very different (and more middle-aged) activity patterns and interests. Middle age is also a time when people may experience the death of their parents (representing the loss of the "child" role as well as reminders of one's own mortality) and the birth of grandchildren. Compared with young adulthood, there may be fewer signposts for movement into middle age. Midlife may be characterized more by transitions within roles (of worker or parent, for example) than by events associated with role change.

An "old" age identity may be associated with retirement and widowhood, representing loss of previous roles. These are the transitions most relevant to our concerns in this chapter, because these changes are often assumed to be signs of dependency. However, findings are mixed concerning the effects of roles and role change on age identity among older persons. Some have found associations between older age identity and retirement (Brubaker and Powers 1976; Bultena and Powers 1978; Mutran and George 1982) or widowhood (Mutran and Reitzes 1981), but others have not. Ward et al. (1988), for example, found that retirement and widowhood had only weak associations with age identity when age and health were controlled.

In summary, we study four specific kinds of roles here, focusing on the central role spheres of family and work: parent, adult child, spouse, and worker. A middle-aged as opposed to young identity is expected to be associated with having children. The parent role as a state for people in midlife stimulates social involvements and concerns associated with having children who are nearing or have entered adulthood. There may also be signposts associated with the parent role in midlife, such as children leaving home or having their own children (beginning the grandparent role), that trigger a shift in age identity from young to middle-aged. Feeling middle-aged may also be associated with the death of one's parents (loss of the "child" role). Having an "old" identity, in turn, may be associated with role changes (losses) represented by retirement, widowhood, and death of one's parents.

Our predictors of age identity include both sociodemographic variables and measures of role incumbency. Sociodemographic predictors include age (in years); subjective health ("How is your physical health at the present time?" coded 1 = very poor to fair, 2 = good, 3 = excellent); gender (1 = male, 2 = female); race (0 = non-black, 1 = black); and income (this is coded at the mean for missing values, and a dummy variable representing missing values is included in the equations). Role variables include dichotomies (0 = no, 1 = yes) representing currently being married, having living children, being retired (as opposed to being employed or keeping house), and having both parents deceased.

Since we wish to be able to examine separately the transition from young to middle-aged and from middle-aged to old, we estimate two separate logistic regression analyses. Means and standard deviations of the variables used in these analyses are provided in Appendix C, table C1.2. Coefficient estimates are presented in Appendix C, table C1.3. These coefficients represent effects of predictors on the likelihood of describing oneself as young rather than middle-aged (column 1) and of describing oneself as old rather than middle-aged (column 2). Persons described as "young-old" are not included. We are interested here in the effects of age, health, and measures of roles; we will not discuss effects of other control variables, which can be found in table C.1.3.

In a logistic regression, coefficients represent the effect of a unit change in the independent variable on the natural logarithm of the odds ("log odds") of using a particular formal service. Richard Alba (1987) shows how the antilogarithm of a logit coefficient can be transformed into an effect on the probability of a "middle-aged" or "old" age identity. This transformation depends on the value of other predictors; in our comparisons, we assume the case of a respondent who would otherwise have the average probability of a given age identity and report the increase in that probability that is predicted. This procedure provides a good intuitive sense of the size of effects, and these results are reported in table 1.1.

The analyses confirm that both age and health are significant sources of age identification. Older persons and persons in worse health are much more likely to identify as middle-aged as compared to young, and more likely to identify as old than as middle-aged. For example, if we look only at people identifying as middle-aged or as old in our sample, the average probability of thinking of oneself as old is .201. Being five years older would increase that probability to .308, while an improvement of one point (in our three-point scale) of subjective health would decrease it to .150.

We examined the effects of health in more detail, using alternative

**TABLE 1.1**

Predicted Probabilities of "Middle-Aged" or "Old" Age Identity

| Compared to the average probability of .749 of identifying as "middle-aged" vs. "young," if a respondent were: | | Compared to the average probability of .201 of identifying as "old" vs. "middle-aged," if a respondent were: | |
|---|---|---|---|
| 5 years older | .812 | 5 years older | .308 |
| In better health | .623 | In better health | .150 |
| Black | .866 | Married | .120 |
| Parent of one or more children | .841 | | |

*Note:* Based on the logistic regression model in Appendix C, table C.1.2.

measures that appear less subjective. The first alternative is based on the question, "Do you have any chronic physical problems that prevent you from doing things you would otherwise do?" The second is based on the question, "How much does your health stand in the way of your doing the things you want to do?" Both of these alternative indicators affect the probability of identification as old (vs. middle-aged). However, neither affects the young vs. middle-aged dichotomy. This may be due to the limited variation in these functional health measures among younger persons, or to a tendency for younger persons to consider functional health problems to be temporary or unrelated to aging. Thus differences in health do help define the generations.

Some roles also make a difference. Having children is associated with a higher probability of identification as middle-aged as compared to young (table 1.1 shows that having children would raise one's probability from the average of .749 to .841—a stronger impact than being five years older). Being married (vs. widowed, divorced, or never married) is associated with a lower probability of identification as old (cutting the probability nearly in half from the average of .201 to .120). However, neither retirement nor the death of one's parents affects the age identification net of age and health. Though both of these variables are correlated with age identification (correlations are between .20 and .35 with dummy variables representing the age categories), this is mainly due to their association with age.

Another way to control for age is to estimate separate models for younger and older persons. Because few young persons consider themselves old, and few old persons consider themselves young, we estimated simpler binomial logit models (not shown in tables) for these two groups. For those under sixty, the dependent variable was the young vs. middle-age dichotomy. Of the four role variables, only having children affected this choice. For those sixty and over, only being married affected the middle-age vs. old dichotomy.

We also explored gender differences in age identity in these analyses, believing that the meaning and consequences of age categories may differ for men and women. There are gender differences in family and work roles occupied over the life course, and men and women may attach different age-related significance to those roles. In addition, a view that there is a "double standard of aging" (Sontag 1972) suggests that women are considered (and may consider themselves) old at earlier ages. Seccombe and Ishii-Kuntz (1991) find that men are perceived to become "old" somewhere between ages sixty and sixty-four, while women are considered to enter this category in the fifty-five to fifty-nine period. Women, they argue, "because they are primarily valued for their physical attractiveness and sexuality, are perceived to age at a much faster rate than men" (1991, p. 533; see also Bell 1970). Though no study has yet shown such gender differences, popular stereotypes imply that women are thought to "age" earlier than men, and that they are more concerned about aging.

But despite speculation in the literature and popular media about the differential meaning of aging for men and women, we find no tendency for women to identify as either younger or older than men, controlling for other factors. Models including interaction terms between gender and other predictors revealed no significant difference between men and women in the effects of other variables on age identification. Women adopt middle-aged and old identification at neither a younger nor an older age than men, they respond no differently to poorer health or role transitions, and they show no difference in the relationship between age identity and well-being. Perhaps the private responses of men and women to aging do not correspond at all to the double standard that appears in public discourse.

## Age and Well-Being

The transition to seeing oneself as old does not occur for the majority of people until age eighty, surprisingly late in life. It is related to poor health and loss of a spouse, both of which could be interpreted as signs of increasing dependency on others. But it is not related to retirement. We turn now to an additional way in which old age might have implications for sense of loss: a decline in well-being. Old age has generally been viewed as a negative experience. We gain some insight into this phenomenon from questions regarding respondents' sense of how society treats persons of different ages. By a large margin and regardless of their own age, respondents singled out middle age as the period of most respect (80 percent) and influence (90 percent), and youth and old age as the periods of least respect and influence. Do older people experience lower well-being as a result?

A number of studies have found that "feeling" old is experienced negatively, as older identities ("old" or "elderly" versus "middle-aged") are associated with lower well-being (morale, life satisfaction, self-esteem), controlling for such concomitants as age and health (Carp and Carp 1981; Mutran and Burke 1979; Mutran and Reitzes 1981; Ward 1977; Ward et al. 1988). Our own analysis of this question is consistent with these previous studies (see Logan et al. 1992). Controlling for age, we find that feelings of distress are greater among persons who self-identify as old. Happiness is greater among the self-identified young. Finally, life satisfaction is highest among those who consider themselves young. Taken together, these results suggest that an older age identification is related to lesser well-being across all age categories.

On the other hand, actual chronological age has exactly the opposite relation to well-being. Gove et al. (1989) report that emotional discomfort declines with age and that life satisfaction increases. In our own sample, older persons report less distress and more happiness and life satisfaction. For example, we asked our respondents, "How satisfied are you with your life as a whole these days?" Figure 1.3 reports the proportion of persons in each age category who rated their satisfaction at seven on a seven-point scale. It increases from just above 20 percent for persons in their forties to nearly 50 percent for persons in their seventies or eighties.

## Age Identity and Generational Self-Interest

We have found so far that it is hard to give a precise meaning to "young" and "old." These terms are loosely related to chronological age, but people vary greatly in where they draw the lines between young, middle-aged, and old, and in when they perceive themselves as crossing one of those lines. Another complexity is that although "old age" is widely viewed as a period when one has little respect and influence, it is also the time when people feel happiest and most satisfied with life. In light of these findings, it is striking that social commentators often speak of the conflicts among generations in political life, as though in this respect the generations were sharply defined. More specifically, the older generation is often depicted as well organized and self-interested, willing and able to mobilize its resources in its own behalf and with little regard to the needs of others.

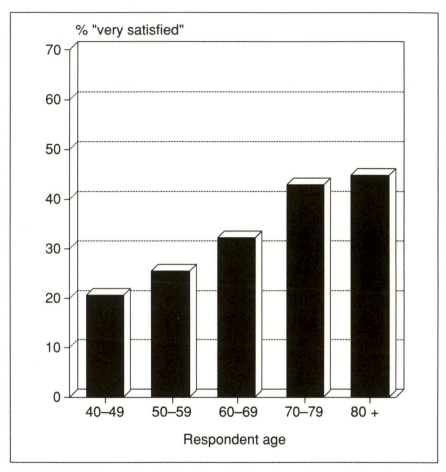

**FIGURE 1.3** Age and Life Satisfaction

This aspect of generational identities is highly charged. Ongoing public debate on the cost of federal programs for older persons has underlined the potential for conflict in intergenerational relations. What are reasonable expectations of support for the older generation? At what point do efforts to meet their needs undermine the well-being of younger people? Of most interest to us is the degree to which these issues manifest the conflicting interests of various age groups. Is there somewhere in the confusing mix of chronological age or age identification a core of solidarity and self-interest in juxtaposition to the interests of people of other ages? Do people's views of the right balance of responsibilities between generations correspond to such a self-interest? Do generations—which are in other respects so difficult to distinguish—define themselves as separate and distinct social categories in this way?

We should point out that in this respect the images of aging that we cited at the beginning of this chapter are quite distinct. The sandwich generation is usually understood as giving and forthcoming toward those who need help. The woman in the middle, as depicted by Brody and others, is a kinkeeper, socialized to accept her responsibilities as mother and daughter and quite prepared to attempt to meet them. Preston offers another view of the human situation. Programs for the elderly, he asserts, receive support inspired by the selfish motives of several kinds of people: the elderly themselves, those who might otherwise have to support an elderly family member themselves, and those who anticipate their own old age. He dismisses the potential impact of altruistic motives for support of either children or the elderly. "We have drifted towards a purely self-interested and adversarial form of government and lost along the way notions of community good," he says (1984, p. 447). We have accepted "a world view that legitimizes calculations based upon individual self-interest" (p. 445).

We might think of Preston's view as the "strong version" of the image of elderly dependency: not only is the older generation vulnerable and dependent, but it *demands support*. This view is compatible with theories of an "aging subculture" or "aging group consciousness." In one early forecast of trends, for example, Arnold Rose (1965, p. 5) noted that political battles over health care had "given many older people a sense of common lot and common interest." Such experience, he believed, could be the catalyst to transform the elderly from a statistical category into a self-conscious social group, capable of mobilizing in its own interest. Indeed, Cutler and Schmidhauser (1975) report that older persons were more supportive than younger persons of federal financing of medical care, with a strong additional effect of subjective age identification (as "elderly" or "senior citizen") among the aged (see also Weaver 1976). Similarly, Williamson et al. (1982, p. 109) find that older persons are politically more conservative, but that on "political issues that are perceived by the elderly as directly relevant to their own interests as older persons, however, they tend to hold more 'liberal' attitudes, often doing so in blatant contradiction to a generally conservative orientation."

Self-interested attitudes, in turn, have been thought to be based on social changes that reinforce aging group consciousness. Living apart from younger family members and general trends of residential isolation of older people help to set them apart as an interest group (Pampel and Williamson 1989; Rose 1965; Weaver 1976; Williamson et al. 1982).

Membership in age-linked organizations, especially senior citizen centers, has been found to be positively associated with support of governmental programs for the elderly (Smith and Martinson 1984; Trela 1971). Trela (1971, p. 123) attributes this effect to age segregation: "To the degree that they are joining the growing number of senior centers and other groups of aged and confining their associations to age peers, they are shielded from cross-generational viewpoints and may increasingly adopt age as a reference point." Pampel and Williamson (1989) argue further that tendencies toward the homogenization of interests of older people—for example, their increasing dependence on the state for retirement support, and reduction in the number of children from whom support can be expected—facilitate political mobilization.

All of these theories posit increasingly distinct boundaries between the generations, reinforced by a sense of self-interest. This thesis has been criticized on several grounds. Binstock (1972), while acknowledging that there are age differences on some political issues, points out that many seniors do not identify as old or do not perceive their problems as stemming from age and that they are subject to competing identifications and interests. Foner (1974) pointed to mechanisms that would normally dampen age-based conflicts, including the prevalence of age-heterogeneous social groups, older people's "sympathy" for younger people's experiences, and anticipation of aging on the part of younger people. Others have noted that the elderly are often reluctant to accept help (Moen 1978). There is also some evidence that older people are less likely to agree that old age in itself should entitle one to government support (Klemmack and Roff 1980) and more likely to agree that persons over sixty-five "get more than their share of government benefits" (Bengtson and Murray 1993).

The literature cited to this point focuses on only one aspect of intergenerational relations: support for public programs. As Bengtson and Murray (1993) point out, self-interest and altruism in the relationships between generations can be manifested at two different levels. In the public arena, claims may be made for governmental programs that specifically respond to the needs of people of different ages. Here the concept of "generation" refers to cohorts of persons born at different times, without taking into account the interpersonal bonds through which people of different ages are interlinked. A second level is within the family, where "generations" are defined by kinship ties. A small but growing research literature has examined the issue of parental or filial obligations, the expectations that older parents and their adult children have about flows of help and support between them.

Within the family itself, even economic models of self-interested behavior now posit some version of altruism. As Becker (1981) formulates this position, people often feel a personal stake in the well-being of a parent or child. Within the family, therefore, sharing of resources (i.e., what appears to be altruistic behavior) often does not conflict with self-interest. Thus Becker suspects that "altruism dominates family behavior perhaps to the same extent as selfishness dominates market transactions" (1981, p. 198). Several studies have documented apparently altruistic attitudes toward intergenerational relations within the family. Not only is there a broad consensus in favor of mutual support among family members, but older people are less likely than younger people to take the "parent's" side on parent-child issues. For example, Bengtson and Murray (1993) report that persons aged sixty-five and above are more likely than younger respondents to agree that "providing care for older parents is too much of a burden for their families." Analyzing the same national survey data, Bengtson and Harootyan (1994, pp. 35–38) conclude that "parents, hoping for the best future for their children, minimize their expectations of support from them, while maximizing their responsibility of support to them." Lye and Nelson (1993), analyzing the National Survey of Families and Households, find that age (ranging from eighteen and up) is positively associated with agreement that parents should pay for children's college education and provide financial assistance to their children. Older people, the parental generation, take this responsibility on themselves.

Conversely, adult children generally express a greater degree of filial obligation than their parents expect of them (Cicirelli 1981). Several studies with small parent-child or three-generation samples have reached this conclusion. For example, elderly parents are less likely than their adult children to think an adult daughter should share her home with a widowed mother (Brody et al. 198; Shanas 1960). Daughters are more likely than their mothers to think that an adult child should adjust her family schedule (but not her work schedule) to care for a dependent elderly parent (Brody et al. 1984), and daughters are less likely than their mothers to say that daughters should expect help with finances and chores (Johnson 1981–82). Hamon (1988) found that parents are significantly less likely than their adult children to agree that children should make room in their home for parents in an emergency, care for the parent when sick, give financial help to the parent, adjust family or work schedules to help the parent, feel responsible for the parent, or coreside with the parent. She concludes that "the desire for independence appears to be the norm for older parents" and that "children may experience some undue anxiety, to the extent that their parents do not

seem to expect as much from them as they do of themselves"
(pp. 20–21).

Are relations between generations based on self-interested group
consciousness or selfless giving? Studies of parental and filial obligation
have emphasized altruism. Theories of aging group consciousness, supported by some empirical research but contested on both theoretical and
empirical grounds, have emphasized self-interest. These findings, however, are inconclusive due to limitations of samples or analytic models.
As noted above, most parent-child and three-generation studies (e.g.,
Brody's Philadelphia study, the Longitudinal Study of Families analyzed by Bengtson and others, Johnson's study of Italian Americans, and
Hamon's research in Harrisburg) are based on small and/or nonrandom
samples. Weaver's (1976) analysis of attitudes toward health care reform
is based on a sample of residents of low-income neighborhoods and
includes controls only for gender, socioeconomic status, and ethnicity.
Smith and Martinson (1984) surveyed participants in a mock "Silver-
Haired Legislative election." Trela (1971) reports only bivariate analyses.
More generally, studies of attitudes toward public programs for the elderly often fail to control for the broader range of political values (e.g.,
attitudes toward other kinds of social programs) with which these views
may be associated. However, Bengtson and Harootyan's (1994, p. 250)
analysis of the 1990 American Association of Retired Persons (AARP)
survey is exceptional among studies of family obligation, in that they
analyze a national random sample with a well-developed multivariate
model. They find a curvilinear effect of age on agreement with norms
of responsibility of parents toward children, and no effect of age on
responsibility toward parents. The unpublished study by Lye and Nelson (1993) also uses a random sample. Their results are also mixed: age
has significant effects in predicting only two of the five attitudes studied.

The Albany survey allows us to replicate the best features of these
previous studies. We draw on a series of attitudes about "appropriate"
parent-child relations (six questions) and governmental programs for
older people (six questions). These indicators are listed in table 1.2.
Questions regarding filial and parental obligations probe attitudes
toward coresidence, help, and contact. Responses have been recoded so
that higher values reflect parents' presumed self-interest: higher values
are assigned to persons who disagree that parents should not expect to
move in with their children, agree that children take less care of their
elderly parents now than in the past, agree that children should stay in
touch regularly with their parents, disagree that children should be able
to depend on parents for financial help, and disagree that children
should expect babysitting help from their parents. Public policy ques-

**TABLE 1.2**
Attitudes toward Family Obligations and Public Programs for Older Persons,
by Age (N = 1,200)

| | Age category | | | | |
|---|---|---|---|---|---|
| | 40–49 | 50–59 | 60–69 | 70–79 | 80+ |
| **Family obligation questions** | | | | | |
| "Parents should not expect to move in with their adult children even if they are having health problems." Disagree or strongly disagree | 69% | 54% | 40% | 45% | 48% |
| "Nowadays adult children do not take as much care of their elderly parents as they did in past generations." Agree or strongly agree | 83 | 77 | 79 | 81 | 73 |
| "Adult children should stay in touch with their parents on a regular basis." Strongly agree[a] | 28 | 19 | 14 | 12 | 14 |
| "If people get into financial trouble, they should be able to depend on their parents for help." Disagree or strongly disagree | 64 | 51 | 42 | 40 | 31 |
| "Children should stay in touch with their parents at least weekly." Agree or strongly agree | 84 | 82 | 82 | 87 | 82 |
| "Children should be able to expect babysitting help from their parents." Disagree or strongly disagree | 82 | 65 | 59 | 53 | 54 |
| **Public policy questions** | | | | | |
| "Are we spending too much, too little, or about the right amount on assistance to the elderly?" "Too little" | 78 | 72 | 66 | 59 | 72 |
| "Old age pensioners have a right to be taken care of in a dignified way even if younger people must contribute their taxes to make this possible." Agree or strongly agree | 96 | 91 | 81 | 80 | 85 |
| "The older person gets a fair break in benefits from our society." Disagree or strongly disagree | 69 | 60 | 48 | 34 | 33 |

*continued*

**TABLE 1.2 (continued)**

| | Age category | | | | |
|---|---|---|---|---|---|
| | 40–49 | 50–59 | 60–69 | 70–79 | 80+ |
| "Programs should be developed which allow older people to continue living at home rather than in a nursing home." Strongly agree[a] | 24 | 23 | 21 | 17 | 30 |
| "Anyone over 65 should be entitled to health care at an affordable cost." Strongly agree[a] | 37 | 27 | 22 | 16 | 20 |
| "Even if it meant an increase in taxes, this area should be provided with a public transportation program for the elderly." Agree or strongly agree | 86 | 86 | 74 | 77 | 79 |

a    Close to 100% of all age groups agree or strongly agree on this item

tions ask opinions about spending levels and provision of programs for older persons. Again, responses have been recoded to reflect the self-interest of the older generation. Persons are assigned higher values who believe "we are spending too little" on assistance to the elderly, agree that pensioners have a right to be taken care of, disagree that the older person gets a fair break in benefits, agree that programs should be developed to allow continued residence at home for older people, agree that older people are entitled to affordable health care, and agree that a public transportation program for the elderly should be provided.

Table 1.2 reports the proportion of respondents in each age group who gave answers reflecting primary concern with the interests of older people. These data show a consistent tendency on both kinds of measures for older people (at least up to age eighty, where the sample size is considerably diminished) to be least likely to adopt the "pro-elderly" position. For example, older people are much less likely than are younger people to agree with the proposition that "anyone over sixty-five should be entitled to health care at an affordable cost," or that "adult children should stay in touch with their parents on a regular basis." Altruism, not self-interest, seems to govern the attitudes of both the younger (that is, middle-aged) and older generations in this sample.

## Age Effects after Controlling for Other Predictors

To facilitate multivariate analyses of these attitudes, indices of "family obligation" and "public policy" have been created as the sum of standardized scores of these indicators (missing values were scored with a value of zero if real values were available for at least three indicators on the scale). There is a correlation of .41 between the family obligation and public policy scales. Thus our decision to treat them separately is based not on their statistical properties but on substantive considerations. First, the research literatures on family obligations and public policy have been generally separate, and one of our purposes is to juxtapose results for the two kinds of attitudes. Second, analyses in which every indicator is treated individually as a dependent variable yield nearly identical results to those where the indices are the dependent variables. Creation of indices is a convenient means of reducing the volume of results to be reported with no distortion of the findings.

We are concerned mainly with the effects of age on these attitudes. Age is coded into approximately ten-year intervals of 40–49 (31 percent of respondents), 50–59 (23 percent), 60–69 (26 percent), 70–79 (15 percent), and 80 or above (5 percent). These categories are preferable to treatment of age as an interval scale because we found some evidence of nonlinearity in its effects: in some equations with individual attitudes, age effects peaked with the 70–79 category. (This nonlinearity cautions us against extrapolating our findings to younger persons—that is, for people in their twenties and thirties who were not included in our sample.) Use of categories also facilitates thinking about age effects in terms of "generations," such as the generation of people in their forties compared to those in their seventies, although of course this is only a loose rendering of the concept. As we found above, if the term "older generation" were based on people's self-descriptions, less than half of respondents even in the 70–79 bracket would be considered "old" or "elderly." Still, self-described age identity is highly correlated with chronological age, and we assume that respondents in the 40–59 age bracket represent—in relative terms—the younger generation, while those in their seventies and above represent the older generation. Those in their sixties might be considered a "swing" category between the two.

Besides age, we incorporate a number of variables that have been employed in other studies of intergenerational attitudes. These include number of living parents and number of living children to represent the respondents' role incumbency. Bengtson and Harootyan (1994) found that those persons with adult children more strongly agree with norms of responsibility toward children. Other measures of demographic background are race, gender, and marital status (a set of dummy variables indicating married [56.8 percent], divorced [14.6 percent], and widowed [21.3 percent], with never married [7.3 percent] as the omitted category). Social class is measured by income (with a dummy variable for missing income as in the equations reported above). Place of residence is measured as two dummy variable representing suburban (21.7 percent of respondents) or rural (11.7 percent) residence, with central city residence (66.6 percent) as the omitted category.

Subjective health is used to represent people's need for age-related assistance. (We have also examined a measure of functional disability similar to the Activities of Daily Living [ADL] scale commonly used in gerontological research, and find similar results.)

Finally, to represent people's political leanings, which presumably have an independent effect on their attitudes toward government programs for the aging, we include two attitudinal variables. The first is a three-point scale of "liberalism" based on the question, "On most domestic political issues, do you think of yourself as more of a conservative, a liberal, or a middle-of-the-roader?" (Higher values represent the more liberal position). The second is an index (the sum of standardized scores) of response to questions about whether "the government is spending too much money, too little money, or about the right amount" on health, education, and assistance to minorities (higher values represent attitudes favoring more spending). It is essential to know whether age differences in the attitudes studied here are only an extension of broader political attitudes (e.g., what has been described as older people's greater conservatism [Williamson et al. 1982]), or whether they are specific to beliefs about intergenerational relations.

In Appendix C, table C.1.4, the effects of all these variables are assessed on an index of family obligation and an index of support for senior citizen programs, using multiple regression. As shown in the first and third columns of the table, the age differences reported above are statistically significant and account for 12.0 percent and 8.0 percent of the variance in the two scales, respectively. In the second and fourth columns, controls are introduced for the other personal characteristics that have been thought to influence family and political attitudes. Introduction of these controls only slightly reduces the age coefficients.

In the multivariate equation for public programs for the elderly, respondents in their fifties have significantly lower scores (compared to those in their forties), with a coefficient of −.860. Coefficients for other age groups (all of which are statistically significant) become increasingly negative up to age eighty: −1.901 for those in their sixties, −2.505 for the seventies, and −2.180 for eighty and above. In the equation for family obligation, a similar pattern is found, with those in their eighties least likely to emphasize adult children's obligations to their parents.

These age effects are illustrated in figure 1.4. We have calculated the predicted value of respondents' attitudes on each standardized attitude

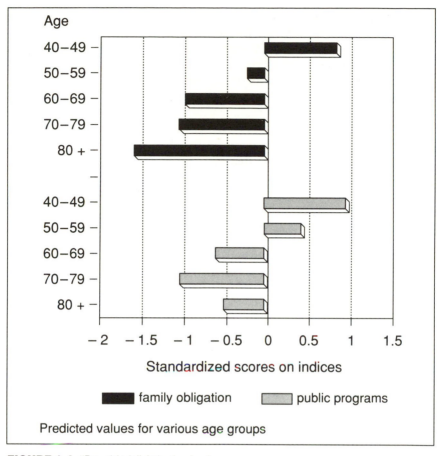

**FIGURE 1.4** "Pro-elderly" Attitudes by Age

scale, taking the average (mean or modal) value for every independent variable. The figure shows plainly that persons in the forty to forty-nine age group are the only ones predicted to have a more positive than average "pro-elderly" score on both indices. They are followed by persons in their fifties, predicted to have nearly the average score on the family obligation index and a higher than average score on the public programs index. Older groups (sixty and over) are predicted to have well below the average score on both indices. Thus the multivariate results confirm what see saw above in the bivariate tables.

Few other variables have significant effects on attitudes. People with more adult children are more likely to adopt attitudes favoring the younger generation. Residents of rural areas have higher scores on the family obligation scale (and also on the public program scale, though barely falling short of the .05 significance level). One might attribute this effect to the more traditional cultural values in rural areas, but the coefficients for suburban residents are also both statistically significant. As would be expected, respondents who consider themselves more liberal and those who favor more spending in other social programs are more supportive of public programs for seniors. Finally, women and blacks are more favorable to senior programs.

Some negative findings in these equations are worth noting. Education has no significant effects. There is no gender or race difference in family norms. Neither health (a possible indicator of needs for assistance) nor marital status (where divorce might have been considered an indicator of family values, and divorce and widowhood might be indicators of needs for intergenerational help) has significant effects. And political attitudes are quite independent of family norms, despite their strong effect on feelings about public policy.

## The "Age Consciousness" of the Older Generation

The findings illustrated in figure 1.4 are exactly opposite of what would be predicted if older people's views were determined by self-interested age consciousness. Nevertheless, it is possible that variables associated in the literature with more "age-conscious" opinions do affect the attitudes of the older people in our sample. We therefore conducted further analyses among persons sixty and above (the number of cases in these regressions, after deletions due to missing data, is 531). These regression equations are presented in Appendix C, table C.1.5. Based on the literature cited above, we included three additional predictors reflecting age consciousness or isolation. If chronological age is only loosely related to subjective age, people's generational consciousness could affect attitudes even if aging does not. "Age identity" is a dummy variable distinguishing those who report themselves as old, elderly, or aged (34.3 percent of this subsample) vs. middle-aged or young. "Age preference" distinguishes those who report a preference for spending time with people their own age or older (36.5 percent of respondents) vs. younger persons. "Center membership" identifies persons who are members of a senior citizen center (18.8 percent).

We also included two indicators of actual relations with children suggested by Finley, Roberts, and Banahan (1988), who hypothesize that physical and emotional closeness between generations is positively associated with feelings of family obligation (though they may not be related to attitudes toward public policy). "Nearest child" is the travel time in minutes to the nearest living child (with a mean of fifty-nine minutes). "Closeness to child" is a subjective report of "feeling of closeness" (values of one to four ranging from not very close to extremely close, with a mean of 2.8), where the value is for the living child to whom the respondent feels closest. Bengtson and Harootyan (1994, p. 251) provide tentative support for these hypotheses based on bivariate correlations.

There are correlations of about .10 among several of these indicators (those who live further from their nearest child are more likely to feel older and be senior center members; those who prefer to spend time with people of their own age or older are also more likely to be senior center members). But only one has a zero-order correlation of .10 or higher with intergenerational attitudes: those who feel emotionally more close to a child tend to have lower scores on the family obligation scale (r = −.16). That is, a parent's affective ties to children seem to be a source of altruistic norms favoring the child's welfare. In a multivariate analysis, even this association drops below a statistically significant value. Thus we conclude that none of these variables—not even age identification or related measures—has a significant independent effect on either the family obligation or public policy index for older respondents. Generational self-interest, whether inferred from chronological age or age identity, seems not to determine people's views about these family or policy questions.

## Where Are the Generation Gaps?

The image of a dependent older generation is undermined by the absence of a clearer dividing line between middle and old age, as we discovered in the first portion of this chapter. Even more revealing is our finding that neither old age, nor any measure of age identity or consciousness or isolation, is associated with claims for greater intergenerational help or attention or more public support. On a broad range of policy and family issues, people's attitudes do not reflect generational self-interest.

Age differences in the attitudes studied here highlight intergenerational solidarity, as older people's attitudes seem to give greater weight to the needs of younger generations, and vice versa. Relations across age groups apparently have an altruistic character—not only in the family, where economists (following Becker's lead) have come to expect it, but also in the impersonal realm of governmental programs. This pattern may have many sources. The social norms evinced by older people may reflect their desire for autonomy and self-reliance, their sense that the proper role of parents is to be givers rather than receivers, and their wish not to become a burden to the younger generation. Older people may also have discovered that aging does not handicap them as much as younger people might expect. The views of middle-aged respondents may be partly based on self-interest. Several observers have noted that these people can anticipate their own aging and that younger persons with living parents may benefit immediately from public programs for the elderly (Foner 1974; Pampel and Williamson 1989; Preston 1984).

It is possible that both altruistic and self-interested motives combine in some way to create the pattern identified here. For example, "anticipatory" or "vicarious" self-interest on the part of younger people would tend to moderate differences between the generations. If in addition older people were looking out for the interests of the younger generation, this combination could explain our results. We believe that the main conclusion from this study is that a simple model of self-interest on the part of both younger and older people is probably incorrect. One must look to other motives. As Bengtson and Murray (1993, p. 113) remind us, our interpretation should not leave out "the two most important predictors of intergenerational behavior and exchange: love and guilt."

These findings are consistent with results from other national and local studies of family obligation. On issues of public policy, the best evidence of self-interested attitudes came from the 1970s studies of attitudes toward federal medical programs for the elderly. Results from Bengtson and Murray's (1993) and Bengtson and Harootyan's (1994) analyses of the 1990 AARP Generational Linkages Survey, by contrast, are more consistent with our finding of intergenerational altruism.

How can these results be reconciled with the perception of intergenerational conflict that has pervaded journalistic, political, and even academic circles? Not only do the relative positions of younger and older people not appear to be self-interested, but also we found a high degree of consensus on most items. Recall that on three items, close to 100 percent in every age category agree or strongly agree on the response that favors older persons' interests. On most other items, there is a strong majority in every age category. Therefore even the differences that we have analyzed are not suggestive of strongly conflicting views.

One possibility is that there has developed a gap between the activities of interest groups and the values of their constituencies. That is, if—as Preston has so effectively argued—the balance of public policy has shifted toward the elderly and to the detriment of children, such a shift may stem from sources other than the values of older people themselves. These may include the effectiveness of political lobbying by organizations representing the interests of the elderly. As Hudson (1978) proposes, the legitimacy of aging programs may largely rest on the continuing support that they enjoy from younger people, and not only on the self-interested support of older people. And perhaps it is the "professionals, providers, and advocates . . . more than the elderly themselves, that have been the motivating force behind these programs" (p. 431; see also Binstock 1972).

Addressing possible responses by aging interest groups to charges of selfishness, Kingson (1988, pp. 771–72) proposes "to view the emergence of the intergenerational equity issue as an opportunity to develop a multigenerational advocacy agenda and strategy." In dealing with such policies as health care reform, where the distribution of costs and benefits across age groups is a central issue, it is often assumed that generations will be at odds with one another (Callahan 1987). The concern that people of different ages apparently feel for one another may instead mean that a multigenerational strategy would strike a responsive chord in the public at large and in the aging lobby's own constituency.

# 2

# Which Is the Dependent Generation?

*With Russell A. Ward*

*The image of frail elderly is misleading for intergenerational relations: help is generally reciprocal, but more is given to the child generation until the point when parents reach about seventy-five years of age. Coresidence of parents and adult children is an example of this phenomenon: the evidence shows that coresidence primarily meets the needs of the child rather than the parent. Also, despite strong assumptions in the literature on gender differences, we find no effects of gender on coresidence, and the gender differences in helping are limited to mothers' greater likelihood of receiving help from adult children—both sons and daughters.*

■ We can hardly identify the older generation. People's application of generational labels varies with their own age, and any attempt to base definitions on patterns of self-identification would classify some fifty-year-olds as elderly and some people in their seventies as middle-aged. Nor is the problem of definition simplified by any tendency for an age conscious mobilization of the elderly in pursuit of their collective interests. The opposite seems to be more true, and our view is that intergenerational relationships are essentially altruistic. Rather than define generations by age categories, therefore, we believe it will be more useful to think about them in terms of family ties between parents and children. The parent is the older generation, and the child—even in middle age—is the younger.

Every parent-child relationship is likely to evolve over time in accordance with the resources and needs of both parent and child. Most often this relationship is lifelong, even though many social scientists think of the nuclear family only in terms of parents and their minor children. As Rossi and Rossi (1990) point out, parents help children throughout childhood and they internalize these helping patterns. They do not stop suddenly when children reach age twenty or twenty-one. On the other hand, by the time parents are near the end of life, they are often frail and may need assistance from children or other people. Thus, a transition often occurs sometime during the life course, although it is not clear at what point it occurs or what factors lead to the change. Gerontological specialists emphasize the period after this transition, and consequently there is a tendency to assume that the older generation is dependent on the younger. This is the image that is often portrayed in the popular media.

In this chapter we evaluate patterns of instrumental support between parents and their adult children, including both interhousehold assistance and coresidence, searching for common trends on which a realistic image of intergenerational relations can be based. Bengtson and colleagues (Bengtson and Roberts 1991; Bengtson and Harootyan 1994) have defined six dimensions of intergenerational solidarity: structural (coresidence or proximate residence), associational, functional (help), affectual, consensual, and normative (feelings of responsibility for other generations). In Chapter 1 we introduced data bearing on normative solidarity, and we will focus on other dimensions throughout this book. Here we analyze their structural and functional dimensions, focusing in particular on patterns of age and gender, the two main pillars of family organization (Rossi and Rossi 1990).

Three recently collected data sets have provided researchers with good sources of data on intergenerational assistance. These are the National Survey of Families and Households (Eggebeen and Hogan 1990; Cooney and Uhlenberg 1992), the Boston area study by Rossi and Rossi (1990), and the AARP study of 1990 (Bengtson and Harootyan 1994). All include measures of whether help is given to and received from parents and adult children in a variety of areas, including some types of instrumental assistance, over a specified time period.

In the National Survey of Families and Households (NSFH), respondents (aged nineteen and over) were asked about three kinds of help during the past month: advice, household services (including babysitting, transportation, car/house repair, and other work around the house), and financial assistance. (The division of tasks among members of the same household is generally treated separately, since coresidence involves a distinctive kind of helping and sharing.) One important finding from these national data is the reciprocity of helping relationships. In fact, reciprocal help is actually more common than help in only one direction (Kulis 1992). This means that the image of helping as "caregiving" to a dependent person, common in the gerontological literature, applies only in exceptional situations. It makes more sense to think of helping as a dimension of interaction between independent people.

A second consistent finding is that the relative balance of help from parents to children and from children to parents changes slowly over the life course. Based on reports from adult children aged twenty to sixty-four, Cooney and Uhlenberg (1992) analyzed the trajectory of support from parents over the adult child's life course. Help from parents peaks when children are in their late twenties and early thirties and falls off after they reach age thirty-five. Analyzing the same data from the parents' perspective, Eggebeen (1992) found that parents tend to give less help as they grow older, but their receipt of help does not show a clear linear pattern with age. Finally, Eggebeen and Hogan (1990) examined help in *both* directions for all respondents with living parents. They suggest that child care is the key element in these exchanges. Adult children with young children of their own have the most exchanges with parents. For example, 40 percent of those adult children who have children under age five receive babysitting help from parents. After the adult child reaches age forty, the balance shifts to helping their parents, rather than receiving help from them (see also Eggebeen 1991; Hoyert 1991).

A third set of findings concerns gender differences. Here the results are less clear. Eggebeen (1992) finds that fathers give more and receive less help from children than do mothers. But other analyses suggest that women both receive and give more help (Eggebeen and Hogan 1990; Bengtson and Harootyan 1994). Data on reciprocal help are also reported for the Boston area by Rossi and Rossi (1990). Their questions encompass help with chores, during illness, and fixing something, as well as advice, comfort, and monetary loans. The reference time period is "the past year or so." Their report on help between respondents and their adult children reveals that mother-daughter pairs experience the highest level of exchange, mainly due to the high incidence of help from daughters to mothers.

Thus both age and gender have been found to be of major importance in organizing reciprocal patterns of assistance. However, since all studies cited above measured help as a dichotomy, the frequency and intensity of help has not been examined. The Albany survey allows us for the first time to assess age and gender effects on these aspects of intergenerational relations. This chapter focuses on interhousehold help and coresidence. Analyses of interhousehold help are based on those respondents who had at least one noncoresident child aged twenty-one or above. We present information on a parent's relations with *all* adult children and on relations with *one randomly selected* adult child.

Previous research has been conducted from three viewpoints: the adult child respondent in relation to his or her parents (e.g., Cooney and Uhlenberg 1992; Eggebeen and Hogan 1990; Rossi and Rossi 1990); the parent respondent in relation to all adult children combined (Eggebeen 1991, 1992; Hoyert 1991); and the parent respondent in relation to individual adult children (Rossi and Rossi 1990; Hoyert 1991). While we could use the first strategy, we do not because our respondents' living parents are old enough (average age in the seventies) that both coresidence and help from parents to respondents is rare. We chose instead both the second and the third strategy. The second provides an overall view of the parents' situation. The third allows us to take into account characteristics of individual children that may affect his or her relations with a parent.

Our data on intergenerational helping are based on questions about "How you manage some everyday activities. For each of the following activities, please tell me who does it. Do you do it yourself, does your spouse do it, a friend, someone you pay, or what?" This question was applied to six tasks: grocery shopping; cooking meals; doing laundry; providing local transportation; doing house repairs, yard work, and similar chores; and cleaning the house. For each task, the respondent was asked if anyone else (up to three additional individuals) helped with each activity. (One might wonder whether asking about only four helpers results in under-reporting of receipt of help. Out of twelve hundred respondents, the numbers reporting four participants in the six household tasks ranged from thirty-four to eighty-eight, a relatively small percentage of the total. Further, since several of these tasks are collapsed into broader categories, it is possible for the respondent to have named more than four persons for two of the broad categories.) For each individual listed, the respondent also was asked how often that person performed each activity—once a day, two to six days a week, once a week, at least once a month, six to eleven times a year, two to five times a year, once a year or less, and only in emergencies (a volunteered response)—these were converted into task frequency per month values. When used as a dichotomy (help vs. not help) all frequencies with the exception of emergency help are combined. We also recorded the respondent's estimate of the hours spent in an *average* week by each person.

In short, information was gathered about help received in the process of finding out how respondents accomplished tasks of everyday living. To measure help given to others, respondents were asked whether the respondent ever helps specified others with each of several household tasks, and if so, how often. The list of tasks included fewer and more inclusive categories, as well as a category for child care. Because we want to compare incidence and time spent in help in both directions, we have combined some categories for help received.

Information on monetary help to and from children was also gathered, but the questions were asked in a nonparallel manner and those data are not analyzed here. Information about giving and receiving advice, as in the NSFH, was not gathered here as it was felt that the distinction between giving and not giving advice is much more arbitrary than is the reporting of instrumental help. While respondents were questioned about personal and sick care, for assessing help to respondents it was asked only who "would" help if such help were needed; thus, it was not possible to incorporate this kind of care into the analysis.

## Generations and Helping

Let us begin by summarizing patterns of helping for each group of tasks. Our sample includes 792 parents who have at least one noncoresident child aged twenty-one or older. We have calculated the percentage who give or receive help to or from *any* of their children, and also the percentage who give or receive help to or from a specific *randomly selected* child. Table 2.1 reports these percentages.

**TABLE 2.1**

Help between Respondent Parents and Noncoresident Adult Children (All Children; Randomly Selected Child) Age 21 and Over (N = 791)

| | Parents receiving help from | | | Parents giving help to | |
|---|---|---|---|---|---|
| | any child | this child | | any child | this child |
| cook meals do laundry clean house | 7% | 4% | housekeeping, cleaning or cooking | 21% | 13% |
| grocery shopping transportation for local errands, appointments, etc. | 14% | 7% | shopping or providing transportation | 24% | 14% |
| home repairs, yard work, or similar chores | 14% | 7% | heavy chores around the house, yard work, repairs, etc. | 13% | 8% |
| | | | babysitting | 38% | 21% |
| any kind of help | 27% | 14% | any kind of help | 58% | 39% |
| mean total hours per week | 1.69 | .61 | mean total hours per week | 3.27 | 1.34 |

*Note:* Based only on respondents with one or more noncoresident adult children.

Parents receive help from children somewhat rarely—only about one-quarter receive household help from any child, and about one in seven receive help from the one selected child. Figures range from 4 percent of selected children helping with housekeeping tasks to 7 percent helping with repairs and yard work. For those children who *do* help parents with a particular task, those helping with housework and those helping with shopping and errands, the median frequency is once a week (not shown in table 2.1). The median frequency for yard work and repairs is once a month. The average amount of help per week from an individual child is well under one hour, while the average amount from all children combined is still less than two hours.

Parents are more than twice as likely to be helping children as to be receiving help from them. In particular, about one in five respondents gives babysitting help to the randomly selected adult child. Altogether, about two in five adult children receive some kind of help from parent respondents in our sample, who spend an average of 1.3 hours per week helping any given child and 3 hours helping all children.

These data support a model of the parent continuing as a caregiver to adult children, an extension of the care children receive in childhood, rather than a reversal. But one wouldn't expect such a reversal until parents become old and frail, or until children decrease their demand for help, perhaps because they have no children of their own who need to be looked after. At what point does this occur? To answer this question we categorize our data by the parent's age, and the results are illustrated in figure 2.1 (see Appendix C, table C.2.1 for the complete breakdowns). We focus first on help exchanged with a randomly selected individual child; shortly we will also present patterns of help exchanged with all adult children by parent age.

The figure shows that help to a parent from a *specific* child is fairly uncommon for most of the age range analyzed here. The percentage of individual children giving any help to parents in a given age group ranges from 5 to 14 percent until parents reach age seventy-five. Errands and heavy work are more common than housekeeping help until the oldest age groups, and even for children with very old parents, the percent giving help with shopping/errands stays substantially higher than that for other kinds of help. About one in four children of a parent seventy-five or over helps with shopping and one in three helps with some chore. This finding makes sense because mobility outside the home is related to age: five percent of the respondents aged seventy-five and over need help to go outdoors, and an additional 12 percent have some difficulty. The average child of respondents over age seventy-five helps these parents just over one hour a week.

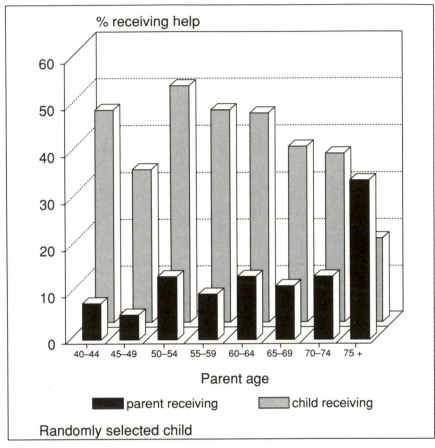

**FIGURE 2.1**  Intergenerational Help by Parent Age

Help from parents to individual adult children is more common. Respondents through their early seventies help children with all kinds of tasks analyzed here, and babysitting is particularly common when parents are at ages fifty to sixty-four (and children are probably ages twenty-five to forty). Babysitting drops off after respondents reach seventy, probably because fewer children have their own young children needing care. Parents help children on average one to two hours per week, peaking when parents are in their early fifties to early sixties. The percentage of parents giving and receiving help is not equal until parents are in their mid-seventies and children are in their early forties (as reported also by Rossi and Rossi 1990). Before that time, clearly the predominant direction is from parents to children.

The same conclusion applies to help between parents and *all* their adult children combined (see Appendix C, table C.2.2). While these figures are, not surprisingly, higher than those for individual children, the patterns are similar to those reported above. Help from parents to children, particularly babysitting but other kinds of help as well, is more common than help from children to parents until parents reach age seventy-five. At this point over half of parents are receiving help from one or more children, although three in ten parents continue to give help to at least one child.

## Gender and Helping

Intergenerational relations do vary across the life cycle. The next question we examine is the role played by women in these relations. How different are the behaviors of sons and daughters, fathers and mothers? More specifically, how unique are the relationships between mothers and daughters (this is the tie emphasized by Rossi and Rossi [1990]) compared to those across genders or between male kin? This topic has been discussed extensively. The implicit model in most treatments has assumed one-way helping, from child to parent. One reason for this emphasis is researchers' concern for the well-being of widowed parents, predominantly women, who can no longer depend on assistance from a spouse. But the spotlight aimed on relations between mothers and daughters has stronger theoretical roots in ideas about gender differences in both the child and parent generations.

### The Adult Child Generation

If married older people receive most of their needed help from the spouse, it has been argued that women in the next generation provide most of the needed assistance for widowed parents (Brody 1981). Numerous studies have shown that daughters provide larger amounts and more diverse kinds of assistance to older parents than do sons (Sherman et al. 1988 ; Stoller and Earl 1983; Horowitz 1985; Montgomery and Kamo 1989; Rossi and Rossi 1990; Dwyer and Coward 1991; Coward and Dwyer 1990).

Several kinds of explanations have been offered to explain daughters' presumed greater involvement in helping (Finley 1989; Montgomery and Kamo 1989; Montgomery 1992; Walker 1992; Lee 1992). These can be summarized into three basic kinds of arguments. First is the cultural assignment of women to perform nurturant and household tasks and to maintain kin relations (Brody 1981; Montgomery and Kamo 1989; Horowitz 1985). This explanation would imply differences in expectations of parents for filial responsibility and adult children's filial attitudes, but evidence as to these differences is mixed (Sherman et al. 1988; Brody et al. 1984; Finley et al. 1988). This assignment can be viewed as originating in gender differences in psychology or socialization, or as part of a gendered division of labor reinforced by differences in resources and power (see Walker 1992; Ferree 1991).

A second explanation gives more weight to the preferences of parents. On some kinds of tasks, parents may have particularly strong preferences about whether a son or daughter helps them. For example, it has been suggested that there may be taboos regarding sons performing tasks involving intimate body contact with parents (Montgomery and Kamo 1989), particularly between sons and mothers, invoking an incest taboo (Lee 1992; Lee et al. 1993). If women prefer help from daughters (and men from sons), demographic patterns would result in a preponderance of daughter caregivers. This is because the vast majority of disabled elderly who do not have spouses to help them are women, due to women's greater longevity and age differences in marriage between men and women.

Third, many researchers have focused on the extent to which men have more competing responsibilities and less time availability than women, due in large part to greater involvement in paid work (Brody 1981; Horowitz 1985, Finley 1989; Matthews and Rosner 1988; see also the review of relevant results in Montgomery 1992). If paid employment limits workers' ability to spend time with parents, and if daughters are less likely to be employed than sons, one would expect gendered patterns of helping behavior (but gender differences would disappear when employment is taken into account).

*The Parent Generation*

While daughters are thought to be most likely to provide help, mothers are believed to be most likely to receive it. Some provocative discussions of this phenomenon are framed in terms of a generational payoff. Women devote more time and energy to the direct care of family members than do men (Walker 1992) and are responsible for the variety of tasks known as kinkeeping (DiLeonardo 1987; Rosenthal 1985). It might, therefore, be expected that this lifetime of caretaking and kinkeeping activities would pay off in old age, through receiving higher levels of social support and assistance: "in old age, it is the woman who reaps the rewards of her investment" (Longino and Lipman 1981). Others have argued the opposite position: that the investment some women made in kinkeeping "was in most cases tragically doomed" (DiLeonardo 1987).

There is, in fact, evidence that older women have higher expectations for help from children than do their male counterparts. Women are more likely than men to think elderly persons should live with children if unable to care for themselves, and are less likely to favor their living in an "old age home" (Seelbach 1977). Their expectations are apparently reinforced by social norms. In a vignette study of attitudes about kin obligations held by the general population, both marital status and gender of the hypothetical recipient were salient in assistance-giving norms. A widowed mother or other unmarried female relative evokes the most obligations for help from kin (Rossi and Rossi 1990).

Due to these assumptions as well as evidence that mothers and daughters are more involved in intergenerational helping patterns than fathers and sons (e.g. Rossi and Rossi, 1990; Sherman et al. 1988; Stoller and Earl 1983), many studies of intergenerational assistance have focused exclusively on mothers and daughters. Many of these studies are also based on nonprobability samples, and few have considered assistance flowing in the opposite direction. (The Rossi and Rossi study, the AARP study, and the NSFH are exceptions to both limitations.) Thus there is a gap here between widely held theories and the actual empirical evidence.

Our approach is to categorize our dyads (linking a parent respondent with a selected adult child) into mother-daughter, mother-son, father-daughter, and father-son pairs. These are classified by age of the parent (unfortunately the number of cases for the oldest group is small, but the patterns suggest the importance of keeping separate those respondents over age seventy-five.) For each type, we present information on help given from the parent to the child and from the child to the parent. These data are reported in Appendix C, Table C.2.3.

Let us consider first the help flowing from children to parents. Figure 2.2 illustrates the percentage of parents in each type of dyad who receive help. For the first two rows in this figure, the pattern contradicts theoretical expectations. The largest percentages are for help from sons to mothers. Only for the oldest parents does the mother-daughter combination stand out, and here it is only marginally different from mothers and sons. (Measured in average hours of help, as shown in Appendix C, table C.2.3, this difference is considerably greater: 2.24 hours vs. 1.09 hours. But even measured in terms of hours of help, the mother-daughter link stands out only for parents aged seventy-five and over.) More clear is the stronger tendency for mothers over age seventy-five to receive help than do fathers of that age. This is the only gender difference in help from children to remain significant in this sample when other characteristics of parents and children are controlled in a multivariate analysis (Spitze and Logan 1992). In particular, we call attention to the

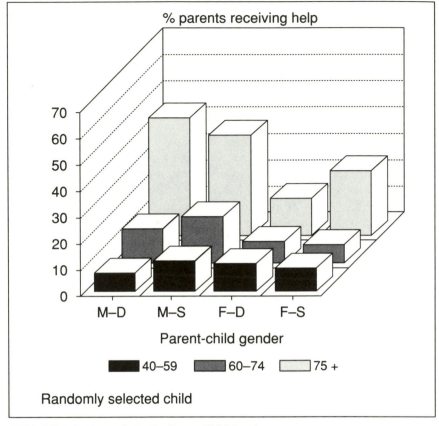

**FIGURE 2.2** Help to Parent by Parent-Child Gender

finding in our multivariate analysis that dyads involving daughters do not show more help to parents than dyads involving sons.

Turning to help from parents to adult children, the gender patterns are even more confused. For parents aged forty to fifty-nine, the highest incidence of parent-to-child help is from mothers to daughters, but the lowest level of help, that from fathers to sons, is not much lower. For the two older categories, the levels of help between mothers and daughters and between fathers and sons are very similar. In fact, in a multivariate analysis there are no significant differences by gender of either parent or child (Spitze and Logan 1992).

Thus, while there is some evidence that mothers *receive* more help than fathers, we find little evidence of differences between help given by daughters and sons, or help given by mothers and by fathers. A breakdown (not shown) by type of task reveals, not surprisingly, that daughters are more likely than sons to help parents with housekeeping, and sons are more likely to help with repairs and yard work. Help with shopping and errands is less gender-typed. The same pattern is found in the kinds of help given by mothers and fathers, though both mothers and fathers babysit in large proportions. Yet these manifestations of gendered activities do not sum up into the overall pattern that the literature and our own preconceptions had led us to anticipate.

This is a surprising conclusion. Is it likely due to some idiosyncracy in the Albany region or a quirk in our sample? We think not. More likely it is a matter of how we designed the study and what questions we asked. The key elements are the kind of sample (a random sample of the population rather than a convenience sample of disabled or frail elderly), the kind of measures (including the usual range of daily tasks required for independent living rather than focusing on intensive caregiving), the collection of information about all family members (male and female), and the inclusion of indicators of other characteristics of both parents and children (to be used in later multivariate analyses.)

In relation to the *receipt* of help, the Albany results are perfectly consistent with our own analysis of national-level data (Spitze and Logan 1990). We turned to the national sample of the Supplement on Aging of the National Health Interview Survey. The SOA provides sufficient information for persons aged sixty-five and over to examine gender differences in both living arrangements (i.e., coresidence with adult children) and the receipt of help from adult children. Here, briefly, is what we found.

1. With respect to coresidence (which we will return to below), we found that gender differences in living arrangements are mainly due to presence or absence of a spouse. Women are more likely than men to live alone or with other relatives. But of those with no spouse, living arrangements of men and women above age sixty-five are similar, and approximately equal proportions live alone or with relatives. Women who live alone live closer to children and receive more phone calls from children than do men, are involved in marginally more visits, and receive no more mail than do men living alone.

2. Women report more needs and functional limitations despite virtually identical subjective health assessments for both genders. They also receive more help in most age groups and living situations. This is true even for married respondents, suggesting that if women do remain married, they receive assistance from spouses and others to a slightly greater degree than men do (or at least they perceive higher help levels). Of course, older women are much less likely to be living with a spouse.

3. Importantly, however, multivariate analysis suggested that the higher levels of help received by women are mainly due to greater reported needs. At a given level of need, unmarried older women receive no more informal help than do older men, and there is only a small difference among married persons.

Thus, it would appear that the gender differences in *receipt* of help that do exist are mainly in the oldest age group, and that they are explained by marital status and direct indicators of need.

In regard to the lack of major gender differences in the *provision* of help, we believe that the key is our focus on routine help in a general population sample in contrast to the focus of many past studies on time-intensive care of frail elderly persons. Despite gender differences in caregiving to frail elderly parents, the kinds of routine help measured in our study are not provided any more by daughters than by sons. What does this result imply about the theories of gender differences outlined above?

First, consider the theory that women are culturally assigned to do certain kinds of household and nurturing tasks. Intensive caregiving, the focus of much of the literature, may be performed primarily by wives and daughters. Among the activities that we studied, there are also some signs of a gender-based division of labor: women do more housekeeping activities and men more repair and yard jobs, with men and women more equally sharing errands and shopping. Our results do not contradict the theory of assignment of specific tasks to women, but rather suggest that the broader category of "helping parents" in the usual form and intensity that this assistance is found is neither a male nor a female role.

Second, parents' own preferences may affect patterns of intensive caregiving. However there are certainly no cultural taboos, incest or otherwise, against sons providing the kinds of help that are most typical for our sample (e.g., shopping and transportation). Therefore the preponderance of women in the parent generation may have limited relevance to such help.

Third is the theory of competing responsibilities. As proposed in the literature, the typical assumption is that sons and daughters participate unequally in parent care but that this difference could be explained by differences in hours of employment. From this perspective, the lack of a gender difference in helping parents implies that outside employment has little impact on helping. This is an issue that we take up in detail in Chapter 4. But here again the key may be the way in which we measured help. It is hard to imagine that full-time employment would not conflict with the demands of being the primary caregiver of a disabled parent, but quite plausible that job demands could be balanced with occasional evening or weekend assistance.

Thus, our findings should be viewed as limiting the parameters within which theories of gender differences apply. In the introduction of their edited book on gender and caregiving, Dwyer and Coward (1992) point out that "caregiving" often refers to "care provided to an elderly person who has some degree of physical, mental, or emotional impairment that limits his or her independence and necessitates ongoing assistance" (p. 10). But, they say, it can also be conceived of as a "lifelong series of interactions between the caregiver and the care recipient" (p. 11). Previous discussions of gender differences in helping behavior, while couched in general terms of kin relations, have been supported mainly by data on caregiving to frail elderly parents. The applicability of these explanations may depend on where, along this continuum of definitions, we are looking. Furthermore, we have focused here on purely instrumental activities, and it is possible that gender differences are more pronounced when more subtle, less visible kinds of support are in question. For example, there may be differences in emotional support or management of help. All of these distinctions imply that concepts such as "help" or "caregiving" should be more finely specified. Theorists might need to distinguish a dimension like "emotional investment in help" from "routine assistance" or "intensive caregiving."

At the least, our findings demonstrate the importance of conducting intergenerational research on both genders, rather than on mothers and daughters only. We echo the admonitions of Horowitz (1992) that study designs include men, that they include a continuum of helping or caregiving situations, and that they study *all* helpers so that a full picture of parent-child helping relations can be provided.

## Living Together

Our examination of intergenerational help emphasized reciprocity, noting that the older generation is the main provider of support until late in life. We turn now to what is perhaps the most intense form of interdependency between generations: living together. Here the direction of support is hard to determine. Probably there is some degree of interdependence in most cases of coresidence. Still, assumptions are often made about which generation is more dependent and whose needs are being met by the living arrangement (Aquilino 1990). Coresidence by middle-aged parents is usually attributed to continuing or renewed dependence of children on parental resources (DaVanzo and Goldscheider 1990). Conversely, coresidence by older parents is attributed to parental dependency, viewing shared housing in the context of support and caregiving to the parent.

Trends in coresidence may shed some light on the relative roles of parent and child needs. The proportion of young adults residing with parents has increased since the 1960s (Glick and Lin 1986). Aquilino (1990) notes that adult children are tending to remain longer in the parental household and are more likely to return. These patterns have been attributed to such factors as rising divorce rates, increasing numbers of births to young unmarried women, slowed economic growth and higher unemployment, and high housing costs (Barber 1989; Glick and Lin 1986; Treas and Bengtson 1987), all of which emphasize child needs.

The implications of trends in parent characteristics, particularly of older parents, are less clear. Population aging, resulting in increased numbers of persons aged seventy-five and older, suggest greater need for shared housing by frail and widowed older parents. However, improved living standards of older persons may have reduced their needs for coresidence while also increasing their ability to assist with the housing needs of their children.

Coresidence by adult children and parents is not a "normative" pattern, as independent living is clearly preferred. Treas and Bengtson (1987), for example, note that older people prefer to live in their own homes and most adults oppose the idea of older people sharing a home with their grown children. Independence is similarly evident in the living arrangements of middle-aged parents and their adult children. The "empty nest," wherein middle-aged parents reside in households from which all of their children have left, has become typical in the twentieth century (Barber 1989). However, studies of housing arrangements show that although coresidence is not typical, neither is it uncommon. National survey data analyzed by Crimmins and Ingegneri (1990) reveal that the proportion of older (over age sixty-five) parents living with a child was 28 percent in 1962 and 18 percent in 1975 and 1984; other localized surveys have found similar proportions of older parents coresiding with an adult child (Kotlikoff and Morris 1990; Suitor and Pillemer 1988).

Aquilino (1990) has analyzed coresidence for a broader age range using the 1987–88 National Survey of Families and Households. Among parents who had a child or stepchild over age eighteen, and who were householders (only about 5 percent of coresident parents were living in a child's household), 30 percent had coresident adult children, including 45 percent of parents aged 45 to 54, 28 percent of those aged fifty-five to sixty-four, and 14 percent of parents aged sixty-five and older. Speare and Avery (1993) report similar figures based on 1984–86 Survey of Income and Program Participation (SIPP) data. Thus, parent-child coresidence declines with parental age. It also declines with the age of the child, from approximately 80 percent at age eighteen to nineteen to 15 percent for those aged twenty-five to twenty-nine (Glick and Lin 1986). But it is a relatively common situation throughout parental middle and later life, and, as Aquilino (1990) notes, the lifetime prevalence of coresidence is understated in these cross-sectional views. DaVanzo and Goldscheider (1990), for example, have found that "returns to the nest" are relatively common, though generally temporary.

Whose needs determine such housing decisions? An emerging literature suggests that it is the needs (or, more broadly, the circumstances) of children that account for coresidence with *both* middle-aged and older parents. This is also our view, based on research with the Albany sample. The key here is our ability to measure the needs and resources of both parents and children, and to use these together as predictors of coresidence. The literature on support networks makes much use of such indicators, and we introduce them as control variables in most of the multivariate analyses presented in later chapters. Therefore, we will discuss them in some detail here as they relate to coresidence.

## Parent Needs and Characteristics

Relevant parent characteristics include age, gender, marital status, family structure, and health and economic status. Gender differences might be expected from the kinkeeping role of women, discussed above. What differences there are, however, favor men. Crimmins and Ingegneri (1990) conclude that older men are more likely to coreside with children after sociodemographic characteristics, need, and child availability are controlled. Our results, based on the SOA cited earlier in this chapter, find no parent gender differences in living with a child after controls for marital status of the parent (Spitze and Logan 1990). Divorced fathers, however, have less contact of any kind with adult children, either social interaction or coresidence, than do their married counterparts (Cooney and Uhlenberg 1990). Moreover, children have limited contact with noncustodial parents (Furstenberg et al. 1983; Seltzer and Bianchi 1988), which may reduce commitments and assistance in later life (Smyer and Hofland 1982).

For older parents, widowhood is associated with living with a child (Aquilino 1990; Cooney 1989; Crimmins and Ingegneri 1990), though recent survey research has shown that children are helped financially by such arrangements as much as are their widowed parents (Waehrer and Crystal 1995). There is strong evidence that mothers in worse health are more likely to live with children (Wolf et al. 1991), and (based on data from the National Long-Term Care Survey) nearly 40 percent of the "frail elderly" share a household with an adult child (Stone et al. 1987). However, the frail elderly are a minority of older parents, and it does not appear that support needs of older parents are typical sources of coresidence. Speare et al. (1991), for example, conclude that although disability is related to living with others, there is relatively little change in living arrangements in response to changes in need for assistance. Aquilino (1990) also finds little evidence that adult children choose to live with parents in order to care for them.

Income is another indicator of parental need (or conversely, parental resources). The low-income elderly are more likely to share a household with others (Bross et al. 1987; Holden 1988), and living with children, particularly in the child's household, is negatively associated with parents' income and education (Aquilino 1990; Crimmins and Ingegneri 1990; Kotlikoff and Morris, 1990). There are racial differences in coresidence, controlling for other factors (Speare and Avery 1993). Further, the role of income and other resources may vary by race and by the resources of the elderly *relative to* those of other family members (Mutchler 1990).

## Child Needs and Characteristics

We have noted that coresidence declines with child age. Patterns in coresidence are also likely to be related to the marital status of children. Unmarried children are more likely to need housing assistance, or at least to have less need for independent housing, and are also more available to assist with parental housing needs. The never-married predominate in coresidence (Glick and Lin 1986; Suitor and Pillemer 1988), and Glick and Lin suggest that women coreside less often than men because of their earlier average marital age. Divorced/separated children are less likely than the never-married, but more likely than married children, to coreside with parents.

Having unmarried children may in fact be the most important predictor of whether older parents live with an adult child (Crimmins and Ingegneri 1990). Aquilino (1990) reports that 45 percent of parents with an unmarried adult child, versus only 2 percent of those whose children were all married, live with a child. He further notes that the likelihood of having an unmarried adult child is high for parents of all ages, ranging from 80 percent of parents younger than fifty-five to about half of parents aged sixty-five and older.

Availability of coresidence as an option for adult children may also be a function of family size. Number of children is positively related to the likelihood that a parent will live with some child (Aquilino 1990; Crimmins and Ingegneri 1990), but it is also likely to reduce the probability of coresidence by any particular child (Wolf et al. 1991). Children whose siblings may need parental housing (e.g., those who have unmarried siblings) may be less likely to live with parents themselves.

Evidence of differences in coresidence by gender of child is mixed. Some studies report that older persons, particularly those who are widowed, are more likely to live with a daughter (Troll et al. 1979), but Cooney (1989) finds that divorced or widowed women aged forty and older are somewhat more likely to live with sons. According to Aquilino (1990), coresidence is positively related to number of sons for parents under sixty-five, but negatively related for older parents. Having daughters is not related to coresidence (Spitze and Logan 1990).

There may be gender differences in the role of marital status, however, as some studies find that unmarried sons are more likely than unmarried daughters to return to the parental home (DaVanzo and Goldscheider 1990; Glick and Lin 1986). Wolf and Soldo (1988) show that older mothers most often live with unmarried sons, followed by unmarried daughters, married daughters, and married sons. Consistent with these results, Speare and Avery (1993) find unmarried daughters less likely to coreside than unmarried sons.

A related, and complicating, factor is whether children have children of their own. Unmarried children with dependent children presumably have greater need for coresidence, but also place additional burdens on parent resources and willingness. Divorced and separated sons more frequently coreside than do daughters, which may be because sons do not have custody of their children (Glick and Lin 1986). Coward and Cutler (1991) report that elders living in two-generation households are more likely to live with sons, while those in three-generation households are more likely to live with daughters. Madigan and Hogan (1990) find no evidence that single mothers move to live with or near kin, suggesting that there are limits to use of the parental home as a "safety net" (see also Speare and Avery 1993).

Other child characteristics relevant to their needs include health, employment, and socioeconomic status. These might either promote or reduce the odds of living with a parent, depending on which generation's needs count more. Children who are in poor health, are unemployed, or have low income have greater need for coresidence, but are also less able to help their parents. There are indications that the child's needs may play the greater role: returning to the parent's home is more common among children with lower incomes and greater financial dependence on parents (DaVanzo and Goldscheider 1990; see also Kotlikoff and Morris 1990).

This suggests that the appropriate question for research on coresidence may not be: Which parents live with adult children?; rather, it may be: Which adult children live with parents? Unfortunately, the evidence on this question is limited by the design of prior research. Research on parents in later life has used the older parent as the unit of analysis, predicting which parents coreside with children (e.g., Aquilino 1990; Crimmins and Ingegneri 1990). Wolf et al. (1991) have noted that such research usually has asymmetric information about parents and children, with details on parents and household members but only limited summary information about other kin (including noncoresident children). This obscures the role of child situations and needs. Research on nestleaving and return (e.g., Glick and Lin 1986; DaVanzo and Goldscheider 1990) has addressed the likelihood that adult children coreside with parents, but these studies focus on young adult children (aged eighteen to twenty-nine) and do not address the situations of older children and parents.

## Frequencies of Coresidence for Parents and Children

We turn now to the results from our Albany study. Figure 2.3 presents the percentage of parents who live with any of their adult children, taking into account the parent's age and marital status (a more complete cross tabulation by gender is found in Appendix C, table C.2.4). Overall, about 35 percent of persons aged forty through fifty-nine coreside with an adult child, falling to 29 percent in the sixties and 15 percent after age seventy. Thus, coresidence is least likely for parents who, by their age, would seem to have the most need for assistance from their children. Furthermore, although differences by marital status of parent are not great, they do not favor unmarried parents. This is also contrary to the pattern one would expect if parent needs were predominant, since presumably unmarried parents are more likely to be in need of company or housing.

In order to be able to take the child's characteristics into account, we again look at our sample of parent-child dyads, where each parent is paired with one randomly selected adult child. Figure 2.4 shows patterns of coresidence by the parent's age and the marital status of the

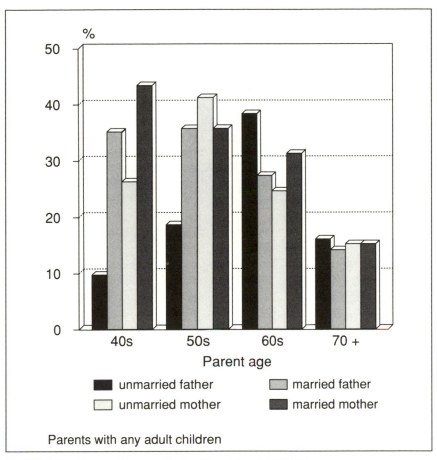

**FIGURE 2.3** Percent Parents with Any Coresiding Adult Child

child. (Appendix C, table C.2.5 provides more detailed breakdowns by the gender of both parent and child). There are dramatic differences between unmarried and married children: unmarried sons and daughters are much more likely to live with parents than are married children.

There is no consistent gender difference in these patterns until parents reach age seventy, when unmarried daughters become much less likely than unmarried sons to live with parents. Nor is there a consistent effect of the parent's gender.

Taken as a set, these findings show that it is relatively common throughout the life course, at least up to age seventy, for parents to live with an adult child. The likelihood of coresidence seems to depend most

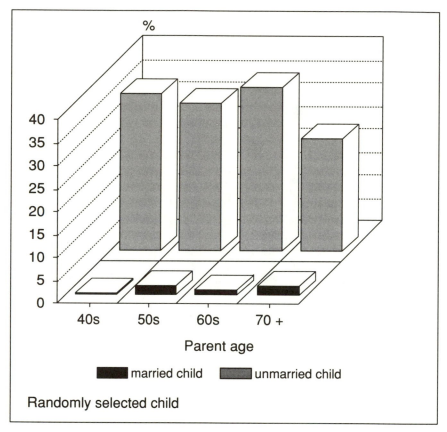

**FIGURE 2.4** Percent Coresiding by Child Marital Status

on the marital status of children. There is little indication, thus far, that parent characteristics and needs are a factor. To draw a more definitive conclusion, we now turn to a multivariate analysis.

Since coresidence is a dichotomous dependent variable, we use logistic regression techniques. This analysis includes indicators of both parent and child characteristics as reported by the parent. For the child, these are marital status, health, employment status, gender, number of minor children, step-relation or noncustodial history, and number of unmarried siblings. Parent variables are marital status, health, employment status, income, race, age, gender, and rural or suburban residence (with urban residence as the reference category). The employment status of both parent and child is represented as dummy variables for full-time and part-time work, with nonemployment as the reference category.

Data are analyzed separately for parents under sixty and sixty or above, to see if there are any changes in patterns over the life course. For example, one might expect child needs to dominate coresidence in earlier stages of the life course, as the child seeks to become established in adult life; later, parent needs might emerge as more important determinants. But if one generation's needs predominate throughout the life course, the same factors would predict coresidence for both younger and older parents.

Means and standard deviations for all variables in this analysis are presented in Appendix C, table C.2.6. Results of the logistic regressions are presented in Appendix C, table C.2.7 (for the likelihood of living with *any* adult child) and Appendix C table C.2.8 (for the likelihood of living with a *particular* child).

We first consider the models for younger parents, whose average age is about fifty-one. The number of unmarried adult children is a strong predictor of coresidence. Married and lower-income parents are more likely to have coresiding children. As we did in Chapter 1, we calculated the change in probability associated with each of these significant logit coefficients, to better understand their meaning (see table 2.2). For respondents under age sixty, the average probability of having any adult

**TABLE 2.2**
Predicted Probabilities of Any Child or of a Randomly Selected Child Living with Respondent

| **Respondents under age 60** | | **Respondents over age 60** | |
|---|---|---|---|
| Compared to the average probability of .356 of any child living with the respondent, if a respondent: | | Compared to the average probability of .236 of any child living with the respondent, if a respondent: | |
| Had one more unmarried child | .469 | Had one more unmarried child | .455 |
| Were married | .531 | | |
| Had an income of $10,000 more | .322 | Compared to the average probability of .116 of a randomly selected child living with the respondent, if the child: | |
| Compared to the average probability of .198 of a randomly selected child living with the respondent, if the child: | | Were married | .010 |
| | | Had one more child < 21 | .076 |
| | | Worked part-time | .419 |
| Were married | .009 | Had one more unmarried sibling | .156 |
| Had one more child < 21 | .117 | | |

child living in the household is .356, but having an additional unmarried child increases that probability substantially (to .469). If the parent is married, that increases the probability even more (to .531). Thus, marital status of parent and children are major factors in the coresidence process, and in both cases the implication is that children's, not parents' needs are being influential. Parental income decreases the probability. Adding $10,000 to the average parent's income would result in a slightly decreased probability of .322 of any child coresiding. This could mean that higher-income parents subsidize their children so that they can reside elsewhere, or that lower-income parents are more likely to desire to share housing with children.

The equation for coresidence with a *randomly selected* adult child allows us to assess more directly the effects of child characteristics. For parents under sixty, no parent characteristic is a significant predictor (see Appendix C, table C.2.8). The strongest predictor is child marital status. A randomly selected child of a parent under age sixty is dramatically less likely to coreside if he or she is married, with a decrease in the probability from .198 to .009. Children who have children of their own are also less likely to coreside with parents; the decrease with an additional minor child (grandchild of the respondent) is to .117, also a substantial effect.

Turning to parents above age sixty (average age sixty-nine), we find that no parent characteristic predicts the likelihood of living with *any child* (Appendix C, table C.2.7). The number of unmarried adult children is the only significant predictor of coresidence. Compared to the average probability of any child living with an older respondent, .236, having one additional unmarried child increases the probability to .455.

Finally, considering coresidence with a particular *randomly selected* child (Appendix C, table C.2.8), we find a pattern similar to that for parents under age sixty. Married children and those with minor children of their own are less likely to coreside. Compared to the average probability of .116 that a randomly selected child coresides, being married decreases that child's probability dramatically to .010. If the adult child has an additional child of his or her own, the probability decreases to .076. If the child works part-time, in comparison to the reference category of nonemployment, the probability increases dramatically to .419. This is surprising, and may reflect unusual and temporary circumstances of a child in school or otherwise in economic need. More surprisingly, however, those with more unmarried siblings are *more* likely to coreside. If the parent has one more unmarried child, the selected child's likelihood of coresiding increases from .116 to .156. We had expected there to be a crowding, or competition, factor operating here, such that those with more unmarried siblings were less likely to be able to find space in the parental home. Perhaps instead there are "family effects" operating, in which groups of siblings remain unmarried or become divorced or separated and remain attached to the parental home.

Taken together, these results suggest that parent needs play little part in coresidence, even for parents in older age groups. Children's characteristics are influential predictors of living with both middle-aged and older parents. This conclusion is reinforced as we investigate the division of household labor between generations in coresident households.

## Division of Household Tasks in Coresidence

Help to and from coresident children is very different from exchanges of help between people living in separate households. When parents and children occupy the same household, it is difficult to determine when the sharing of household tasks can be defined in terms of intergenerational help, or is simply normal and expected. Nevertheless, the division of household labor between parents and coresident adult sons and daughters is an indicator of their contributions to the household. We assume that coresidence is meeting parents' needs if children do a substantial share of housework, but that children are the beneficiaries if parents do most of it. This detailed information on arrangements within the household has not been included in previous studies of coresidence.

Frequencies of household tasks performed by the respondent (who is the parent), the respondent's spouse (if any), and each child are based on the total of all tasks performed per month (summed across six categories of tasks). The share of household tasks performed by the child were computed by dividing the child's housework task total by the sum of the respondent's, spouse's, and all coresident children's total household task frequencies.

The results of these calculations are presented in figure 2.5. Regardless of the parent's age and the gender of the adult child, we find that children do considerably less than a quarter of household tasks. Daughters perform more tasks than sons, but even for daughters the contribution is far below that of parents. Perhaps most telling, the total number of tasks performed by parents—even very elderly parents—is greater for those with a coresident adult child than for comparable parents who have no child living at home (not shown in figure; see Ward et al. 1992).

These data are consistent with other recent analyses. South and Spitze (1994), using NSFH data, report that coresident adult sons increase mothers' housework time by two hours per week, while daugh-

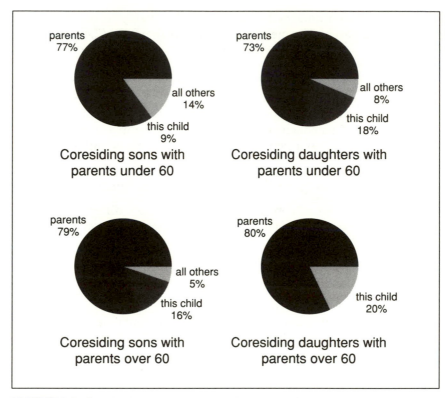

parents
77%

all others
14%

this child
9%

Coresiding sons with
parents under 60

parents
73%

all others
8%

this child
18%

Coresiding daughters with
parents under 60

parents
79%

all others
5%

this child
16%

Coresiding sons with
parents over 60

parents
80%

this child
20%

Coresiding daughters with
parents over 60

**FIGURE 2.5** Contributions to Housework by Parents and Children

ters decrease mothers' and fathers' time by two hours. However, these are minor adjustments compared to the hours performed by parents, particularly mothers. Spitze and Ward (1995), using the same data set, find that in households with only one coresident adult child and no other nonparental adults, the parent reports the adult child to do between 13 percent (sons) and 22 percent (daughters) of total housework. Again, these figures are strikingly similar to those in figure 2.5.

## Discussion

Our results bear strongly on the tendency in the gerontology literature to characterize routine relations between adult children and their parents as typically more dependent and unidirectional than they are. A number of studies of "caregiving" have used that term very loosely and imprecisely (see discussion in Cantor 1991). Sometimes a caregiver is defined as anyone who provides any service to an elderly parent (e.g.,

Walker et al. 1989), and parents are assumed to be dependent on such care. Earlier we discussed the range of activities that could be viewed as caregiving, including, in its broadest sense, a "lifelong series of interactions." (Dwyer and Coward 1992). We found that parents are much more likely to help adult children with housekeeping and errands and about as likely to help them with heavy repairs and yard work than to receive such help, for most of the ages studied here. One would not, however, think of describing these relations as ones in which the older parent is a caregiver for the healthy adult child. A certain amount of infrequent but regular help with tasks of everyday living characterizes many of these relationships, and such help is not necessarily predicated on frailty or inability to do the task oneself.

Help, whether it takes the form of shared housing or interhousehold assistance with tasks, is frequently a normal component of relations involving regular interaction. Parents and children may shop together, build a deck together, or cook a meal together just as they might sit down in the living room and chat. Helping occurs in a range of situations varying from care for a totally dependent elder (or adult child, or infant grandchild) to the incidental help that occurs as people interact. It clearly occurs in many situations that do not involve dire need or frailty. A suspicion that this was so led to our decision to gather information on help to the respondent by asking how the respondent gets things done, rather than by prefacing it with a question about difficulty or need, as was done, for example, in the 1984 Supplement on Aging to the National Health Interview Survey. Restricting data-gathering on helping to those expressing needs unnecessarily narrows the focus of research on helping, and on intergenerational relations in general. It also biases that research toward a focus on help to the frail elderly, since much of parents' help to children probably would not be measured were such a screening question used.

Our main purpose in this chapter is to reinforce our argument that older parents are not generally the demanding, dependent partner in intergenerational relations, as popular and scientific accounts sometimes portray them. Recent research on caregiving and on "women in the middle" often implies that parent care is a typical and expected part of the filial relationship, a "normative family experience" (Brody 1985), and much recent attention has been devoted to "caregiver burden."

Parents' help to adult children is more common than children's help to parents for most ages. Although part of this difference is explained by the fact that babysitting goes only in one direction, babysitting cannot be discounted and there are differences in some other kinds of help as well. This finding is consistent with an image of continuity in the parent-child relationship over the life course. Parents' efforts to meet children's needs in childhood are continued in many cases throughout life, while children may never be called upon to help parents to the same degree. We acknowledge that children's help to parents during emergencies near the end of life would not show up in an analysis of routine help patterns such as this. But such assistance should not overly determine our sense of what parent-child support is all about. First, we have limited evidence of the incidence and duration of such help. Second, there is every reason to believe that parents have offered similar emergency help to children in earlier years, not measured in our study. Third, financial assistance, not studied here, has been shown to follow similar patterns (Rossi and Rossi 1990, p. 414).

Analysis of coresidence reinforces this point of view. With few exceptions, such parent characteristics as health, marital, and employment status have little bearing on coresidence in either middle or later life. Child characteristics are more important predictors of coresidence. In particular, regardless of parent and child ages, never-married and, to a lesser extent, divorced or separated children dominate coresident situations. It is children who show the greater need for parent's help in providing shelter, or who have less reason to desire independent housing, who are most likely to coreside with middle-aged and older parents. Information on division of labor within the household also clearly reflects whose household is being shared and whose needs are being met.

Recognition of a primary role for child needs does not exclude a role for other factors, including parental need. There are significant effects of parent age on help to and from children and of the parent's gender on help from child to parent. These partly reflect parents' needs. Clearly also there are situations in which coresidence represents caregiving for older parents (though this appears to be a minority situation). Researchers should look more carefully at the prevalence of this form of coresidence and at the factors that distinguish it from the more typical situation. Nonetheless, it appears to be the needs and circumstances of adult children that most often trigger coresidence.

A second major finding in this chapter is that gender effects are more mixed and more modest than we had expected based on past literature. Gender effects differentiate between fathers and mothers rather than highlighting the mother-daughter pair. Further, coresidence patterns show no clear-cut gender patterns. Unmarried mothers are no more likely than unmarried fathers to coreside, and unmarried daughters coreside in similar numbers to unmarried sons until parents reach age seventy. Beyond that point, they are less likely to coreside than are sons. This is not surprising in light of our findings regarding help. Since coresidence seems to reflect help to children more than the reverse, and the only gender differences we found in help were to older mothers, there is little reason to expect gender differences in coresidence by gender of parent or child.

The lack of gender differences raises as many questions as it answers. Doesn't the number of children, and especially daughters, affect a parent's chances of having contact and exchanging help with the younger generation? Don't daughters play a special role in these exchanges, and isn't their participation undermined by the broad social changes— divorce and changing gender roles—that are often thought to disrupt the family as a whole? In the next two chapters we will analyze how family size and composition, women's labor force participation, and divorce affect intergenerational contact and help. As we probe these effects, we will gain a much clearer view of the role that gender plays in structuring intergenerational relations.

# 3

# Family Composition and Intergenerational Ties

*Sociologists have speculated that having more children, particularly daughters, has a payback in old age. Declining family size, therefore, is expected to reduce the chances of receiving assistance in later life. We show that sons and daughters are about equally important to visiting with and helping parents. In contrast, daughters talk on the phone more with their parents. There are effects of number of children on the total amount of contact and help experienced by parents, but these are partially compensated by closer ties with only children.*

■ The American family is changing quickly, as manifested in declining fertility, rising divorce rates, and changes in gender relations such as the increase in women's employment. How do these changes affect relations between parents and adult children? We start in this chapter with family composition. How might decreases in the average number of children in a family, coupled with changing expectations regarding gender roles, affect relations between parents and grown children?

This issue is important for both theoretical and practical reasons. Theoretically, the question is how the composition of a group (here, the family) affects the behavior of its individual members. This question has been raised by sociologists from Georg Simmel to Peter Blau. On the policy side, it has been argued that aging parents who have few children or no daughters are at a disadvantage in the receipt of informal services and emotional support and will require more formal services (Horowitz 1985; Montgomery 1992). This thesis predicts acute policy impacts when people with low or declining fertility approach old age early in the twenty-first century (Dwyer and Coward 1992; Eggebeen 1992). But most parents today still have several children. In our Albany sample, 85 percent had at least one living child. Of those respondents who had at least one *adult* child, about half (50.7 percent) had either two or three children, and only about 10 percent had just one child (and we find the

56

same result if we turn the sample around to ask how many siblings our respondents with living parents have).

Peter Townsend (1968; see also Crimmins and Ingegneri 1990) raised the issue of family structure almost thirty years ago in relation to living arrangements. In the U.S. case he found some evidence of what he termed "compensation" across both gender and number of children. For example, those with an only daughter were particularly likely to share her household. What is the origin of such effects, if they exist? To organize our thinking, we draw on two models of how alternative potential helpers interact, taken from the theoretical literature on support systems for the elderly (Cantor 1979; Dono et al. 1979). For simplicity we discuss these models as though the parent were the recipient of children's help, or the beneficiary of coresidence. They are presented this way in most studies. But we have already shown that help flows in both directions, and these models can also be applied to help from parents to children.

The *additive model* presumes that different providers are functionally equivalent. If more are available, there is a higher probability of getting help from at least one of them. Applied to our problem, this would suggest that the main effect of family structure would be through size: the larger the family, the more help and contact a parent would receive. At the extreme, of course, a person with no children can find no support from this source, but there may be noticeable differences even between people with one and two children. If the behaviors of each child are independent of one another, the parent with an only child has a greater risk that the child will have moved out of the area, will have other competing commitments, or will not be interested in helping the parent.

The *substitution model* suggests that behaviors of each provider are not independent after all. If there is more than one potential provider, each is presumed to fill in where needed, and if one is unable to help, then another will substitute. Applied to family composition, this model predicts much smaller effects of family size. Even an only child may meet parents' needs for contact or help, in the absence of a potential substitute. As Townsend (1968, 1973) put it, "a child in a small family tends to 'make good' the inadequacy of numbers." This concept is at the heart of the principle of substitution. To the degree that substitution is operating, the main effects are not on what the parent receives but on the burden placed on each child. Each child in a larger family would be expected to have less responsibility.

Let us see what happens when we add gender to our discussion. Most theorists believe that there is a hierarchy of potential helpers, based on the recipient's preferences and on the capacities of helpers (Litwak 1985). Suppose (despite the absence of gender effects in the previous chapter) that there is a preference for help from daughters (or that daughters are more willing to help than are sons). In the additive model, the implication would be that number of siblings is less consequential than number of daughters. A parent with more daughters would be expected to receive more support. (The behavior of each child would remain unaffected by family composition, either defined in terms of number or gender of children.) In the substitution model, however, a son might be expected to fill in when a daughter is not available. Therefore again, neither family size nor number of daughters would have strong effects on total helping. But the hierarchy of preferences would mean that children with sisters will help less than children who have no sister.

Substitution of sons for daughters could occur even where there are strong norms related to gender roles. Suppose that gender differences are due to differential socialization of male and female children regarding gender or filial norms. Some researchers have suggested that family structure would influence the degree of sex-typing in that socialization (White and Brinkerhoff 1981). If there are no daughters, sons might be more likely to be socialized into nurturant roles, and to be expected to perform traditionally female-typed jobs around the house. Or, from another direction, suppose that daughters are emotionally closer to parents than sons. It might also be the case that sons in families with no daughters also tend to become closer to parents.

Now let us consider the application of these models to help from parents to children and to social contact that does not imply helping, in the form of phoning and visiting. Parallel hypotheses could be developed to link a parent's help to children to the number of children. An additive model would anticipate more total help given by parents with more children. A substitution model, by contrast, might recognize some ceiling on a parent's time and resources and expect the amount of help given to any particular child to depend on the number of other children. For example, Aldous and Klein (1991) describe a "familistic" model, according to which parents of large families value family contact and thus would, if anything, have as much or more contact with each child in such a family as in a smaller family (this leads to the same expectations as the additive model). On the other hand, their "size constraints" model presumes that large families—because of the pressures of managing a complex household—are less nurturing and lead to weakened ties between parents and children in adulthood. We do not focus on these social psychological processes here, but we will provide some information on the relation between family size and family norms and sentiments later in this chapter. Size constraints could reduce a parent's attention to each of many children, even without differences in family values.

## Previous Evidence of Structural Effects

Effects of family composition can be studied at two levels. More important from a policy perspective is the total social support enjoyed by parents. This is the bottom line on which the need for formal supports may hinge (see Chapter 6 for an explicit analysis of the relation between informal and formal support). From the standpoint of sociological theory, we are more interested in the processes underlying the bottom line result: how is the behavior of one sibling contingent on the number and gender of other siblings? The evidence is somewhat limited at both levels.

One of the earliest studies building on Townsend's discussion of family structure was by Matthews (1987b). She approached the question as a set of choices in how sibling groups divide the labor involved in helping parents. She identified four patterns: no one helping; all helping equally; unevenly divided, with all helping; and unevenly divided, with not all helping. She found that larger families and families including brothers were more likely to fall into the latter two categories (Matthews and Rosner 1988.) These results imply both a size effect (in larger families, some siblings rely on others to provide care) and a gender effect (brothers, it is assumed, may rely on their sisters to provide care). In a later study using a sample of lone sisters and their brothers, Matthews (1995) found that sisters were typically considered to be in charge and that, to some extent, contributions to brothers were discounted.

More recently, several other researchers have investigated structural effects on help to elderly parents (Coward and Dwyer 1990; Dwyer and Coward 1991; Spitze and Logan 1990), as well as help and contact between samples including middle-aged and older parents and their adult children (Aldous and Klein 1991; Eggebeen 1992; Rossi and Rossi 1990).

We analyzed the effects of family structure on total support exchanged between parents and adult children using the 1984 Supplement on Aging, based on parents aged sixty-five and over (Spitze and Logan 1990). We included as dependent variables the frequency of visiting and of telephone contact, and receipt of regular help by parents from all children, as well as the likelihood of coresiding with a child. Results varied among these forms of social support. We found that having at least one daughter is key for receipt of assistance, but that additional children (male or female) made little difference. For phoning, apparently a female activity, having more daughters leads to more contact.

Having more children, both daughters and sons, positively affects the frequency of visiting and the probability of coresidence.

A more recent paper by Eggebeen (1992) analyzed data from the National Survey of Families and Households (NSFH) for respondents with one or more noncoresident adult children (aged nineteen or above). Thus, his sample was more diverse in age than the Supplement on Aging. His dependent variable was whether the respondent has received any help with transportation, repairs to home or car, or other work around the house from any child during the past month. Predictors included a set of dummy variables to represent family composition: an only daughter was the reference category, with other codes representing only son, two or more sons, two or more daughters, two or three mixed, and four or more mixed. All categories of children provided significantly more help than only daughters, with the exception of two or more daughters. Eggebeen concluded that "number of children is more important than their gender composition." It should be noted that this is a subsample including many middle-aged and healthy parents. The results of this and the previous study differ somewhat on gender patterns, but both show some evidence of positive effects of having more children on some forms of support.

Also using the NSFH, Montgomery and Hirshorn (1991) report percentages of respondents receiving household help by race, gender, and composition of children. Like Eggebeen, they find clearer effects of number than gender, although those with an only son appear to be particularly disadvantaged.

Using their Boston-area data for parents and adult children from three generations, Rossi and Rossi analyzed both contact and helping behavior. They found generally negative effects of family size on contact between parents and individual adult children and nonsignificant effects of family size on help to parents. They suggest that a large family may provide a different experience for parents than for children (1990, p. 494). For parents, it may imply closely spaced pregnancies, financial strains, and limited time for marital interaction or interacting with each child. From the child's point of view, however, Rossi and Rossi find that those who grew up in large families assess them retrospectively as having been more cohesive than smaller families.

For additional evidence on the helping behavior of individual children, we turn again to research on elderly parents (the National Long-Term Care Survey and the National Survey of Informal Caregivers). Coward and Dwyer (1990; also Dwyer and Coward 1991) analyzed both caregiving time and involvement in specific tasks of daily living (the ADL and IADL scales, indices heavily weighted toward personal caregiving). They categorized families as having an only son, only daughter, single-gender (sons), single-gender (daughters), and mixed-gender composition. They found both gender and size effect differences. Only children are much more likely to provide support than others (as predicted by the substitution model), but daughters are more likely than sons to do so even in only-child or single-gender networks (thus revealing a gender preference).

### Results from the Albany Study

The Albany survey allows us to replicate previous studies of the effects of family composition on support exchanged between parents and all children combined. This is our starting point. Subsequently we will focus on relations between a parent and a particular child. We measure social support in three ways: personal contact between parents and children, telephone contact, and help to or from adult children with routine daily household tasks. These represent two of the dimensions in the Bengtson model: functional and associational solidarity (Bengtson and Harootyan 1994). We focus on noncoresident adult children (aged twenty-one and above) because our measures of contact and help presuppose separate residences.

Helping was discussed in the previous chapter. To measure contact, we asked respondents how often they visit with the parent or child in question "in your home or his/her's or somewhere else?" We also asked how often they talk to the parent/child on the telephone. Because each question was asked about each of a potentially large number of parents and children, we chose not to ask about who initiated the contact, which would have doubled the number of questions. These questions are similar to those used by Rossi and Rossi (1990), and somewhat different from those in the NSFH. The latter survey asked how often the respondent saw the parent/child during the past twelve months, and how often the respondent contacted a parent (was contacted by a child) by letter or telephone call during that period. Some researchers using these data have analyzed visits and calls or letters separately (e.g., Bulcroft and Bulcroft 1991), while some have combined all forms of contact into one measure (e.g., Cooney and Uhlenberg 1990).

We also gathered data on sending and receiving cards and letters from each adult child, but have chosen not to analyze these data here for the following reasons. First, the frequency of mail contact is much lower than other contact; for example, mail from respondents to parents has approximately the same frequency per year as do phone calls per month. Second, while one might suspect that sending mail is an alternative to other forms of contact due to distance or cost, in fact the correlation between mail and phoning is near zero and nonsignificant, and the correlation with visiting is low and positive. Third, when we ran regressions using mail contact as the dependent variable, explained variance was extremely low. Therefore, we focus here on telephone contact and visiting in person.

## Respondents' Reports on Relations with All Adult Children

The first set of analyses concerns parents' reports about contact and help exchanged with *all* adult children. We use the same sample of respondents who have one or more noncoresident adult children as in Chapter 2, yielding a sample size of 792. Dependent variables for contact and help are coded as follows. The frequency of visits in person (at either the respondent's home, the parent's home, or elsewhere) and frequency of telephone conversations between respondent and parent were originally gathered in eight categories, ranging from never, to once a year or less, up to once a day or more. We recode them here to represent monthly number of interactions with each adult child. We then sum monthly contacts across adult children to derive measures of total contact. The other two dependent variables represent weekly hours of help from the parent to each adult child, and from each adult child to the parent. These are also summed across adult children.

Key independent variables for this analysis include number of noncoresident adult children (we also decompose this into number of sons and number of daughters) and family composition categories (only son, only daughter, one son and one daughter, two or more sons, two or more daughters, and three or more of mixed gender).

Other independent variables include respondent's gender and marital status (in four dummy variable combinations), respondent's age, health (coded from 1 = very poor to 5 = excellent), family income (in $1,000s), employment status (full-time, part-time or nonemployed), race (black vs. nonblack), and urban (vs. rural or suburban) residence.

First, we present basic information on patterns of contact and help by family structure. In table 3.1 we show that amount of contact appears to increase with number of children in almost a linear fashion. (This relationship is displayed very clearly in figure 3.1, for visiting.) Patterns for help given and received are not so linear. Respondents receive approximately the same amount of total help from any number of children ranging from one to five; the figure for six or more is slightly higher (despite the deletion of one outlier). They give less help in the case of an

**TABLE 3.1**

Mean Monthly Contact and Weekly Hours of Help to and from All Noncoresident Adult Children, by Number of Noncoresident Adult Children

|  | Visit | Phone | Help parent | Help child | N |
|---|---|---|---|---|---|
| One child | 6.42 | 10.38 | .99 | 1.75 | 174 |
| Two children | 12.26 | 22.72 | 1.28 | 3.41 | 246 |
| Three children | 17.06 | 30.52 | 2.20 | 3.01 | 168 |
| Four children | 22.91 | 37.65 | 1.45 | 3.61 | 91 |
| Five children | 32.86 | 55.02 | 1.20 | 6.45 | 50 |
| Six + children | 36.67 | 55.91 | 3.00 | 4.04 | 43 |
| Total | 16.09 | 27.57 | 1.53 | 1.75 | 772 |

only child, but there is little difference in help given between families with two children and those with more than two.

Results for contact are more consistent with the additive than the substitution model. But on the whole, we see only slight evidence of additive effects for helping. It seems, rather, that parents receive about one or two hours of help per week, and give about three hours of help per week, regardless of the number of children.

Let us see how these results are affected by taking into account the gender of children. Table 3.2 compares various categories of number and gender of children. Now there are not only differences between contact and help, but also differences between visiting and phoning. Parents with one son or with one daughter report the least number of visits; those with both a son and a daughter report about twice as many; and those with three or more children report about four times as many visits. Visiting conforms to an additive model with no gender hierarchy (see figure 3.2). By contrast, phoning reveals an additive model in which gender also counts. Parents with one daughter report more calls than those with one son; those with two daughters report more calls than those with a son and a daughter (in turn, more than those with two sons), and those with three or more children report the most calls. (We will return to the issue of gender and telephoning at a later point in this discussion.) Again the averages for helping show no consistent trend.

Next we turn to a multivariate analysis of contact and help between parents and all adult children. The mean values of relevant variables are provided in Appendix C, table C.3.1. The average parent respondent, who is sixty-one years of age, has 2.7 noncoresident adult children and experiences sixteen visits a month and twenty-seven telephone calls

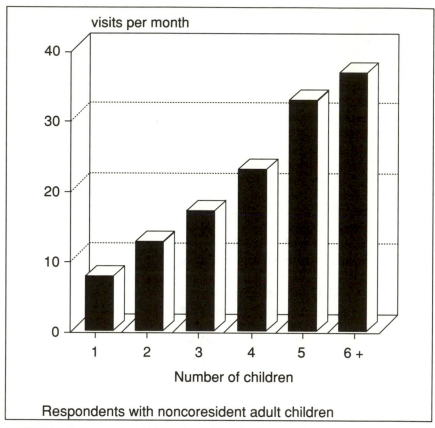

**FIGURE 3.1** Respondents' Visits with Children by Number of Noncoresident Adult Children

from all adult children combined. (These visits may include some combined visits involving more than one child at a time.) Respondents give three hours of help a week to adult children and receive under two hours.

Appendix C, table C.3.2 reports coefficients for regression equations in which the indicator of family structure is number of noncoresident children. The significant linear effect of number of children in every equation is supportive of an additive model. For each additional noncoresident adult child, parents experience five to six more visits per month and nine more phone calls, and they give and receive approximately one-half hour more of help each week.

**TABLE 3.2**
Mean Monthly Contact and Weekly Hours of Help to and from All Noncoresident Adult Children, by Family Structure of Those Children

|  | Visit | Phone | Help parent | Help child | N |
|---|---|---|---|---|---|
| One son | 6.11 | 8.60 | 1.19 | 2.29 | 91 |
| One daughter | 6.75 | 12.33 | .77 | 1.17 | 83 |
| One son, one daughter | 12.36 | 21.67 | .71 | 3.44 | 135 |
| Two + daughters | 16.81 | 33.08 | 2.65 | 3.81 | 82 |
| Two + sons | 10.93 | 19.19 | 1.24 | 2.40 | 80 |
| Three + mixed gender | 24.27 | 40.43 | 1.98 | 3.99 | 301 |

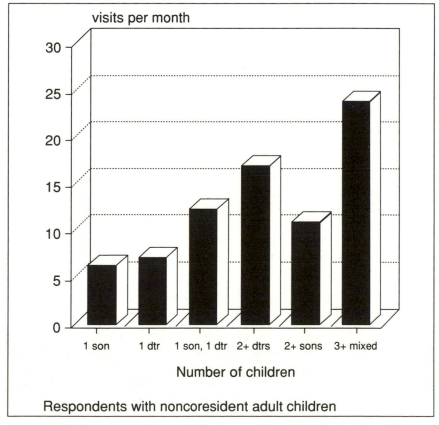

**FIGURE 3.2** Respondents' Visits with Children by Number and Gender of Adult Children

Do gender effects appear in the multivariate analyses? These are tested in two ways in the equations reported in table C.3.3. First, number of children is decomposed into number of sons and number of daughters. This procedure uncovers a gender difference in phoning, with a much larger coefficient for daughters than for sons, but no gender difference for visiting or helping (the differences in coefficients for daughters and sons are small and in opposite directions).

Second, dummy variables representing family composition (as in table 3.2) are introduced, where all categories are compared to the "one son and one daughter" reference group. These confirm previous results regarding visiting and phoning. Compared to the "son and daughter" reference group, parents with only a son or only a daughter have six or seven fewer visits per month, those with two or more sons or two or more daughters have the same number (neither coefficient is significant), and those with three or more children have significantly more visits. This is a straightforward additive effect. But results for phoning show a strong gender bias in which both genders count but daughters count more than sons. Results for help are less conclusive. Having two or more daughters is the only structure that provides parents with significantly more help than the reference category of one son and one daughter (though the coefficient for three or more children is in the same direction), and neither "only child" category has a negative coefficient. Only daughters receive less help from parents than the reference category (here, the coefficient for only sons is in the same direction but not significant).

In brief, the multivariate analyses reinforce the patterns seen in the bivariate tables (3.1 and 3.2). The additive model applies clearly to visiting and phoning, with an evident gender effect for phoning. Gender differences do not appear in the exchange of help. Number of children affects help given and received by parents, but not in the simple linear pattern presumed by the additive model.

## Respondents' Reports on Relations with Randomly Selected Adult Children

We conclude from these results that, at least for a sample including the whole age range of parents with adult children, family size has important effects on contact, but much less clear effects on the exchange of help. Phoning is the only activity measured here that we find to be gender-typed (though surely if we looked more closely at types of assistance, comparing house cleaning to yard work for example, other gender differences would be evident). We now confront the question of what micro-level processes underlie these patterns. Specifically, is the contact between a parent and a given adult child unrelated to family composition, thus yielding the additive effect of number of children? And more important, is the weakness of the additive model for helping a consequence of substitution, where children give and receive less help if they have more siblings?

To deal with these questions, we analyze information on specific parent-child pairs, randomly selecting one adult child for each parent respondent. This means that children in smaller families are more likely to appear in our analysis, but it avoids the tendency in some studies for parents to report on a favorite, or particularly helpful, adult child.

The following analyses are parallel to those reported above, with two exceptions. First, we are able to report separate results for sons and daughters, since we are focusing on individual children now. As noted above, the frequency of visits in person (at either the respondent's home, the parent's home, or elsewhere) and frequency of telephone conversations between respondent and parent were originally gathered in eight categories, ranging from never, to once a year or less, up to once a day or more. Appendix C, table C.3.4 provides the frequencies of visiting and phoning at this level of detail for both sons and daughters in our sample. In our analyses, these are translated into contacts per month.

Second, we can include the adult child's characteristics as predictors in the multivariate analysis. These include travel time between the parent's and child's residence, in hours; dummy variables representing the child's marital status (married, reference category; never married; divorced/separated/remarried; and widowed); health; employment status (full-time, part-time, nonemployed as reference category); child's number of minor children at home; whether the child was ever noncustodial with reference to this respondent parent; and whether this child is a stepchild of the respondent. We include measures of the child's sibling structure, which are parallel to those in the above analysis except that these measures refer to all siblings rather than simply those who are adult and noncoresiding (that is, we test the effect of existence of other children, even minor children who live with the parent, on the given child's relationship to the parent).

Again, we begin by examining overall averages of contact and help for different family sizes. Table 3.3 shows that parents report no more visits or phone calls with only children compared to children with various numbers of siblings. As figure 3.3 illustrates for visiting, only sons have about as many visits as any other category of sons, and only daughters have the highest average number of visits. But this is far from a linear pattern. Among sons, the highest number of visits is for those

**TABLE 3.3**

Mean Monthly Contact and Weekly Hours of Help to and from Randomly
Selected Noncoresident Adult Child, by Number of Siblings

|  | Visit | | Phone | | Help parent | | Help child | |
|---|---|---|---|---|---|---|---|---|
|  | Sons | Dtrs | Sons | Dtrs | Sons | Dtrs | Sons | Dtrs |
| Only child | 7.19 | 9.12 | 10.15 | 14.31 | 2.37 | 1.61 | 2.54 | 1.44 |
| One sibling | 4.11 | 6.44 | 7.66 | 14.57 | .32 | .73 | 1.68 | 1.90 |
|   Brother | 3.55 | 5.93 | 7.44 | 13.64 | .06 | .24 | .76 | .84 |
|   Sister | 4.58 | 6.90 | 7.85 | 15.42 | .53 | 1.23 | 2.44 | 2.92 |
| Two siblings | 6.58 | 6.41 | 9.74 | 12.37 | .56 | .75 | 1.64 | 1.65 |
| Three siblings | 3.97 | 6.97 | 5.87 | 13.25 | .22 | .38 | .77 | .63 |
| Four siblings | 7.28 | 7.92 | 9.85 | 15.35 | .24 | .31 | .57 | 1.19 |
| Five + siblings | 4.25 | 6.92 | 8.55 | 10.07 | .10 | .35 | .48 | .44 |
| Total | 5.30 | 7.00 | 8.38 | 13.32 | .41 | .51 | .94 | 1.04 |

who have four siblings; among daughters, the highest number of phone
calls is also for those with four siblings. Our interpretation of these data
is that there are no real differences on these dimensions of social support.

There is, however, some evidence of a substitution effect on help to
and from parents. For both sons and daughters, an only child is reported
to provide substantially more help than is a child with other siblings.
There is also a tendency for only sons to receive more help from parents
than do sons with one or two siblings, and the average value drops further for those with three or more siblings.

Looking more closely at who these siblings are, brothers or sisters,
allows us to explore more directly the gender preferences that may oper-
ate in intergenerational ties—or more precisely, the substitution of sons
for daughters. Let us suppose that there were a bias toward contact and
help with daughters rather than sons. A gender-specific substitution
might imply that a son who has no sisters would fill in for the missing
daughter by providing more contact and help. There is no such pattern.
If anything, both sons and daughters with a single sister help parents
more and receive substantially more help than do those with one
brother, and they also (though the differences are smaller) have more
contact with parents.

Let us see how these findings hold up in a multivariate analysis. We
report means and standard deviations for this analysis in Appendix C,
table C.3.5. Parent characteristics were discussed in relation to the earlier
analysis. The average adult child has 2.4 siblings (including nonadult

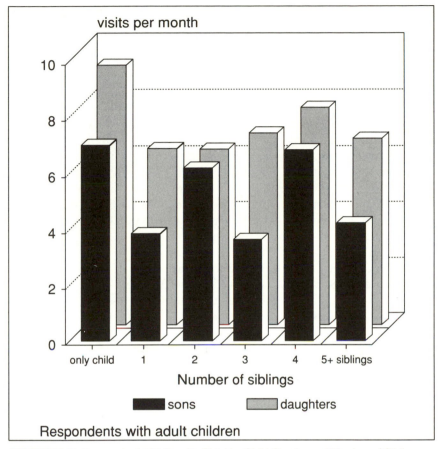

**FIGURE 3.3** Respondents' Visits with Child by Child Gender and Number of Siblings

siblings, in this analysis), and the majority are married. The average travel time to an adult child is around three hours, but this reflects a skewed distribution; the median travel time is one-half hour. The means reveal slight differences in favor of daughters for visiting and greater differences for phoning, but help to and from children is similar across gender of child.

We present the regression equation for daughters in Appendix C, table C.3.6, and the regression equation for sons in Appendix C, table C.3.7. The regression equations provide information on the effects of a wide range of variables, including several (employment, marital status, custody of children, etc.) that we focus on in Chapter 4. Here we limit our attention to the family structure variables. There are no effects of number of siblings on visiting or phoning for sons or daughters. Children do not visit or phone their parents less if they are part of a large family, or more if they are part of a small family. This result is consistent with the tabulations reviewed above, and with the strong additive effects of number of children for parents' total contact with children.

Both sons and daughters receive less help from parents if they have more siblings, however, suggesting that there is a kind of ceiling effect on the total amount of time that parents will choose to devote to helping their children. And sons give less help when they have more siblings, which is in conformity with substitution (though it is unclear why there would not be a similar substitution effect for daughters). These effects offer some explanation for the very small impact of number of children on total help received by parents: the more children there are, the less each son does. (Conversely, the fewer children there are, the more each son does, compensating for small family size.)

As in the earlier analysis, we experimented with several different ways of taking into account the gender composition of families. Appendix C, table C.3.8, presents results for three alternative approaches, in which sons and daughters have been combined into a single sample and interaction terms between gender and sibling structure are introduced. In the first panel, family composition is measured simply as number of siblings. In the second panel, it is decomposed into number of sons and number of daughters. And in the third panel, it is represented as a set of dummy variables (only child, one brother, one sister, and two or more siblings of either gender).

No new results emerge from these analyses. Differences between sons and daughters are found mainly for phoning. Family composition variables have effects mainly for exchange of help. There are no theoretically interpretable interactions between family composition and gender, and certainly nothing that would reflect gender-specific substitution.

## Respondents' Reports on Relations with Parents

Another way to examine these questions is to focus on those survey respondents who have living parents, and to base the analysis on their reports of contact and help exchanged with their parents. This sample only partly overlaps with the sample analyzed in the preceding sections, and it is considerably smaller (460 cases compared to nearly 800 in the preceding analyses). We have decided to present results for this sample despite some reservations: the sample is smaller and therefore less reliable, it does not encompass a full age range of adult children (it excludes those under forty), the analytical steps are a direct replication of material that we have already reported and may therefore seem unduly repetitive, and the results do not fall into a neat pattern.

On the other hand, when respondents are treated as adult children, we can take advantage of survey information on their values and sentiments, which some theorists have considered to be central to any potential effects of family size. Where results from this sample conform to those found above, we can gain confidence in the robustness of conclusions. And where findings differ, we must consider whether the contradictions reveal problems with measurement that might lead parents to report different relations with children than do children with their parents.

We define the sample as persons with living biological parents who did not coreside with parents (this excludes thirty-eight respondents who share households with parents). Thirty respondents have parents who are separated or divorced from each other. We decided to exclude these cases as well, because they unduly complicated the measurement of both help and contact. For married parent couples (122 cases), help and contact were measured jointly, while for separated parents, we would have had to sum such contact or to calculate its average value. Given the small number of cases involved, it seemed more reasonable to focus on a single parent household.

Only three dependent variables are considered. We do not include a measure of help from parents to respondents, because these parents, whose average age is seventy-seven, rarely help their adult children. For reference, the frequencies of visiting and phoning in the original detailed categories (from never to daily or more) for sons and daughters are provided in Appendix C, table C.3.9.

The key independent variables are measures of the number and gender composition of respondents' siblings, parallel to those used in the above analyses. Control variables include characteristics of parent and of respondent, with only minor differences from the variables introduced in previous equations. Income here refers to the adult child rather than the parent, and parent's employment status is not available. Because contact with married parents is considered jointly, two parent characteristics (oldest parent age and health of parent in worse health) take this into account.

Before presenting results for the dependent variables representing contact and help, we take a slight detour in order to return to a question raised early in this chapter. We suggested that if there were structural effects stemming from a combination of gender and number of children, there were several processes through which they might be produced. They might be based in the present-day situation of the adult sibling structure. Or they might be due to childhood socialization or childhood-based differences in feelings of closeness. To test for such differences, we need measures of attitudes toward filial responsibility and feelings of closeness to parents, measured from the adult child's point of view. We have been able to use three such measures: reported feelings of closeness to parents (which we refer to as closeness), a scale of attitudes toward appropriate filial relationships (which we refer to as norms), and an indicator of whether sons and daughters have the same responsibilities toward helping parents (see Appendix B for additional details on these measures).

Does family composition affect children's feelings of filial responsibility and closeness? We find no effects of any measure of sibling structure on any of the three dependent variables measuring attitudes or closeness (tables are not reported here). Nor is there any significant interaction between gender and any of the sibling structure measures in these three equations. Thus, gender and number of siblings are unrelated to feelings of closeness or attitudes toward filial responsibility. This suggests that if sibling structure has effects on relationships of adult children with their parents, these effects are not attributable to the kinds of feelings and attitudes measured here. Attention should be focused instead on the possibility that sibling structure is important principally because it determines the number of other children who may potentially be available to interact with parents.

Appendix C, table C.3.10, supplies mean values of the variables involved in this analysis for men and women respondents. These provide important background information for interpreting the results. Since all respondents are over the age of forty, the average age of their living parents is relatively high, around seventy-seven. In more than half the cases, only the mother is living; in another 15 percent of cases, only the father is alive. On average, respondents' parents had 2.5 other living children and live between three and four hours' travel time from respondents. Again, this reflects a skewed distribution; the median travel time is just over one-half hour.

Consistent with results based on parents' reports, daughters report more visits per month with parents and substantially more telephone calls than do sons. They also provide more help per week (2.1 versus 1.3 hours), contrary to the earlier results. Parent characteristics for this sample may account for some of this difference between sons' and daughters' helping. The parents here, compared to those in the analyses above, are older. Presumably some are more needy, and they are more likely to be women. Indeed, when we control for these characteristics below, the only remaining difference between sons and daughters is for telephone contact.

In table 3.4 we present mean monthly visits, telephone calls, and weekly hours of help to parent by the adult child's number of siblings. Most striking in our view are the dramatic differences between only sons and only daughters, especially for visiting (this is illustrated in figure 3.4). Only sons have much less contact with parents and they provide them much less routine help than do only daughters. These contrasts are so striking that we wondered whether they were caused by a small number of extremely deviant cases. There are fourteen only sons in our sample, and although this is a small set it is also quite consistent. Six visit with parents monthly, while the rest range between never (two cases) or once a year to nearly once a month. Only two speak with parents more than once a week by phone. By comparison, the only daughters in this sample describe unusually close ties to parents. This difference between only sons and only daughters, revealed in their own reports, was not reported by parent respondents.

For those with one or more siblings, as found before, amounts of contact and help are similar across sibling size, with a slight dropping off between one and two siblings in some cases. Whether we interpret the pattern as additive or substitution hinges on gender. The value for only sons is so low compared to all other categories that one might view results for sons as additive. Values for only daughters are so high that a substitution model might be applied for daughters, not only for helping (as above) but also for contact.

**TABLE 3.4**

Mean Monthly Contact and Weekly Hours of Help from Respondents to Parents, by Number of Siblings

| | *Visit* | | *Phone* | | *Help parent* | |
|---|---|---|---|---|---|---|
| | Sons | Dtrs | Sons | Dtrs | Sons | Dtrs |
| Only child | .55 | 13.84 | 4.41 | 16.86 | .36 | 5.07 |
| One sibling | 4.43 | 7.37 | 11.03 | 11.39 | 1.07 | 2.30 |
| Brother | 4.17 | 7.58 | 11.55 | 9.31 | .55 | 3.21 |
| Sister | 4.61 | 7.14 | 10.65 | 13.67 | 1.46 | 1.27 |
| Two siblings | 4.73 | 4.93 | 7.89 | 10.59 | 1.25 | 1.40 |
| Three siblings | 5.11 | 5.61 | 4.60 | 10.35 | 1.68 | 1.26 |
| Four siblings | 2.45 | 5.64 | 3.30 | 14.24 | 2.05 | 2.30 |
| Five + siblings | 4.39 | 3.29 | 6.55 | 4.78 | 1.30 | .97 |
| Total | 4.07 | 6.40 | 7.13 | 10.86 | 1.11 | 1.53 |

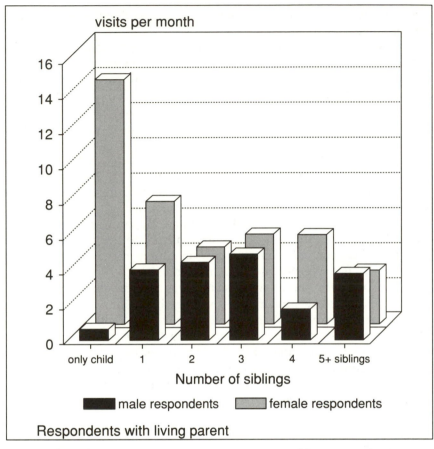

**FIGURE 3.4** Respondents' Visits with Parents by Number of Siblings and Gender

Looking at family structure in terms of its gender composition offers some new information. Here again we find the difference between only children and others opposite for sons and for daughters. The behavior of sons who have one sibling seems little affected by whether the sibling is a brother or sister. (Those with a sister provide somewhat more help to parents than do those with a brother. This suggests not gender substitution but just the opposite. Perhaps a sister prompts sons to help more, or offers a positive model to be imitated.) Daughters' visiting is the same regardless of whether they have a brother or a sister. Those with a sister talk with parents more frequently by phone than do those with a brother, but they help parents less.

As our final step, let us see whether these average differences are still found when other personal characteristics are taken into account. (The relevant tables for sons and daughters are found in the Appendix C, tables C.3.11 and C.3.12). In these analyses the indicator of family composition is the number of siblings. We will discuss the effects of key control variables, such as employment and marital status, in the next chapter.

In fact, differences found in the bivariate tables are not clearly replicated in the multivariate analyses, possibly because the bivariate tables were so strongly affected by the values for only children. For daughters, the sole significant effect of number of siblings is for visiting. Contradicting analyses based on parents' reports, the negative coefficient here signifies that daughters with more siblings visit their parents less often. Coefficients for phoning and helping are not significant, however. For sons, the large difference in visiting that we saw in the earlier tables between only sons and others proves not to be statistically significant. There are two significant effects of number of siblings, but these are in opposite directions. Those sons with more siblings have *less* frequent phone contact with their parents, but they provide more help.

The effects of alternative measures of family structure are presented in Appendix C, table C.3.13. Here sons and daughters are combined into the same sample, so that the net effect of gender can be estimated. Further, interactions between gender and family structure are tested.

One clear result from all of these analyses, confirming conclusions that we drew earlier, is that there is a significant net difference between sons and daughters for telephone contact. Controlling for all other factors, daughters talk to their parents by phone about four times more per month than do sons (this is about the same difference as revealed in our analysis of parents' reports). But they do not visit more often or provide more assistance to parents.

Other results in these equations are more difficult to organize and report. Our first step (parallel to the analyses that we conducted based on parents' reports) is to measure family composition simply as number of siblings. These equations are found in the first panel of table C.3.13 in Appendix C. We find negative direct effects for visiting and phoning, but not for help—just the opposite of results shown in Appendix C, table C.3.8 based on parents' reports. Introduction of gender interactions recalls the pattern displayed in the bivariate tables for visiting and help: a negative effect of number of siblings that is found solely for daughters (but not for sons, perhaps due to the very low values for only sons).

The second panel shows the effects of number of sisters and number of brothers coded separately. Consistent with the first panel, there is no effect of number of brothers or number of sisters on helping. Having more brothers (but not sisters) decreases visits and telephone calls significantly, and this effect does not differ by gender of respondent. This is unexpected; if filial contact were more normative for daughters than sons, one would expect any substitution effect to be more influenced by the presence of sisters. Adult children might be expected to fill in with more phone calls when they had brothers and do less when they had sisters. (However, this assumes that such contact is initiated by the adult children.)

In the third panel, we examine variables reflecting number and gender of siblings in more detail. Having one sister and no brothers is the omitted reference category. In relation to that group, respondents who are only children visit and help more, and the interaction term suggests that this effect is much greater for women than men. Our bivariate analysis showed that in fact only sons do substantially less than any other group. For helping, the positive effect of one brother offers the only indication of a gender-specific substitution effect: children with one brother help more than those with one sister.

Taken together, these findings based on children's reports show that gender effects are limited to telephone contact. Unlike our previous analyses based on parents' reports, they offer some evidence that availability of other siblings reduces contact with parents and may also decrease helping (for daughters) or increase it (for sons). But these effects are inconsistent and they depend on the child's gender and on the particular gender composition of the siblings. There is no consistent tendency for either brothers or sisters to have the greater impact.

## Discussion

What have we learned here about the importance of family size and gender composition on parent-child relationships? First of all, family size does not affect children's closeness to parents, attitudes about filial responsibilities, or attitudes about gender-typing of those responsibilities. These postulated effects, all of which have been said to be rooted in one way or another in childhood socialization, do not occur. Our thinking about sibling structure should focus instead on the sharing of filial responsibility in adulthood: when more children are potentially available for contact and support to parents, how does each child adjust his or her own behavior? Put simply, the additive model postulates no such adjustments, while the substitution model suggests that adult children will modify their contact and help to parents in relation to available siblings, perhaps particularly in relation to the availability of sisters.

Results from the parts of our analysis of contact and helping, using the parent's perspective and then the adult child's perspective, seem incompatible when inspected closely. For visiting and phoning, we find more support for the additive model when analyzing parents' reports and more support for the substitution model when focusing on children's. For helping, the pattern is reversed. Why might children's reports lead to different findings than parents' reports? It is possible that this difference is due to a bias in our sample of parents: older persons who were institutionalized or too frail to be interviewed were not included. Or there may be bias in reporting by either parents or children. When parents are interviewed regarding relations with each of their children, they may tend to report those relations as being more similar than they actually are, due to their feeling of "generational stake" (Bengtson and Kuypers 1971; see also Giarrusso et al. 1995) or to norms against favoring certain children. Or possibly only children (at least if they are daughters?) feel some social pressure to report more frequent interaction with parents (although such pressure, if it exists, does not result in reports of greater emotional closeness). Perhaps it is necessary to interview separately parents and all children in a family network to obtain an accurate picture of what is going on.

We should not overemphasize the differences, however. To the extent that children may increase or reduce their contacts with parents to adjust for the number of siblings, these adjustments are small. For example, the largest negative coefficient in predicting visits for either number of siblings, number of brothers, or number of sisters is about −.75 (found in Appendix C, table C.3.11, based on daughters' reports). But the average number of visits per month reported by daughters is greater than six. Thus, even if the daughters' reports turned out to be more accurate than parents' reports (which showed no substitution tendency at all), it would still be the case that parents with more children experience many more visits. That is, the additive model would still be essentially correct, regardless of whose reports are relied on.

Even when we consider nonlinear effects, such as models in which an only child is contrasted to other categories, we reach similar conclusions. In the first sample, an only child is estimated to have about 3.5 more visits than a child who has a sister, for example. This is a substantial difference; it greatly reduces the predicted difference in visits between parents with one compared to two children. But it does not reverse the conclusion that parents with more children (especially those with more than two children) experience more visits. In the second sample, differences in favor of those with two children compared to those with only daughters are not great, but parents with three or more children would experience substantially more visits than other groups.

Conclusions regarding help to parents depend more strongly in their details on the sample and model specification. Again, however, the non-linear models point toward substantial differences between only children and other categories: differences of more than one hour per week based on parents' reports, and more than two hours per week based on children's reports (we refer here to the coefficients for the last panel in tables C.3.8 and C.3.13 in Appendix C, without interaction terms). These are very large differences in relation to the overall averages, reported as less than one hour per week by parents and in the range of one or two hours per week by children. Effects of this magnitude on the behavior of an only child are more than enough to outweigh the potential advantages for a parent who has two or three children. This may explain why our first table in this chapter showed no clear relationship between number of children and total help reported by parents.

Next we turn to our conclusions regarding gender and gender-specific substitution. We find two patterns. For visiting and for help to parents (as well as help to children in the first analysis) there are small gender differences that disappear in the multivariate analysis. This is consistent with some past studies of help exchanged with healthy middle-aged and older parents and is not surprising considering that for most kin networks, visits often involve the whole family. Even if arranged by individuals, get-togethers are likely to involve spouses and children. And given the low levels of help exchanged in our sample, and our conclusion that this may occur in conjunction with visiting, it seems logical that this would also involve sons and daughters in similar amounts.

On the other hand, there are consistent differences in telephone contact between sons and daughters (Rossi and Rossi 1990). Although the means differ slightly depending on which sample we analyze, in both cases we find that daughters talk on the phone with parents four more times per month, or once more a week, than sons do. Given the much greater frequency of telephone contact than visiting in person for parent-child pairs not living in the same immediate neighborhood (we will discuss the issue of geographic distance more in chapters 4 and 6), this may reflect an important difference in the maintenance of intimate ties and the function of kinkeeping.

These gender differences are consistent with Fischer's (1992) discussion of the diffusion of the telephone as a form of social interaction earlier in this century. He concluded that women talked more on the telephone with kin and friends than did men and that households with more adult females were more likely to have a telephone during the earlier period. He considers three plausible explanations for this difference. First, women might use the telephone to counter isolation during the day. This is of course more relevant to the time period he is studying, when more wives were full-time homemakers and more people lived in rural areas. Second, women may use the telephone in their family role as social manager and kinkeeper: making appointments, arranging social events, keeping family members informed about others. And third, women are considered to be more comfortable in some types of intimate social interactions than men, and the phone fits their style of interaction. The second and third explanations seem consistent with a scenario in which daughters have more intimate conversations with parents (especially mothers) and help to arrange family gatherings.

Our results regarding gender-specific substitution are largely negative. We anticipated that when daughters are not available, sons might "fill in." This appears not to occur. One reason may be that, in terms of personal visits and helping, relations of adult children with parents are not different for sons than for daughters. For a behavior with no gender differences, the absence of a daughter leaves nothing special for a son to compensate for, as compared to the absence of another son. In regard to phoning, however, the culturally based reasons for men to feel less comfortable with this form of contact may make it difficult for a son to "substitute" for a daughter. Another reason for the overall lack of gender substitution may be that both sons and daughters influence each other's behavior. Such a mixture of influences may be difficult to capture with simple family-structure variables.

We do not intend to imply that effects of family composition are due solely to choices made by children. Due to the emphasis in the gerontological literature on samples of frail elderly, there is a tendency to view adult children as the agents in this process, as choosing to be or not to be filially responsible. It is as though parents are thought to sit back and wait for their children's attention. Yet as Aldous (1987) cogently documents, middle-aged and elderly parents make their own choices about the types of relationships and extent of contact they wish to have with their children. Aldous shows that parents initiate contact and give assistance to children differentially, responding to children's needs and their feelings of closeness. The same point is made by Coward and Dwyer (1990) in their discussion of their research on caregivers' sense of burden. They suggest that we need to know more about how these patterns come about, how sons or daughters come to be "chosen" as caregivers, who is asked and who refuses. We should, therefore, consider the possibility that social support derives from reciprocal choices: when there are more children, both the children and the parent may adjust their expectations and behavior in relation to the structure of the sibling group. This is the social process that we believe most likely underlies our findings.

This chapter has provided new evidence, albeit mixed, regarding potential effects of current and future demographic trends. As family sizes decline, a larger proportion of parents will have no daughters. We conclude that these parents should not be disadvantaged in terms of in-person contact or occasional help, at least as long as their needs do not require more intensive help than is typical in this sample. They may, however, be involved in fewer telephone conversations, with a possible resulting decrease in maintenance of intimacy, than they would if they had daughters. Regardless of children's gender, parents with small families, particularly those with only one child, may have somewhat less total intergenerational contact but may receive no less of the routine kinds of help reflected here.

# 4
# Intergenerational Effects of Employment and Divorce

*Neither the child's employment nor the child's divorce decreases contact with or help to parents, contradicting expectations based on theories of role conflict. There is some evidence that parents provide additional support to divorced daughters who have custody of minor children. Parents have somewhat weaker ties with children who were at one time noncustodial. Thus, divorce may intensify some intergenerational ties and weaken others.*

■ Family composition is one route through which emerging demographic trends might affect relations between adult children and older parents. From the parents' point of view, larger family size leads to more contact (but not necessarily more exchange of help). Therefore, it is reasonable to project that declining fertility will result over time in a diminution of intergenerational ties as experienced by the parent generation. This result is partially compensated by the fact that adult children in smaller families tend to have more contact with their parents. We now consider two other social trends that have been believed to have a similar impact: rising levels of female employment and the explosion of rates of divorce.

Discussion of these trends has emphasized the role of daughters, based on evidence that daughters are more likely than sons to be the primary caregivers for the frail elderly. We focus not on caregiving but on the more usual range of ties between parents and their adult children, and we find limited gender differences in these ties (see Chapter 2). Therefore we are led to give equal consideration to effects of employment and divorce on both daughters and sons. As women expand their participation in nonfamily roles, particularly in the workforce, this fact might well reduce the time and energy that can be devoted to care for, or interaction with, parents (Brody 1979; Lang and Brody 1983; Horowitz 1985). In principle, the effects of work responsibilities on relations with parents are also salient for men, even though men have often been excluded from studies of the effects of employment and divorce, and

81

they are less often portrayed as facing conflicts among competing demands.

Marital disruption is more common today than at any time in the past; nearly two-thirds of recent first marriages will end if current levels persist (Bumpass 1990; Martin and Bumpass 1989; Norton and Moorman 1987). The effect of marital disruption on divorcees, their children, and divorcees' relations with their young children is well documented (Demo and Acock 1991; Kitson and Morgan 1991; Spanier and Thompson 1984) and is not treated here. We are interested in two kinds of impacts: the effects of the child's divorce on their relations with parents, and effects of the parent's (earlier) divorce on relations with adult children. Regarding the first, there has been considerable speculation (Cicirelli 1983a; Duffy 1982; Johnson and Vinick 1982), but the investigation of this impact has produced inconsistent results. Still, some scholars (e.g., Smyer and Hofland 1982), projecting current divorce rates into the future, have expressed worries about the ability of divorced children to meet the needs of their parents (especially widowed mothers). Others are concerned that divorced fathers will find themselves isolated from their children in old age, given increased levels of divorce and the general pattern of maternal child custody (Goldscheider 1990; see also Eggebeen 1992; Smyer and Hofland 1982; Uhlenberg and Myers 1981).

Many of the early empirical studies on these topics were based on convenience samples or on women only, or have lacked comparison groups. More recently, a few have been based on high quality data sets such as the NSFH and the AARP study. Here we take advantage of the Albany survey's random population base and its inclusion of both sons and daughters, mothers and fathers to assess such consequences as are being felt by both generations in the present.

## The Effects of Employment

How might employment be expected to influence an adult child's relations with parents? First, employment may promote the formation of social ties (especially to coworkers) that could compete with familial ones. This could lead to decreased feelings of closeness to parents and other kin. Second, employment may influence attitudes toward filial responsibility. For women, employment is a less traditional role than full-time homemaking and may be associated with less traditionalism in attitudes regarding the duties and responsibilities of adult children. Third, employment might have a simple and direct effect on filial relations due to time constraints. Time spent on the job is not available (except in rare instances) for simultaneously visiting with or helping parents, and in most cases only limited personal telephone conversations can be carried on at work. If employment influences filial contact without influencing feelings of closeness or filial attitudes, we will assume it is due to time constraints.

Many researchers have speculated on potential effects of employment among adult sons and, particularly, daughters on help to aging parents (e.g., Brody 1981, 1985; Treas 1977). One type of study has drawn samples of working people, asking how many provide some form of caregiving to a dependent relative or friend and what conflicts these persons experience between the worker and caregiver roles (e.g., Enright and Friss 1987; Gibeau and Anastas 1987; Neal et al. 1987). In a synthetic review of seventeen such studies, Gorey et al. (1992) found estimates ranging from 2 percent to 46 percent of paid workers providing caregiving to a dependent adult. These studies typically had very low response rates, and higher estimates come from those with the lowest response rates. Therefore, Gorey et al. conclude that caregivers are overrepresented in samples with low response rates, and they suggest that a more accurate estimate for paid workers who are also caregivers is in the 7 to 12 percent range.

Several studies compare help of employed and nonemployed women to elderly mothers. Lang and Brody (1983) report that employed women provide fewer total hours of help to mothers than the nonemployed. Brody and Schoonover (1986) find no significant differences in most kinds of help in their sample of three-generation female triads. But they do find that employed daughters help parents less with personal care and meal preparation (both of which are time-intensive, daily tasks), and in these areas the employed daughters also hire more help and receive more help from other family members than do nonemployed daughters. Comparing fifty pairs of employed and nonemployed sisters in a volunteer sample, Matthews and Werkner (1985) report no overall difference by employment status in nine help areas. But among those with parents in poorest health, who have the greatest needs for assistance, employed sisters helped less. Both of these studies imply that intensive caregiving conflicts with paid employment.

Studies including *both* male and female (adult child) respondents or reports on both sons and daughters are more likely to be based on population samples. Stoller (1983) conducted 502 interviews with *helpers* of persons aged sixty-five and over, and of these 47 percent were adult children. Employment of the helper significantly reduced hours of help received by the parent for those with son helpers only, by twenty-three hours a month. Employment did not reduce daughters' help. Stoller speculates that daughters simply increase their work weeks to help parents. In contrast, Houser and colleagues (1985) found that for a sample of 499 sons and daughters of elderly white widows, hours of employment affected daily caretaking help to mothers significantly, and sex differences in helping were explained by employment hours. Finley (1989) drew a sample of 325 male and female respondents with living mothers. She studied the probability that the child was the primary provider of help in those areas where the mother received help. This variable was not related to the child's employment status. In their recent analysis of the AARP study data, Lawton, Silverstein and Bengtson (1994) report that adult children who were employed were in fact *more* likely than others to help parents.

Using a life-course perspective, Moen et al. (1994) examined caregiving experiences of white women surveyed in 1956 and again in 1986 in relation to their employment patterns. Their focus was broader than most other studies cited here, in that the term "caregiving" was defined by the respondent and might be short-term, and recipients of care were not restricted to parents. However, they found no evidence of conflict between the two. Over three-fifths of the women reported having been caregivers at some point, most often between the ages of forty-five and sixty-five, and those who were employed were as likely to become caregivers as the nonemployed.

Finally, the only published research (previous to our own) examining effects on interaction as well as helping was conducted by Steuve and O'Donnell (1989). They studied eighty-one women with parents aged seventy and over. Full-time work (as compared to part-time work or full-time homemaking) appeared to constrain helping and interaction (other than telephoning) for those living within an hour's drive of parents. Small numbers of cases, however, make these results only suggestive; for example, only sixteen respondents worked full-time and lived within an hour's drive of parents.

Thus, most research on potential conflicts between employment and filial relations has focused on help given to frail elderly parents, and not on the relations involving both contact and less time-intensive helping that characterize the vast majority of adult child-parent pairs. Limitations in research designs, particularly in sampling, make the results of some studies unreliable, and the results in any case are mixed. Yet the hypothesis that child's employment affects intergenerational relations—particularly for those with older parents—has many adherents, and it deserves a more systematic test.

## Findings for Employment

In Chapter 3 we presented three sets of analyses based on respondents' relations with all children, with randomly selected children, and with living parents. In each analysis we included the employment status of parent and/or child, although in the third analysis the employment status of elderly parents, average age seventy-six, was not considered relevant. We decided to code employment status as a trichotomy (full-time, part-time, not employed) for the sake of consistency. Although we had information on paid work hours of respondents, we did not have this information for children. (We will also refer to results of Spitze and Logan's [1991a] research in which employment was coded in hours worked per week.) Thus, we have several sources of evidence regarding effects of employment on the family relations of both men and women.

First, we consider the notion, introduced above, that any effect of employment on intergenerational relations may be due to a relationship between attitudes toward filial obligation or feelings of closeness to parents and employment status. We have both kinds of measures for respondents in relation to their parents. (The question about closeness was asked about each parent separately, even for married parent couples. However, the correlation between respondent's closeness to mothers and fathers, when both were living, is .770. Therefore we predict the mean closeness rating for those with two parents.) We found no effects of employment on either closeness or filial attitudes, nor did we find any significant effects of weekly hours of employment on these dependent variables in our previously published work (Spitze and Logan 1991a). Thus, if employment has any effect on relations with parents, we will view it as a direct result of time conflicts rather than an indirect one stemming from subjective feelings or attitudes.

Is there such an effect of employment status on contact and help patterns? These results are fairly easy to summarize. Figure 4.1—based on parents' reports about children—shows no relationship between child's employment and visiting; results are the same for phoning and helping (see Appendix C, tables C.3.6 and C.3.7, for the multivariate results). Surprisingly, the multivariate analysis reveals that parents who are employed full-time *receive* significantly more help from children (see Appendix C, table C.3.2); the difference is approximately one hour per week. This finding suggests the image of an active, busy parent whose child helps out occasionally when schedules get tight, rather than a frail older parent needing help.

Comparable results based on children's reports are found in Appendix C, tables C.3.11 and C.3.12. There are no effects of employment on contact with or help to parents from women respondents. There is, however, a significant negative effect of male respondents' full-time employment status on help to parents. This amounts to approximately one and a half hours less help per week. Note, however, that the comparison

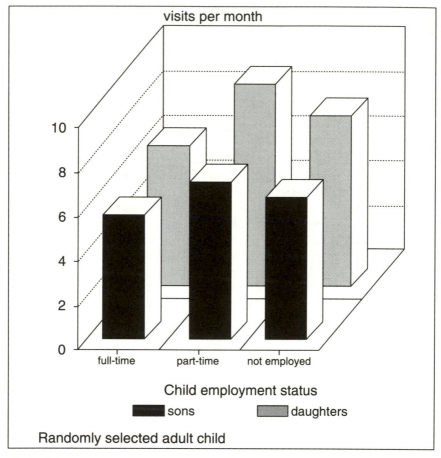

**FIGURE 4.1** Respondents' Visits with Adult Children by Child's Employment Status

group here is men who are not employed, whether due to unemployment, disability, retirement, or some other reason, and there are only twenty-four such men in the sample who have living parents.

Thus, our general conclusion is that there is very little evidence of a conflict between employment and relations with parents during most of the adult years. In attempting to explain the null effects of employment on contact and help, one might posit that, given the typically low or modest parental needs for help (see Hess and Waring 1978; Troll et al. 1979; Spitze and Logan 1989) or due to long distances between parents and children, regular help is seldom needed or possible. Thus, for the low average levels of help found in the general population, it is unlikely that paid work and assistance will conflict. Neither is regular interaction likely to conflict with paid work, since such contact can occur during leisure hours.

In our earlier published work (Spitze and Logan 1991a), we tried several alternative methods of looking for effects of respondents' employment on relations with their older parents to guard against the error of rejecting a hypothesis that may be true for some subgroups in the population. First, we posited that, for those at great distances, regular helping is not possible. We selected respondents using two different cutting points, those living within four hours' travel time and those within one hour. We then evaluated both contact and helping for men and women within these subgroups. There were no significant effects of work hours on contact or help to parents for men or women living within four hours travel time from parents. For men within one hour of parents, there was a marginally significant (p = .06) negative effect of work hours on hours of help, although its magnitude (unstandardized coefficient = −.05) suggests a very small tradeoff of three fewer minutes of help per week for every hour of work.

As a further test, we selected those respondents who have at least one parent in fair, poor, or very poor health, and who live no more than one hour from the parent (N = 135). These would be the people for whom help to parents is both more likely to be needed and also possible on a regular basis. Even for this group there are no significant effects of hours of employment on any measure of helping behavior for men or for women.

One might suggest that the cases in which parent care would conflict most with employment would involve shared living and are thus being missed here. Our measures of visiting, telephoning, and helping precluded the inclusion of persons sharing housing with parents, since contact measures have ambiguous meaning when a household is shared and it is impossible to separate help from simple sharing of housework in that situation. We did examine separately, however, those thirty-eight cases of shared living. We found, first, that the probability of living with a parent was unrelated to hours worked for men or women (using logit analysis). Although we did not have histories of living arrangements for those currently living together, the distribution of parental health (twenty-nine of thirty-eight are in fair, good, or excellent health) suggested that caregiving is not the motivation in the majority of cases. Thus, we conclude that we are not missing a large cluster of cases in which employment and caregiving conflict.

## The Effects of Divorce

As we noted earlier, divorce may have two kinds of intergenerational effects: effects on the divorced child's relation with parents, and effects of the parent's divorce on later relations with children. We will discuss each of these in turn, along with results from our study that provide relevant evidence.

*Respondents' Experience of Children's Divorce*

How many parents experience a child's divorce? To our knowledge, this question has not been addressed before now based on a probability sample. For example, the National Survey of Families and Households has information on adult children but not on their marital history, so it would not be possible to replicate this table using those data.

Table 4.1 presents information on parents in various age groups. First, a bare majority of respondents in their forties have an adult child, while the vast majority of respondents in other age groups have such children. Similarly, having a married child is somewhat uncommon for respondents in their forties, but common for the vast majority of parents above age fifty. (The slight dropoff for respondents above age seventy probably represents lower fertility of respondents who were of child-bearing age prior to the baby boom period.) Thus it is mainly after fifty that parents are "at risk" of having divorced children.

The third row in table 4.1 presents the proportion of parents who have experienced any child's divorce. For respondents in their sixties and above, this is fairly common, including well over a third. From this table we could calculate the percentage of those with ever-married children who have experienced a child's divorce. For example, among those in their sixties this would be 41 percent in comparison to 83 percent, or 49 percent of those with ever-married children. The figure for those seventy and above would be 48 percent. (These figures are slightly lower

**TABLE 4.1**
Marital History of Respondents' Children

|  | Respondent age | | | | |
|---|---|---|---|---|---|
|  | 40–49 | 50–59 | 60–69 | 70 + | Total |
| **Percentage of all respondents who have:** | | | | | |
| An adult child | 55% | 88% | 89% | 77% | 76% |
| An ever-married child | 20% | 71% | 83% | 74% | 59% |
| An ever-divorced child | 3% | 24% | 41% | 36% | 24% |
| A currently divorced or separated child | 4% | 20% | 28% | 24% | 18% |
| A remarried child | 1% | 10% | 22% | 21% | 13% |
| N | 365 | 275 | 308 | 246 | 1,194 |

than the percentage of marriages ending in divorce because divorces have a slight tendency to cluster in families.) We also present, for the reader's information, percentages of respondents with *currently* divorced or separated children and remarried children.

Of particular interest is the parents' experience of an adult child's divorce leading to noncustody of the child's children. Such situations may affect grandparent-grandchild contact. We find (not in tables) that one in ten respondents in their sixties currently have grandchildren not in their own adult child's custody, with smaller percentages in other parent age groups. Of respondents in their sixties *who are grandparents*, 14 percent have a minor grandchild not in the adult child's custody. Of the smaller number of grandparents (41 percent) who have a child with children from a marriage that ended in divorce, 33 percent have a grandchild not in the child's custody. These figures may underrepresent the extent to which such situations have *ever* been experienced, since we asked only about current arrangements.

*Previous Studies on Adult Children's Divorce*

Thus, middle-aged and older parents have nearly a fifty-fifty chance of having one or more children who divorce. How has the research literature viewed such situations? The predominant view in the literature is that divorce debilitates the adult child. Researchers expect that children undergoing divorce, especially daughters, experience severe demands on their time and energy, due to financial constraints (sometimes leading to part-time or full-time employment for women) and to single parenthood. Both sons and daughters are assumed to need more help from parents (financial, household, child care, and emotional support) and to be less capable of providing parents with the help *they* may need (Cicirelli 1983b; Johnson 1988a; Smyer and Hofland 1982; Spanier and Hanson 1982). If interaction and emotional support to parents require time and energy (Cicirelli 1983b; Smyer and Hofland 1982), this also would imply decreasing contact and feelings of closeness to parents following an adult child's divorce.

While this perspective is consistent with much that has been written on adult children's divorce, there are also reasons to expect no discernible impacts. First, while these processes would imply increases in help to children (especially daughters) and decreases in help to parents, they would not necessarily affect contact levels or feelings of emotional intimacy. Help in either direction might increase closeness *or* create strain, and the net effect on closeness or contact may be null. Second, to the extent that helping patterns are often reciprocal and arising out of interaction (e.g., shopping together) rather than need or inability to do a task oneself (Spitze and Logan 1992), one might expect any change in help levels to and from parents and adult children to be in the same direction (i.e., both increase or both decrease help). Third, parent-child relationships over the life course have been characterized as exhibiting a great deal of continuity (Rossi and Rossi 1990). An adult child's divorce, while at least temporarily traumatic for the immediate family, might not be expected to have a major impact on a relationship with such a long history as that between the divorcing adult child and his or her parents.

Empirical research has probed effects of adult children's divorce on emotional intimacy, levels of contact, and helping relations. One potential response to divorce involves coresidence between a divorcing adult child and a parent, which presumably would also result in increasing levels of contact and mutual help. Our focus here, however, is on relations between noncoresiding parents and adult children. Results of studies of such situations are decidedly mixed.

Some studies suggest divorce places a strain on the *quality of the parent-child relationship* (Cicirelli 1983b; Cooney and Uhlenberg 1990; Johnson 1988b; Umberson 1992), particularly between mothers and daughters (Johnson 1988a), while some argue that it brings them closer (Ahrons and Bowman 1982). Divorcing adult children may seek emotional support from a variety of sources, including parents (Aldous 1987), but also may become less emotionally available to parents and seek support from friends if they do not perceive kin as supportive (Milardo 1987). If they become more dependent on parents for financial support or a residence, this may create strain due to returning to a dependent status (Johnson 1988b).

Some researchers report that the quality of the the adult child-parent relationship and *amount of contact* are maintained or even increased following a divorce (Ahrons and Bowman 1982; Spicer and Hampe 1975). Umberson (1992) finds no significant impact on contact with father or mother, while divorced adult children experience higher levels of strain and less emotional support from parents. Cherlin and Furstenberg (1986) report that most grandparents maintain levels of contact with grandchildren at or above levels before the breakup, but some, especially parents of an adult child who does not have custody of the grandchildren, decrease contact. They also argue that divorce strengthens intergenerational ties along maternal lines.

The gender of the divorcing child is believed to have a significant impact on the timing of how divorce affects interaction with parents (Ahrons and Bowman 1982; Leslie and Grady 1985). There is suggestive evidence that contact with the parent tends to increase for perhaps a year following a divorce for both sons and daughters, but over time the contact decreases back to the level prior to the divorce for sons and remains high for daughters (Ahrons and Bowman 1982). This gender difference may relate to the fact that more sons than daughters remarry and to the imbalance in custody patterns and in financial situations.

Fewer studies have examined patterns of *help by divorced adult children to their parents*. Dwyer et al. (1992) looked at changes in help given to elderly parents and found no effect of a child's change to a "not married" state (not distinguishing between divorce and widowhood). Cicirelli (1983b, 1983c) found adult children with disrupted marriages gave significantly less total help to parents than those with intact marriages, primarily because of lower perception of parental needs during this time, less feeling of filial obligation, and because of conflicting job responsibilities. Stoller (1983) reported still a different pattern, that married adult children helped parents less than unmarried ones. However, she did not separate divorced from never-married and widowed adult children, as this was not her primary focus, so it is difficult to draw any conclusions about divorced persons from her study. Brody et al. (1994), using her sample of mothers and daughters, compared help provided by daughters in five different marital statuses. Reinforcing Stoller's result, the married and remarried daughters helped the least, although the total help received by their mothers equalled amounts by other mothers; the difference was made up by other helpers, including husbands and children of the married daughters. Never-married daughters helped the most, by far, with divorced and widowed daughters falling in between.

Several studies have provided suggestive evidence that divorced persons, particularly daughters, receive more practical *help from their parents* than do nondivorced persons, particularly financial and child-care help (Johnson 1983, 1988a; Leslie and Grady 1985; Spanier and Hanson 1982; Spanier and Thompson 1984). The presence of grandchildren significantly increases the possibility of parental support (Spanier and Thompson 1984), particularly from grandmothers (Presser 1989). These findings suggest a process of role budgeting through which parents of adult children decide how to allocate attention and help to each child, taking neediness (arising from divorce and family responsibilities) into account (Aldous 1987).

### Our Findings for Adult Children's Divorce

We have evidence on these effects from both the adult child's and the parent's point of view, based on descriptive tables and on multivariate analyses presented in the previous chapter. (Although we do not have longitudinal data that would allow us to examine changes over time with changes in marital status, we do control for other factors that might be expected to affect both marital status and these relationships.) For adult children, in contrast to analyses in the previous chapter, we separate divorced adult children into those with and without custody of minor children (the latter also includes those with no children or older children).

In table 4.2, we present mean levels of contact and help by child's marital status, separately for sons and for daughters. Clearly there are small Ns in some cells, but daughters with custody appear to experience higher levels of visiting, telephone contacts, and help in both directions. In particular, they have high levels of babysitting help from parents, averaging ten times per month, and experience twenty calls and eleven visits per month. (Their levels of visiting are illustrated in figure 4.2.) Divorced daughters with custody, although few in number, do contrast sharply with other daughters.

Returning to the multivariate analyses of the previous chapter for evidence on these patterns (Appendix C, tables C.3.6 and C.3.7), we find no significant differences between married adult children and those in

**TABLE 4.2**
Mean Contact and Help by Gender and Marital Status of Randomly Selected Adult Child, as Reported by Parent Respondents

|  | Visit/ month | Phone /month | Help to parent hrs/week | Help to child hrs/week | Babysit/ month |
|---|---|---|---|---|---|
| **Sons** |  |  |  |  |  |
| Married | 5.36 (211) | 9.12 | .72 | 1.38 | 1.86 (123) |
| Divorced/sep. |  |  |  |  |  |
| with custody | 1.53 (7) | 7.65 | .29 | .33 | 4.47 (7) |
| Divorced/sep. |  |  |  |  |  |
| without custody | 6.36 (31) | 9.34 | .10 | 2.37 | 5.22 (9) |
| Remarried | 6.23 (32) | 7.40 | .88 | 1.03 | .90 (26) |
| Never married | 4.68 (114) | 7.10 | .23 | 1.15 | 3.66 (11) |
| **Daughters** |  |  |  |  |  |
| Married | 7.34 (233) | 14.11 | .83 | 1.59 | 3.00 (124) |
| Divorced/sep. |  |  |  |  |  |
| with custody | 11.15 (15) | 20.67 | 1.13 | 2.00 | 9.67 (10) |
| Divorced/sep. |  |  |  |  |  |
| without custody | 6.88 (19) | 11.37 | .61 | .58 | .50 (4) |
| Remarried | 8.14 (29) | 15.66 | 0.0 | 1.43 | 3.63 (10) |
| Never married | 4.42 (83) | 10.24 | .24 | .75 | 3.21 (16) |

*Note:* Numbers of cases in parentheses (babysitting only for those with minor children).

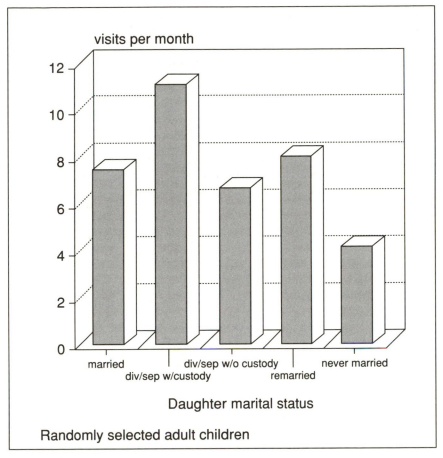

visits per month

**Daughter marital status**

Randomly selected adult children

**FIGURE 4.2** Respondents' Visits with Daughters by Daughter's Marital Status

other marital status categories. When we reanalyzed these equations, separating the divorced into those with and without custody of minor children as represented in table 4.2, we found one significant difference: divorced daughters with custody talked to parents more on the phone than married daughters. (The unstandardized coefficient of 6.01 almost identically corresponds to the difference in means in table 4.2.) Yet other differences are not significant.

In our previously published work, using a more complex form of analysis that took into account all adult children of each respondent and adjusted for dependence among cases (Spitze et al. 1994), we found more significant differences among these categories. In particular, we found that divorced daughters with custody experienced more visits and telephone calls with parents, and received more babysitting and other types of help from parents, than did married daughters. These significant differences parallel bivariate patterns found here. Yet because these differences are not robust across methodologies and samples, we are not certain how to interpret them. However, we do think the patterns for divorced mothers with custody are striking and worthy of further investigation. We would suggest that other researchers, using larger and longitudinal data sets, delve further into the conditions under which an adult child's divorce increases contact with parents.

Previous literature had suggested that there may be effects of adult children's divorce that change with the passage of time, and in particular that divorced sons increase contact with parents for only a year or so before going back to previous levels of contact. To check this possibility for both sons and daughters, we selected currently divorced or separated adult children and tested the effect of years since the divorce or separation occurred on contact and help. There were no significant effects for either sons or daughters. We were, however, unable to compare the specific difference between the first year and later years due to small sample sizes. Thus, again, we would urge others using data sets with a larger number of divorced adult children to focus on issues of timing.

The effect of an adult child's divorce can also be examined using our analysis of respondents' relations with their own parents. In this sample of adults ages forty and over with living parents, the issue of whether divorced women have custody of young children is not nearly as salient, and we will simply compare patterns of contact and help across marital status categories of the respondent (adult child). In table 4.3 we show descriptive results for contact and help for each gender. While some categories have very small Ns, divorced or separated women appear to have similar relations with their parents compared to those of married women. Divorced men are, if anything, in slightly more frequent contact with parents than are married men. Results for the remarried and never married are mixed, while widowed women, although few in number, have particularly high levels of contact with parents.

Returning to our multivariate analyses of these same data (Appendix C, tables C.3.11 and C.3.12), we find that few of these differences are significant. Remarried women do have significantly fewer phone contacts with parents, with a coefficient representing a difference of five phone calls a month. Never-married men have significantly fewer visits with parents, as well as helping them fewer hours in an average week. But the divorced and separated are not different from married respondents.

Thus, combining these results with those for respondents and their

**TABLE 4.3**
Mean Contact and Help to Parents by Gender and Marital Status of Respondent

|  | Visit/ month | Phone/ month | Help to parent hrs/week | N |
|---|---|---|---|---|
| **Sons** | | | | |
| Married | 4.61 | 6.93 | 1.54 | 100 |
| Divorced/sep. | 6.39 | 8.04 | 1.83 | 18 |
| Remarried | 2.40 | 5.67 | 1.73 | 26 |
| Never married | 2.33 | 9.96 | .63 | 19 |
| Widowed | 1.80 | 6.67 | 2.67 | 3 |
| **Daughters** | | | | |
| Married | 6.12 | 11.34 | 1.83 | 132 |
| Divorced/sep. | 6.17 | 11.13 | 2.43 | 63 |
| Remarried | 4.83 | 5.87 | 1.73 | 26 |
| Never married | 4.58 | 7.42 | 2.50 | 12 |
| Widowed | 11.82 | 13.99 | 2.00 | 22 |

adult children, we would conclude that divorce of an adult child does not decrease visits with and help to older parents. If the adult child has young children, the divorce may enhance contact and temporarily increase parents' help to the daughter, but among middle-aged women, being divorced does not appear to change these relations. In particular, we find no evidence of decreased help to parents among divorced women (or men). Having divorced *and remarried* may decrease contact, perhaps in some cases because a new set of parents enters the network. Among middle-aged men, it is the never married who have the least contact with parents.

## Effects of the Parent's Divorce and Remarriage

The final issue about family disruption is the long-term consequence of a parent's divorce on later-life relations with adult children. Smyer and Hofland were among the first to raise the issue of intergenerational consequences of increasing divorce rates. They suggested that "the support of children may not be readily available to stepparents or divorced parents. In exchange terms, the older adults may not have built up enough 'credit' through affection and interaction earlier in life" (1982, p. 70). Goldscheider (1990) elaborated on the issue at length, particularly for future cohorts of older men. She argued that parents of the baby boom and later cohorts, particularly fathers, are at risk of having very low rates of contact with adult children who did not live with them during parts of childhood due to divorce and maternal custody.

Two recent studies have looked for such effects. Bulcroft and Bulcroft (1991) use NSFH data for respondents ages fifty-five and above (mean age sixty-eight) who have been married at least once, and who have a noncoresiding adult child from their first marriage. For fathers, they report that having divorced from the child's mother has a negative effect on geographical closeness, visiting, and phone contact with that child, particularly for men who divorced when the child was young. Results for mothers were negligible, presumably because they rarely lose contact with children through custody arrangements. Cooney and Uhlenberg (1990), focusing only on males from the NSFH but with a different age range (fifty to seventy-nine; mean age sixty), report that those who have been divorced have lower levels of contact with adult children, are less likely to have an adult child in their household, and are less likely to name an adult child as a potential source of support if needed. Both studies interpret the effect of divorce in relation to usual custody patterns. Because we have information as to whether each child was ever not in the respondent's custody for any reason, we can test this part of the process more directly.

It is also possible for divorce to have some effects unrelated to custody. Cooney (1994) looks at effects of later-life parental divorce on parent-child relations, selecting young adults for whom custody was not an issue because their parents divorced after they left home, and finds negative effects for fathers only. Using a similar strategy, Aquilino (1994) finds effects for both parents but stronger effects for fathers. Thus, effects may stem from different aspects of the divorce process. Perhaps children are pressured to side with one parent against the other, or are estranged from both in a later-life divorce.

We also examine differences between relations with biological children and with stepchildren. The creation of stepfamilies is clearly another potential consequence of parental divorce. We take advantage here of data on relations with stepchildren as well as other children. Although many studies have examined problems and strengths of stepfamilies (e.g., Furstenberg and Spanier 1984; Coleman and Ganong 1991) and the strains in second marriages that are associated with the presence of stepchildren (White and Booth 1985), few have examined relations between adult stepchildren and their stepparents (see discussion by Uhlenberg and Myers 1981; Smyer and Hofland 1982; Goldscheider 1990). Using NSFH data on respondents' relations with all adult children, Eggebeen (1992) used percentage of stepchildren as a predictor. He found that a presence of stepchildren decreased overall exchange of help.

In our earlier multivariate analyses of respondents and their adult children (Appendix C, tables C.3.6 and C.3.7), we included a variable representing whether or not the child had ever been noncustodial (presumably in most cases due to divorce). Approximately 6 percent of (randomly selected) daughters and 8 percent of sons had not been in the respondent's custody at some time. When we looked at these patterns by gender of respondent, we found that 12 percent of men and 5 percent of women have adult children who were ever noncustodial. We found surprisingly few effects of noncustodial history on parent-child relations. Daughters who were ever noncustodial talk on the phone with parent respondents fewer times per month (the difference is 6 calls), but there are no other differences for sons or daughters (see Appendix C, tables C.3.6 and C.3.7). We did, however, find that parents feel less close to adult children who were ever noncustodial (not in tables). Thus, at least in early adulthood, children who were involved in noncustodial situations may experience their emotional ties with parents differently, perhaps resulting in less frequent telephone calls. But they do not have measurably less contact in person with those parents. At this point perhaps help is in small enough amounts that any effect of diminished affection does not show up in helping patterns either. These findings may change in later life or in situations where a parent needs a great deal of help.

In these multivariate analyses we also included a variable representing whether a child was a stepchild or not. Six percent of sons and 9 percent of daughters were stepchildren. Respondents report no differences in contact or help to and from stepchildren in comparison to other children. They do, however, report feeling less close to stepdaughters (but not stepsons) than to other daughters (not in tables). Again, the effect of this divorce-related status shows up in attitudinal but not behavioral measures, and more for daughters than sons. We will return to the implications of these results shortly.

## Effects of Other Variables

Both this chapter and the previous one have been largely based on regression analyses presented in the tables in Appendix C, discussing first family structure variables and then turning to effects of employment and marital status history. Before concluding this chapter we comment briefly on two other sets of predictors included in those equations. First are measures of family structure that represent the gender and marital status of the parent generation and the presence of grandchildren. Second, we discuss more fully effects of geographical distance.

Effects of other control variables not discussed here can be seen in the Appendix tables.

We have found mixed results for gender of adult child: daughters talk on the telephone more with parents than do sons, visiting patterns are similar, and help to healthy middle-aged and older parents is fairly balanced between sons and daughters, beginning to tilt toward daughters for older parents. What about the gender of the *parent*? Respondents as adult children report no differences in contact or help given according to whether the living parent is a single father or mother, or part of a married couple (Appendix C, tables C.3.11 and C.3.12). When respondents are questioned about relations with children, however, unmarried (i.e., mostly divorced) fathers report fewer phone calls with daughters than do married couples or unmarried mothers, and married fathers are involved in more visits with daughters than unmarried mothers (see Appendix C, table C.3.6). The difference for phoning is consistent with what we reported above for noncustodial children.

Another indicator of family structure is the presence of children (i.e., grandchildren) in the adult child's home. It might be suggested that children would promote intergenerational bonds, or that they would create time demands that would compete with interacting with older parents. Looking at our multivariate analyses, we find that women who have minor children at home talk on the phone with their parents more than do other women (Appendix C, table C.3.11), but there are no other effects of presence of children on respondents' relations with parents. Looking at respondents' relations with their own adult children, there is no appreciable effect of grandchildren on relations with sons or daughters. Of course, we saw a hint of such an effect among divorced daughters.

One predictor that is highly consistent in its effects, however, is geographic distance between parents and adult children. Rossi and Rossi (1990, p. 458) also report the strongest and most consistent set of effects for geographic distance. As they put it, "there may be great pride in seeing a child earn an advanced degree and take an important position several hundred miles away, but it will be the child who left school earlier, took a local job, and remained in the parents' community who will be the primary source of comfort and assistance in the parents' declining years."

We measured distance in travel time (hours) as reported by the respondent. (Respondents were asked to report travel time in their choice of metric: minutes, hours, or days, and we recoded it to hours.) In our multivariate analyses, respondents reported fewer visits and phone calls with both sons and daughters as distance increases, and give less help to daughters who live farther away (Appendix C, tables C.3.6 and C.3.7). In relation to their own parents, both male and female respondents reported fewer visits and calls and less help with greater distance (Appendix C. tables C.3.11 and C.3.12). In order to examine these patterns in more detail, we present descriptive data in tables 4.4 and 4.5 (see also figures 4.3 and 4.4).

We find that approximately one in seven adult children of respondents lives within five minutes' travel time; figures for respondents and their own parents are similar. About one in three adult children lives within fifteen minutes' travel time, and about half live within one-half hour. These numbers are striking; previous literature has often reported the percentage of parents having *any* child within a particular distance, but we find also that a typical child lives a short distance away from parents.

We compare patterns of contact and help across six different distances, ranging from five minutes' travel time (this could represent a short walk of a few blocks or a drive of a couple of miles) to more than four hours. Beyond four hours probably represents a distance too great for a comfortable weekend trip, so we do not distinguish among greater distances in these tables. Not surprisingly, distance plays a major role in contacts involving visits in person. Those within five minutes see each

**TABLE 4.4**
Mean Contact and Help to and from Adult Children by Distance (in Travel Time) from Parent Respondent

|  | Visits/ month | Phone/ month | Help to child hrs/week | Help to parent hrs/week | N |
|---|---|---|---|---|---|
| **Sons** |  |  |  |  |  |
| ≤ 5 min. | 14.36 | 14.44 | 3.58 | .71 | 52 |
| 6–15 min. | 9.50 | 11.75 | 1.95 | .89 | 77 |
| 16–30 min. | 4.82 | 11.23 | .58 | 1.44 | 78 |
| 31 min.–1 hr. | 3.44 | 8.28 | 1.19 | .69 | 42 |
| > 1 hr.–4 hrs. | .74 | 3.36 | .03 | .48 | 58 |
| > 4 hrs. | .38 | 3.11 | .00 | .43 | 69 |
| **Daughters** |  |  |  |  |  |
| ≤ 5 min. | 14.80 | 17.28 | 3.45 | 1.04 | 58 |
| 6–15 min. | 10.65 | 18.19 | 1.83 | 1.46 | 96 |
| 16–30 min. | 7.52 | 15.74 | .36 | 1.17 | 72 |
| 31 min.–1 hr. | 5.70 | 15.84 | .27 | .85 | 33 |
| > 1 hr.–4 hrs. | .58 | 8.22 | .05 | .35 | 62 |
| > 4 hrs. | .57 | 3.72 | .00 | .05 | 57 |

**TABLE 4.5**
Mean Contact and Help to Parents by Distance
(in Travel Time) from Child Respondent

|  | Visits/ month | Phone/ month | Help to parent hrs/week | N |
|---|---|---|---|---|
| **Sons** |  |  |  |  |
| ≤ 5 min. | 12.18 | 11.70 | 2.66 | 29 |
| 6–15 min. | 4.73 | 10.91 | 2.00 | 27 |
| 16–30 min. | 5.32 | 11.38 | 2.61 | 23 |
| 31 min.–1 hr. | 2.57 | 3.98 | .50 | 14 |
| > 1 hr.–4 hrs. | .68 | 4.05 | .16 | 43 |
| > 4 hrs. | .31 | 2.03 | .33 | 32 |
| **Daughters** |  |  |  |  |
| ≤ 5 min. | 18.82 | 17.52 | 5.50 | 32 |
| 6–15 min. | 9.50 | 19.11 | 2.54 | 48 |
| 16–30 min. | 8.36 | 14.45 | 2.43 | 47 |
| 31 min.–1 hr. | 4.78 | 11.82 | 2.91 | 22 |
| > 1 hr.–4 hrs. | .49 | 3.73 | .30 | 47 |
| > 4 hrs. | .53 | 2.44 | .34 | 53 |

other every other day, on average. Those over four hours see each other on average five to seven times a year. Gender differences in visiting are not great, as we have seen before.

Patterns for telephoning are related to distance, but not as dramatically. There is a gradual decrease for sons between talking every other day to talking almost every week, across distances. Daughters appear to talk with parents slightly more often than every other day, at any distance up to one hour (possibly within the same calling area?), declining to twice a week at one to four hours apart and once a week at greater than four hours' distance.

Helping patterns are less linear, perhaps reflecting need as well as convenience, but beyond one hour, help is fairly rare. For example, among adult children living one to four hours from parents, only 2 of 120 children are reported to help parents in an average week, and 14 are reported by parents to be receiving regular help. Among the 128 at distances above four hours, none help parents regularly and 8 are reported to receive regular help.

Similar relationships are found from reports by children, surprising because they are based on reports about different pairs and different age cohorts. However, there are two differences between tables 4.4 and 4.5 worth noting. First, average levels of help given to parents by both

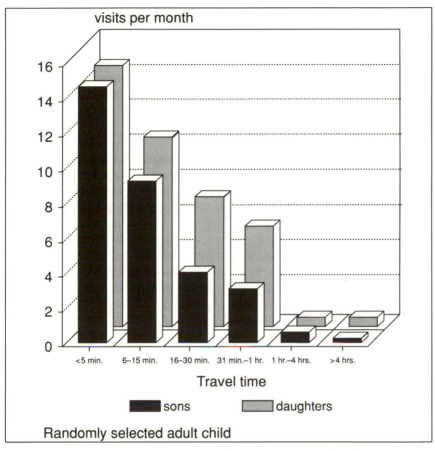

**FIGURE 4.3** Respondents' Visits with Adult Children by Distance from Child in Travel Time

sons and daughters living within an hour are higher in table 4.5. This is probably due to the substantially older average age of parents in this part of the analysis, and the fact that the parents in question are much more likely to be widowed mothers. Second, particularly among those living near parents, there are greater differences by child gender in reports by adult child respondents. This may be due to differences in point of view discussed in the previous chapter, but is more likely due, again, to age of parents and increasing help by daughters to older mothers who are alone. Most strikingly, daughters living within five minutes of parents report helping 5.5 hours per week, an amount greater than we have seen previously for any subgroup in these data. Of these thirty-two

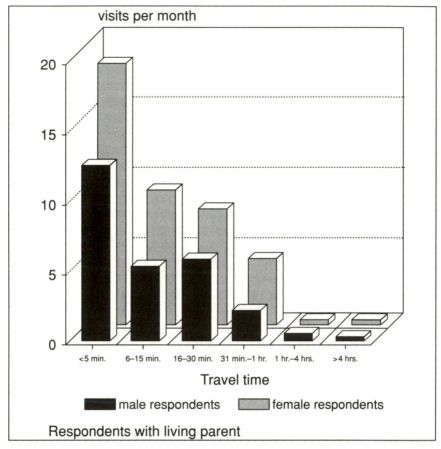

**FIGURE 4.4** Respondents' Visits with Parents by Distance from Parent

daughters, twenty-four help parents in an average week, in amounts ranging from one to twenty-five hours. However, there appears to be no relationship between amount of help and parent health status. Conversely, of those eight providing no regular help, four have parents in good or excellent health and four have parents in fair or poor health. These cases support our earlier view that help is a form of interaction as much as it may be a response to need (see also Hogan and Eggebeen 1995).

These patterns of contact in relation to distance are as expected and are consistent with results of other studies. We will return to the issue of distance in Chapter 6 when we focus on family members who live in the respondent's neighborhood.

## Discussion

We expected, as have others, that employment would conflict with helping parents and maintaining contact with them, thus creating a negative relationship between hours of employment and our dependent variables measuring assistance and interaction. Our data suggest that paid work does not conflict with interaction or feelings of closeness. We found a significant effect of employment in only one equation: a slight decrease in employed male respondents' help to parents. Otherwise the evidence is entirely inconsistent with predictions of a conflict between employment and intergenerational relations. Those who do help parents (fewer than half of respondents) typically spend very few hours a week doing so, thus creating no major conflict with paid work. Adult children's help to respondents is not affected by the child's employment. It is slightly increased when the respondent is employed, suggesting an image of a busy healthy parent rather than a frail needy one.

There has been much recent public discussion about the detrimental effects of increases in women's paid employment on receipt of needed care by the elderly. Our results suggest that there is a small proportion of aging parents that need enough care to conflict with paid employment by the caregiver. We do not wish to minimize the major conflicts and potential stress that are involved with full-time care of a frail, dependent elderly person. Public policy should indeed address the needs of these people. There is no evidence, however, that this is a typical experience of employed middle-aged persons. We also address a broader question, whether future increases in female employment are likely to change the *nature* of filial relationships. Few adult children provide intensive amounts of assistance to their parents, but many have close, loving relationships and frequent interaction. Such interaction does not conflict with employment.

Another purpose of this chapter is to examine effects of divorce. Both theory and past evidence are inconsistent as to possible effects of an adult child's divorce on relations with parents. Some fear that divorced children may require more help and may be able to give less. Alternatively, it seems likely that effects of divorce are not discernible, since relationships with parents are expected to exhibit continuity over the life course.

Our descriptive results suggest that an adult child's divorce is a fairly common experience for parents. About half of parents above age sixty who have at least one ever-married child have experienced at least one child's divorce or separation. The experience of having grandchildren not in the adult child's custody is much less common, but affects slightly over one in ten parents in their sixties. (Of those at risk, due to having a child who has children from a previous marriage, the figure is closer to one-third.) The latter results are, however, cross-sectional and may underestimate the experience of having had noncustodial grandchildren in the past.

We find some evidence (in descriptive tables and in our earlier published work based on multiple adult children) that divorced daughters with custody of their own minor children have more contact with parents and receive more babysitting help than do other daughters. However, except for telephoning, these differences are not statistically significant when tested in our multivariate model based on randomly selected adult children. Thus, we are uncertain as to how to interpret these differences. What is clear, however, is that divorced daughters help parents no less than do married daughters. Nor do divorced female respondents with living parents help those parents any less than married female respondents. Thus, we see no basis for fears expressed in the literature on this issue.

Although we would argue that our test of these issues is superior to previous ones, a remaining unanswered question concerns the extent to which these effects can be replicated using panel data. Some issues of selectivity cannot be controlled here. For example, if divorced women receive more child-care assistance than their married counterparts, it is conceivable that these women also received more help even while married, for other reasons not able to be detected here. On the other hand, it is possible that changes in feelings of closeness actually do occur upon the child's divorce, but that these differences are cancelled out by other preexisting differences.

Thus, our overall conclusion, while tentative and awaiting better tests with longitudinal data, is that an adult child's divorce has a selective and small impact on relations with parents. Many recent discussions have warned that increasing levels of divorce will disadvantage elderly parents who need help from daughters whose own resources are diminished. Our findings suggest that, at the least, a daughter's divorce will not weaken the reciprocal helping relationships between parents and daughters. They may actually increase them. And perhaps more important, the effects found were small, suggesting a great deal of *continuity* in these relationships.

Our evidence about the long-term impact of parental divorce on contact with adult children is based on cohorts that have not experienced the same levels of divorce as will baby boomers (few of whom were represented in our survey). However, our evidence suggests that having lost custody of a child at some point during childhood, an experience more common for fathers than mothers, does not appreciably affect patterns of visiting or the kinds of helping typical for most parents and adult children. This history decreases telephoning only for daughters, a reflection of its effect for both genders on feelings of closeness. These results are only suggestive, are inconsistent with studies based on the NSFH, and are clearly based on fewer cases than those studies. However, they suggest a need to specify the process through which any long-term effect of divorce takes place (e.g., to collect data on custodial histories). Further, to the extent that joint custody becomes a more common arrangement, such effects would be mitigated in the more distant future.

In this and the previous chapter, we have tested implications of demographic processes that have been making observers nervous. Concern has been expressed about the extent to which shrinking family sizes, increasing women's employment, and increasing divorce rates will lessen the likelihood that future elderly cohorts will receive adequate care from adult children. While our results do not speak directly to the availability of intensive caregiving, we do not find any evidence that would fuel these fears.

What about the consequences for the adult child generation, particularly for women who are caught among multiple, stressful demands on their time and energy due to the same trends discussed above? If the needs of the elderly *are* met under these conditions, how will this affect the well-being of their children? In the next chapter, we turn to this question.

# 5
## Role Conflicts for the
## Generation in the Middle

*The "sandwich generation" is depicted as caught between conflicting demands from dependent parents and children. We show that the various roles that middle generation people must deal with typically become intense at different times in their lives rather than converging at one time. Further, we demonstrate that demanding roles can have both positive and negative effects on well being, and there is little evidence that conflicts due to competing roles are the source of unusual levels of perceived burden, stress, or life dissatisfaction for either women or men.*

■ The idea that combining middle generation roles is particularly problematic originated in Elaine Brody's highly publicized work on the group whose name she coined, "women in the middle" (1981). Brody focused on women who combine marriage, parenting of younger or adult children, employment, and care of elderly parents. She argued that taking care of parents is becoming a "normative experience" for middle-aged persons (1985).

Although Brody called attention to a potentially serious problem in the lives of some middle-aged women, her data were based on a nonprobability sample of women who were much more likely to be taking care of frail mothers than the average middle-aged woman. In her sample, 20 percent had a mother living with them and 51 percent provided a mother with needed services. A substantial proportion of these women combined the roles of spouse, parent, employee, and adult child caregiver.

How typical is the "woman in the middle" as described by Brody (1981), and how "normative" is parent care (1985)? As Rosenthal, Matthews, and Marshall (1989) point out, the notion that middle-aged women in the United States are caught between multiple, stressful demands has become widely accepted in both the research literature and the popular press. For example, as we noted in the Preface, a recent *Ms. Magazine* article suggests that the average woman will spend more years caring for aged parents than dependent children. It quotes an Older Women's League president that "the empty nest is nothing more than a myth." In addition, it chronicles problems experienced by caregivers: "depression, anxiety, frustration, helplessness, sleeplessness, and sheer emotional exhaustion" (Weinstein 1989; see also Gross 1989).

Clearly the picture presented of the situation of middle-aged women today is not an attractive one. What is its basis in fact? Is the woman in the middle a "myth in the making?" (as put by Stull et al. 1994). Most studies of caregiving are based on convenience samples of frail elderly and their primary caregivers. In our view, the experiences of those caregivers, stressed as they may be, are far from reflective of the typical American experience. Part of the problem is the inexact use of the term "caregiver" in both research and popular publications. It may be used to denote a range of activities, from anyone who ever helps a parent (or other relative) in any area, to someone who provides full-time intensive care for a frail elderly person. Discussions of caregivers often fail to define the term and jump from statistics based on one definition to another, implying that provision of intensive long-term care is a typical experience. This is the very image of dependent elderly that we devoted so much attention to debunking in Chapters 1 and 2 (see similar critiques by Matthews 1988; Abel 1990b).

Another concern that we have with this literature is its exclusive focus on women. We do know from previous research on housework (reviewed by Ferree 1991) and "his and hers marriages" (Bernard 1972) that the content of roles, such as spouse, may differ greatly by gender. But while sociologists have found that the majority of persons providing intensive care to the frail elderly are women, mostly wives and daughters, we know less about the filial behavior of men who have living parents, or about the constellation of roles experienced by middle-aged men. Are they at risk of being caught "in the middle?" We recall that in our own research so far (particularly as reported in Chapter 2) we have found limited evidence of gender differences in the behavior of adult children.

Finally, while much literature assumes that the constellation of demands associated with being a "person in the middle" is taxing, there is only weak evidence of such effects. The notion that combining various life roles may create stress is a familiar one to most individuals in a complex society. It would be difficult to find a person who has not at one time or another experienced conflicting demands from two roles. A child is sick on an important day at work. One's cousin and one's good friend are getting married the same day in different cities. One's parent doesn't like the way one's spouse is raising the grandchildren.

Therefore it is not surprising that the consequences of occupying particular roles or role combinations have long been of concern for sociologists. One early view characterized roles as burdensome (see Coverman 1989; Goode 1960), encouraging later researchers to search for negative consequences of multiple roles for psychological well-being (see the discussion of this issue in Moen et al. 1989). This has been the thesis of most gerontological literature on caregivers, as well as much writing about women as kinkeepers. But roles and role combinations have also been viewed positively, as providing benefits (Marks 1977; Moen et al. 1992; Sieber 1974) or buffering stress from other roles (Thoits 1983, 1986). Most recently, the effects of both specific roles and of role combinations have come to be viewed as dependent on the specific situation (Moen et al. 1989), on attitudes and preferences of role incumbents and those around them, on whether their timing is normative (Menaghan 1989), and on the specific combinations of roles held (Barnett et al. 1992; Menaghan 1989; Wheaton 1990). What is surprising is that until very recently no study based on a large random sample has evaluated the effects of the specific group of roles experienced by middle-aged persons who have both living parents and children.

## How Common Are Middle Generation Roles?

To our knowledge, Rosenthal, Matthews, and Marshall's research was the first attempt to evaluate, using a probability sample of a population, the typicality of a variety of role configurations for women (1989). They present preliminary evidence based on a sample of middle-aged women in a Canadian city. Analyzing the existence of living parents, children, husbands and jobs for women ages forty to sixty-nine, they find that a minority of middle-aged women experience three or more of these roles at any age over forty. Multiple roles are most likely for women under 55, who are more likely to have living parents, but whose parents tend to be younger and healthier. Those with older, less healthy parents have fewer competing commitments. Based on data from an even smaller subsample of these women, they estimate that a maximum of around one-third may provide long-term care to parents at some point in their lives, but not necessarily concurrently with other responsibilities.

Our Albany survey offers an opportunity to replicate these findings with a larger sample and including a wider range of roles. We are also able to study the experiences of both women and men. Let us begin with a review of frequencies of individual roles, taken singly, for both men and women in middle age. We use some measures of simple incumbency in a role and others that reflect more active pursuit of the role. For example, besides whether people have living parents, we report those who actually live with a parent, and those who help a parent on a regular basis. We then report the percentages of our respondents who experience particular role combinations and examine the effects of combined roles on their well-being.

### Individual Roles

In table 5.1 we present data for "middle-generation" women (that is, women in age categories ranging from forty to forty-four through sixty to sixty-four) for several different roles. These include several role indicators analyzed by Rosenthal: number of living biological parents, number of children, marital status, and employment status. To these we add the number of parents-in-law and whether the respondent has grandchildren.

We find that the majority of women in all age categories are currently married, but increasing numbers move from the married to the widowed category with age. Through age fifty to fifty-four, the majority of women have at least one living parent. At older ages, it is more common to have no living parents, and extremely unlikely to have more than one. In age group forty to forty-four, the majority of women also have living parents-in-law, while after this the numbers drop off fairly rapidly (due partly to divorce). The vast majority of women of all ages have living children. The youngest group, the beginning of the baby boom generation, is somewhat more likely to be childless than older women. The majority have grandchildren by age fifty to fifty-four.

**TABLE 5.1**
Percentage of Middle-Aged Women with Various Roles, by Age

|  | 40–44 | 45–49 | 50–54 | 55–59 | 60–64 |
|---|---|---|---|---|---|
| Married | 65% | 60% | 58% | 56% | 56% |
| Living parents | 86% | 77% | 60% | 42% | 31% |
| Living in-laws | 55% | 41% | 33% | 26% | 9% |
| Living children | 82% | 92% | 89% | 91% | 91% |
| Grandchildren | 11% | 30% | 55% | 81% | 79% |
| Job |  |  |  |  |  |
| Full-time (35+ hours) | 61% | 62% | 56% | 35% | 27% |
| Part-time | 22 | 15 | 19 | 10 | 15 |
| None | 17 | 23 | 25 | 55 | 58 |
| Number of cases | 125 | 86 | 93 | 77 | 102 |

Finally, through age fifty-four the majority of women are currently employed full-time, with that number dropping off dramatically at older ages. Thus, for most of the roles examined thus far, percentages are highest in the age group forty to forty-four, as found by Rosenthal, and most of these roles remain typical through age group fifty to fifty-four. After this, some roles begin to drop off rapidly.

Next, we compare these experiences to those of men in the same age groups (table 5.2). Not surprisingly, three-quarters of men are married in all age categories; marriage does not fall off with age as it does for women. Men are less likely to survive their spouses than are women, and some remarry after widowhood or divorce. For men, having no living parents becomes the dominant situation by age group fifty-five to fifty-nine, just as for women, and the proportion with parents-in-law also declines with age. Men are slightly more likely than women to be childless in the youngest and oldest age categories. And by age fifty-five, half or more men have grandchildren.

Men's rates of full-time employment are considerably higher than women's, and they drop below 50 percent only in the age category above sixty.

Taking all of these results together, it seems that middle-aged people (both women and men) tend to occupy the roles of adult child, parent, spouse, and employee simultaneously (in their forties and early fifties). At these ages, every one of these roles is held by the majority of both men and women. Normal life cycle changes (death, divorce, retirement) reduce these proportions, and by their early sixties the only roles occupied by more than half of men and women are those of spouse and parent/grandparent of a noncoresident child. We might well conclude,

**TABLE 5.2**
Percentage of Middle-Aged Men with Various Roles, by Age

|  | 40–44 | 45–49 | 50–54 | 55–59 | 60–64 |
|---|---|---|---|---|---|
| Married | 74% | 70% | 76% | 74% | 80% |
| Living parents | 88% | 69% | 55% | 36% | 29% |
| Living in-laws | 67% | 59% | 47% | 32% | 27% |
| Living children | 74% | 92% | 91% | 88% | 85% |
| Grandchildren | 8% | 25% | 42% | 50% | 73% |
| Job |  |  |  |  |  |
| Full-time (35+ hours) | 89% | 87% | 82% | 74% | 36% |
| Part-time | 3 | 5 | 4 | 4 | 5 |
| None | 8 | 8 | 15 | 22 | 58 |
| Number of cases | 93 | 61 | 55 | 50 | 55 |

therefore, that early middle age is the period of greatest cross-pressures among potentially competing roles.

There are two flaws in such reasoning, however. First, simply "having" a role does not necessarily mean that the role is demanding. Second, although many roles are held by a majority of persons aged forty to fifty-five, this does not necessarily imply that the same persons hold multiple roles. Therefore, let us take a closer look at our respondents' situations.

To deal with the intensity of roles, we use additional information from respondents on their relationships with parents and parents-in-law and with their adult children. We also include whether the respondent has a child living in the household. As we found in Chapter 2, women who help parents regularly (slightly under half of all women) spend a median of three hours a week doing so. Our activity measures are based on this standard of three or more hours a week. While the use of this cutoff point is somewhat arbitrary, we consider it to be a fairly liberal definition of what might be considered an "active" relationship, and we apply it to help to parents, help to parents-in-law, and help to adult children in table 5.3. Another indicator in this table is whether any parent or parent-in-law coresides with the respondent.

Table 5.3 distinguishes between women (the top panel) and men (the bottom panel). We note to begin with that, apart from simply having

**TABLE 5.3**

Percentage of Middle-Aged Men and Women with Various "Active" Roles, by Age

|  | 40–44 | 45–49 | 50–54 | 55–59 | 60–64 |
|---|---|---|---|---|---|
| **Women** | | | | | |
| Help adult children (3 + hrs) | 7% | 19% | 32% | 36% | 27% |
| Children at home | 70% | 62% | 54% | 31% | 34% |
| Help parents (3 + hours) | 21% | 12% | 9% | 8% | 15% |
| Help in-laws (3 + hours) | 5% | 6% | 2% | 3% | 1% |
| Parents or in-laws at home | 3% | 6% | 6% | 8% | 7% |
| Number of cases | 125 | 86 | 93 | 77 | 102 |
| **Men** | | | | | |
| Help adult children (3 + hrs) | 3% | 11% | 22% | 18% | 24% |
| Children at home | 67% | 69% | 56% | 36% | 31% |
| Help parents (3 + hours) | 11% | 11% | 5% | 10% | 4% |
| Help in-laws (3 + hours) | 4% | 5% | 0% | 4% | 5% |
| Parents or in-laws at home | 2% | 3% | 4% | 0% | 9% |
| Number of cases | 93 | 61 | 55 | 50 | 55 |

children at home, in no case do more than half of men or women at any age have what we are calling an active relationship with parents or children.

For women, help to parents peaks at age forty to forty-four, when only 21 percent provide regular help of three or more hours per week. The early peak may be because the younger respondents are more likely to have living parents (see table 5.1). The percentage declines with age but then rises somewhat for those aged sixty to sixty-four, perhaps because their surviving parents are more likely to be of an age when they need assistance. (The mean age of living parents increases from seventy to eighty-six between the youngest and oldest age groups; mean subjective health of parents, however, is not related to the child's age.) Help to parents-in-law is much less common than help to parents and falls off with age. Living with any parent (biological, step, or in-law) is also rare at any age, never as high as 10 percent.

Through age fifty-four the majority of women have at least one child at home, while after fifty-five the percentage tails off to about one-third. Help to adult children living elsewhere is more common than help to parents, representing the experience of about one-third of the women between ages fifty and fifty-nine. Younger women are more likely to have children still at home and therefore less likely to be providing this type of assistance. Much assistance to children probably relates to being a grandparent (e.g., babysitting), which becomes the dominant situation by age fifty.

Compared to women, middle-aged men are equally likely to be living with a child, but considerably less likely to be helping adult children (perhaps because they are less likely to care for grandchildren). Differences in help to parents and parents-in-law are smaller (except in the forty to forty-four age group). Perhaps only for the very few providing large amounts of help to parents are there striking gender differences. Montgomery and Kamo (1989) present evidence that sons who take on the role of primary caregiver make more limited time commitments than do daughters, and that sons who provide personal care (as opposed to other kinds of assistance) are a highly select group. Like women, men are also unlikely to live with parents at any of these ages.

An important age pattern in these data is summarized in figure 5.1, which shows the percentage of women who experience either of the two more common relationships in table 5.3: helping parents or adult children. We focus on women because they are more involved in these ties than are men. As the figure shows, there is an inverse relationship between these two kinds of activities. At ages forty to forty-four, when women are most likely to be helping their parents actively, they are least

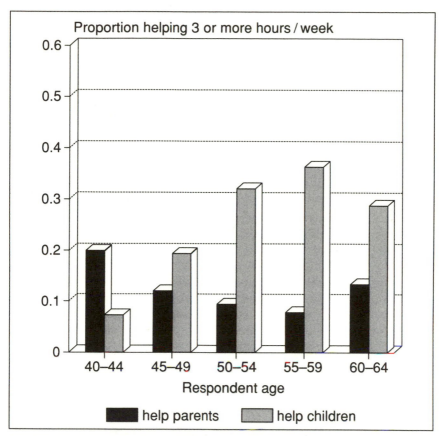

**FIGURE 5.1** "Active" Roles of Middle-Aged Women

likely to be helping their adult children. Then, as one active role becomes less frequent, the other grows.

Thus far these data do not tell us much about configurations of roles, but only that certain roles tend to be typical for the same age groups. Let us now look at specific role combinations. We will start with three major roles: being employed (having a full-time job), being involved with parents (either helping them three or more hours a week or living with a parent), and being involved with children (either helping adult children three or more hours a week or living with a child of any age). We do not include marriage here because we have no measure of the demands involved in marriage and because marriage may provide, as well as require, social support. Appendix C, table C.5.1 lists the frequency of every combination of these three roles, from none to all three, for men and women, grouped by age.

Table C.5.1 shows that the various combinations of roles are very closely associated with age. For example, for both women and men the percentage of persons with none of these three "active" roles is very small at ages forty to forty-four (about 5 percent) but rises to above 30 percent by ages sixty to sixty-four.

At the other end of the spectrum, the percentage with all three roles—presumably the most difficult situation to manage—is highest at age forty to forty-four (about 16 percent of men and 8 percent of women) and declines to near zero at age sixty to sixty-four. The specific combination emphasized in much of the intergenerational literature is when a person is "actively" a parent and adult child helper at the same time. (In table C.5.1, these are the rows for "child and parent" and for "all three roles.") The incidence of this combination is depicted in figure 5.2 for women and men separately. The percentages are almost identical for the two genders: a maximum of about 18 percent at ages forty to forty-four, declining to about 10 percent at sixty to sixty-four.

For both men and women, the combination of supporting children and full-time work is more common than any other combination during their forties and early fifties. This is particularly true for men, due to their higher rates of employment (although they are less likely to be doing the extra household work that children's presence adds in cases that involve coresidence rather than help to adult children). Nearly two-thirds of men in their forties combine these two roles (sometimes in conjunction with supporting parents). Women are less likely to combine children with work, and more likely than men to be supporting children as the only one of these roles.

Only a small proportion of women are working full-time and helping parents at the same time (about 15 percent at age forty to forty-four, diminishing considerably at older ages). Some might explain this as a product of previous conflicts between those roles, which led to quitting the job. Past research on this issue has presented conflicting results (e.g., Stoller 1983; Brody and Schoonover 1986; Finley 1989). Our own analyses have found essentially no effects of hours of employment on the amount of help men or women give to aging parents (see Chapter 3). Those women who had recently stopped working for pay helped parents no more than other women, suggesting that intensive caregiving did not explain the change.

We are now in a position to draw stronger conclusions about potential role conflicts for middle-aged people. First, the roles of being a parent/grandparent, having living parents, being married, and working are very common, though all but parenthood tend to fall off at older ages.

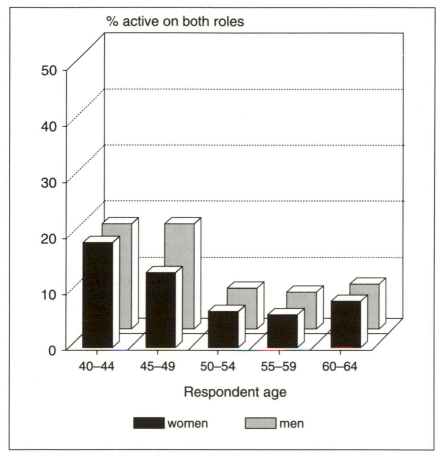

**FIGURE 5.2** Combining "Active" Parent/Child Roles

This fact provides the main basis for discussions of "women in the middle." Second, role "incumbencies" are often not very active. Most people who have adult children or who have living parents do not coreside with them or help them as much as three hours per week. Helping adult children is the most usual "active" role, and it reaches its peak for women at a time when they are least likely to be helping parents or working outside the home. Third, as a result, it turns out that the intergenerational squeeze experienced by women who are actively supporting children and parents at the same time is uncommon. No more than 20 percent seem to be in this position at ages forty to forty-four, with an overall average closer to 10 percent. Even fewer combine these roles with full-time work. And—surprisingly in terms of the emphasis on women in the literature—men are equally likely (perhaps more likely) to report these competing roles.

## Effects of Middle Generation Roles

Although it is uncommon for either women or men to have to deal with both routine care for their parents and the active roles of parent and worker, it is still important to identify the consequences of these role combinations. To the extent that they represent difficult burdens even for a minority of people, they may be a significant social concern. Being "in the middle" may be rare, but nevertheless consequential.

Two bodies of empirical literature have analyzed consequences of roles for their incumbents. First, research on family and work roles has analyzed how the roles of paid employee, spouse/partner, and parent of young children, both singly and in combination, affect men's and particularly women's well-being. This literature, largely focused on issues of gender, has been stimulated by recent increases in women's labor force participation and concerns about both inequity and stress that might arise as women add the paid worker role to other more traditional roles without a concomitant decrease in other responsibilities. In general, effects of these roles have been shown to be *neutral or positive*, with the possible exception of parenting young children.

A second body of literature, largely separate from the first, has examined roles experienced by middle generation persons, including that of adult child of aging parents and, to a lesser extent, parent of adult children. Here the focus has been largely on daughters and on stresses that arise when an adult child provides intense caregiving for a frail elderly parent (Brody 1981, 1985). This literature has considered how the amount of help given to parents may be limited by, or create stress in combination with, other roles held by the adult child helper. Some studies have also examined how parents of adult children are affected by their children's problems or by coresidence following crises such as divorce (Suitor and Pillemer 1988; Ward and Spitze 1992). These relations have received a great deal of public attention, perhaps in part because baby boomers are reaching the point when their parents are aging and their children are simultaneously reaching young adulthood. This second body of literature has emphasized possible *negative* consequences from these middle generation roles in combination with other roles.

Here we combine the concerns of these two sets of literature. We investigate the consequences of "middle generation" roles (adult child and parent of adult children) for men and women, as well as testing whether there are interaction effects created by combining these with other roles (paid worker, spouse, parent of younger children) or with each other. Very few previous studies have examined these particular role combinations. Is the negative view of middle generation roles, in contrast to the generally neutral or positive findings regarding other roles, warranted? In the next section we will review past research on the role of parent and adult child, and we will describe briefly those few studies that have attempted to focus on these roles in combination with others.

## Being a Parent

Research has found that parenthood is stressful, particularly when children are very young, and particularly for women. Parents of both genders have lower psychological well-being and marital quality than nonparents (McLanahan and Adams 1987, 1989). However, the picture is actually more complex. Umberson (1989a) points out that classical theorists and popular belief view parenting in a positive manner, as an important component of healthy maturation and a major source of life satisfaction and social integration (Ishii-Kuntz and Seccombe 1989). While empirical studies have found mostly negative effects, they have been small. Umberson concludes, just as have other role researchers, that the context is crucial, and that parenting can be a source of both benefits and stress depending upon factors such as life cycle stage, living arrangements, economic situation, and marital status of the parent. Umberson and Gove (1989) find that parents with children at home have higher life meaning but lower life satisfaction and higher levels of agitation. This is particularly true for mothers, who report higher levels of demands by children (Umberson 1989b).

There may be differences between having young children at home and having coresident *adult* children. The latter, while requiring less care and attention than young children, still tend to receive some services from parents, particularly from mothers (Ward et al. 1992). They may also be positively selected, such that those who do not get along well with parents or who do not provide some form of exchange with parents, are less likely to stay (Aquilino 1991; Aquilino and Supple 1991; Ward and Spitze 1992). On the other hand, coresidence with parents during adulthood is likely to imply some form of failure to attain adult status or a crisis such as divorce or unemployment, and thus may create stress for parents (Brubaker 1991; Ward and Spitze 1992), particularly mothers who are expected to provide household services to these children.

Having *non*coresident adult children has been found to increase well-being, particularly for mothers, who tend to be in more contact with those children (Umberson and Gove 1989; but see Umberson 1992). This is consistent with White and Edwards's (1990) finding that marital happiness and overall life satisfaction go up when children leave home, but only when there is frequent contact with noncoresident children and when young teens are still in the household (interpreted to indicate recency of others leaving). Thus, the contextual issues of adult child coresidence and contact appear to be key. In contrast to the focus in this literature on *contact* with adult children, we find no evidence regarding potential effects of providing *help* to adult children on older parents' well-being.

*Being an Adult Child*
Some studies of the adult child role have been motivated by concerns about the potential effects of demographic trends on whether frail elderly persons will have their needs met and whether their adult children will be overburdened by multiple roles. A large literature on caregiver stress has focused heavily on adult children as well as spouse caregivers (e.g., Miller 1989; Miller and Montgomery 1990; Pruchno 1990), generally using convenience samples of caregivers providing large amounts of assistance (see critique in Barer and Johnson 1990).

However, we are reluctant to focus on the role of "caregiver" per se. The adult child role includes a variety of forms of contact, including both giving and receiving occasional help, and intensive caregiving is comparatively rare (Rossi and Rossi 1990). As Umberson pointed out recently (1992), few studies using general population samples have examined the consequences of the adult child role in its more usual form of a relationship between healthy parents and children for the adult child's well-being.

*Combining Middle Generation Roles*
Umberson (1992) finds that relations with parents can increase or decrease depression, depending on their content. Only a few studies have measured effects on psychological well-being of the adult child role *in combination* with other roles. Using data from a sample of elderly respondents, Stoller and Pugliesi (1989) conducted interviews with respondents' primary helpers to study whether the caregiver role becomes more or less problematic when combined with other roles (spouse, parent with child at home, and employee). They found, somewhat surprisingly, that although a caregiver's sense of burden increases with hours of help, distress and depression *decrease* with higher numbers of hours.

There were no significant interactions between hours of help given and the other three role variables.

Stoller and Pugliesi took an important first step in applying sociological thinking about role combinations, but their study had several limitations. First, since the sampling design was based on elderly persons and their helpers, the helpers were not a sample of any identifiable population group. (About half were adult children, while the rest had other relationships with the elderly persons.) Second, the sample of helpers was limited in size (N = 173). Its distribution by gender was not reported, nor were gender interactions considered. Third, while the content of the caregiver role was measured in some detail, the other roles were measured dichotomously. Another recently published study found no effects of multigenerational caregiving on psychological well-being (Loomis and Booth 1995). It had the advantage of longitudinal data on well-being, and the disadvantage of measures of caregiving that were subjective (based on obligations "taking a lot" of one's time and energy) rather than concrete. Two other studies (Barnett et al. 1991; Brody et al. 1992) provide some evidence of buffering of the effects of the adult child caregiver role for married persons, but have other important limitations (women only, no measures of employment or parenting).

The Albany study, by comparison, is well suited to determine how the roles of adult child and parent of adult children *combine with* those of paid worker, spouse, and parent of younger children to affect middle-aged men's and women's psychological well-being. Although much of the roles literature has focused on women, we will examine how roles are experienced by both men and women. We use two measures of psychological well-being (a scale measuring distress and self-reported life satisfaction), as well as a measure of perceived family burden. Our measures of roles capture both role incumbency and level of involvement in the role.

## Measuring Effects of Roles

The literature on roles and well-being has used two related but separate kinds of scales to measure well-being. On the one hand, many studies use multi-item scales measuring symptoms of anxiety or distress (e.g., Barnett, et al. 1992; Brody et al. 1992; Kandel et al. 1985; Thoits 1986; Umberson 1989b; Wheaton 1990). Other studies have used single-item scales measuring happiness or life satisfaction (e.g., McLanahan and Adams 1989; Spreitzer 1979; Umberson 1989a, 1889b; White and Edwards 1990). We use both types of measures. We also include a measure of perceived family burden, which may provide a reflection of how the respondent experiences the multiple family roles on which we focus.

The family burden measure is a single-item scale asking respondents if they strongly disagree, disagree, agree, or strongly agree with the statement: "I sometimes feel overburdened by my family's demands on me." This is somewhat similar to Gove and Geerken's (1977) "incessant demands" scale. We include this measure as an indicator of what might be viewed as role overload, without intending for it to be a direct measure of well-being. (Its correlation with distress is .22; with life satisfaction, − .08.) It should be kept in mind that someone with few or no family ties would automatically disagree with this statement.

Distress is measured by a scale based on the following ten statements, which the respondent indicated were true or not true: (*a*) Things keep getting worse as I get older; (*b*) I have as much pep as I did last year; (*c*) Little things bother me more this year; (*d*) As I get older I feel less useful; (*e*) I sometimes worry so much that I can't sleep; (*f*) I get upset easily; (*g*) I am as happy now as I was when I was younger; (*h*) I am afraid of a lot of things; (*i*) I get mad more than I used to; (*j*) I take things hard. Initial responses were 0 = no and 1 = yes. The ten items were then coded so that a value of 1 represented higher distress and were summed into a scale with possible values ranging from 0 to 10 where high distress was coded 10. Alpha coefficients for the scale are .75 for men and .78 for women.

Our single-item indicator of subjective well-being is self-reported life satisfaction (this indicator was introduced in Chapter 1, where we found that older people were more satisfied with their lives). Respondents were asked to rate their satisfaction with their life as a whole on a scale of one to seven, with higher numbers indicating greater life satisfaction. While the responses are somewhat skewed toward higher numbers, we concluded for two reasons that this is not a problem for our analysis. First, we found that this variable is significantly related to several role and control variables for both men and women. Second, when we recoded the less common, lower range of responses (1–3) to the middle response (4), we found that some significant effects disappeared, suggesting that these responses in the lower range are meaningful.

Ordinary least squares (OLS) regression is used to determine the effects of roles on well-being. While the use of cross-sectional data might pose questions about the causal ordering between role variables and well-being (those who are healthier might take on more roles), we would argue that this is not a problem for the roles considered here. They generally represent transitions that were undertaken in the distant past (e.g., having a child) or that were not voluntarily undertaken (having living parents). Well-being is measured currently. We would have more of a concern regarding causal ordering if we were examining roles that are highly voluntary and tend to fluctuate frequently (e.g., club membership).

Means and standard deviations of variables in these analyses are presented in Appendix C, table C.5.2. The main effects of roles (measured in two ways) are estimated for each dependent variable, for female and male respondents separately, and are reported in Appendix C, tables C.5.3 and C.5.4. We then add two-way terms representing combinations of roles. These effects are reported in Appendix C. table C.5.5. Positive interaction terms for burden or distress and negative interaction terms for satisfaction are interpreted as indicators of role strain, while interactions in the opposite direction are understood in terms of one role buffering or compensating for the effects of another. Effects of control variables are as expected and consistent across the two tables; we do not discuss them here.

Simple measures of role incumbency (see table C.5.3) have several significant effects on well-being. Being married has positive effects on life satisfaction for women and men. At the same time, it increases feelings of family burden for women. It is interesting, although perhaps not surprising, that marriage has these mixed effects for women but only a positive effect for men. This is consistent with the concept, originated by Jessie Bernard (1972), of "his" and "hers" marriages.

There is no effect of employment on any dependent variable. However, our measure of employment is admittedly crude, and others have done a better job of measuring the content of the paid work role (e.g., Barnett et al. 1992). Our data were gathered to study intergenerational relations, and few questions were devoted to other roles.

Having living parents or parents-in-law also has no impact on well-being for either women or men. But having children (including children of all ages together) substantially increases women's family burden, and it increases distress about equally for both women and men.

Effects of the more active role measures are reported in Appendix C, table C.5.4. The spouse and worker roles are unchanged from the previous table. One modification from before is that we now find an impact of helping or coresiding with parents (or parents-in-law) on women's burden. But unexpectedly, the association between having children and greater distress disappears when we use the more restrictive definition of having coresiding children or actively helping adult children. What remains in this table is the impact of children on women's sense of family burden.

These results are illustrated in figure 5.3, which presents the pre-

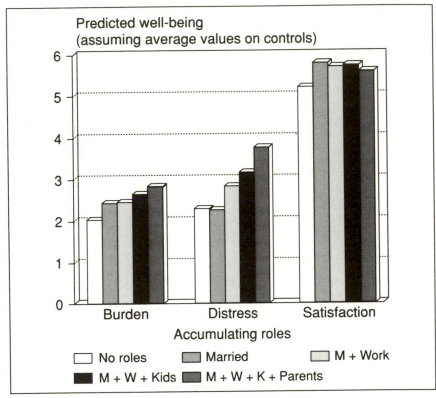

**FIGURE 5.3** Active Roles and Well-Being for Middle-Aged Women

dicted values of burden, distress, and satisfaction for women. We assume average values on the control variables (i.e., women who are fifty-one years old, "good" health reported as four on a five–point scale, and $35,000 income). The figure shows that, compared to having none of the active roles studied here, married women are noticeably higher in both burden and satisfaction. The accumulated effects of adding additional roles are to increase burden and distress (though the latter effects are not statistically significant), but there is no further impact on satisfaction once marriage has been added.

These analyses have estimated only the simple additive effects of various roles. The heart of the matter is whether specific combinations of roles have stronger and more uniformly negative impacts (the role strain or overload hypothesis), or whether they have no impact or actually increase well-being (the buffering hypothesis). To evaluate the effects of role combinations, we add six interaction terms to the four "active" role measures in table C.5.5. Because all roles are measured as dichotomous variables (coded 0 and 1), each interaction term has a value of 1 for people who have the specific combinations of roles being tested and 0 for people who have only one or neither role. For example, the "married + work" term has a value of 1 for people who are both married and working. If it has an effect in any equation, it should be understood as the effect of the role combination over and beyond the simple effect (or main effect) of marriage or working taken separately.

We find no evidence of consequences of role combinations, negative or positive, for men. For women the picture is a bit more complicated. We find two opposite kinds of effects. In the model for women's distress, we now find a significant and *positive* main effect of children. But there is also a significant and approximately equal *negative* effect of the interaction term representing the combination of being married and dealing with children. This means that there is no net effect of children for married women, and the increase in distress holds only for unmarried (mostly divorced or widowed) mothers. This is an example of how one role (being married) appears to facilitate another role (being a parent). There are two examples of negative impacts, both for women. The combination of work and children adds to burden. (Note that here the main effects of dealing with parents and children described previously disappear. We have no explanation for this shift.) And the combination of work and marriage adds to distress.

We also tested for higher-order effects (that is, for the effects of specific combinations of three roles or all four together) and found no significant coefficients. Elsewhere, exploring different ways of operationalizing active roles, we found a similar pattern of counterbalancing interaction effects: some indicating that role combinations reduce well-being, and others indicating a positive impact (Spitze et al. 1994). But only a small fraction of two-way interactions were significant, and there were no consequences of combining three or more roles. In light of these results, we feel confident in concluding that there is little evidence of problems from combining middle generation roles for either women or men.

## Discussion

Our conclusions here bear on two questions. First, how typical are "women [or men] in the middle?" Second, what are the effects of this and similar situations on people's experience of life?

We find that the four major roles discussed by Brody and analyzed by Rosenthal et al.—spouse, paid worker, adult child of aging parent, and parent—are typical of people in their forties and early fifties, but most roles fall off rapidly after that point. Men are equally or more likely to experience each of these as are women, and marriage remains typical for men in older ages. When we examine measures that represent more active involvement in these roles, we find much smaller percentages of women or men participating at any given age, and the most likely ages for helping parents occur before help to adult children (and being a grandparent) becomes most common.

The situation described by Brody is hardly typical of middle-aged women or men in the United States today. On the contrary, only a small percentage of people at any given time are trying to juggle parent care on top of child care, paid work, and marriage. This is not to say that the latter three roles do not present conflicts for many persons today, but rather that for most persons, child care is not a major demand at the same time parent care is. And, at any given time, a very small percentage of men or women are actively providing parent care.

To be fair, Brody never asserts that the situation she describes is experienced by a majority of women in any given age group. She presents the woman in the middle as a "prototype." However, she offers statistics on her three-generation sample that would suggest that juggling this variety of roles *is* typical (1981; p. 474), and clearly these data from her purposive sample of women have been greatly over-interpreted by others.

We do not have data on the long-term prospects for parent care, nor have we seen any such estimates. It may be the case that, at some point during adulthood, the majority of women or men provide some care for a frail elderly parent. Apart from employee surveys, which are also cross-sectional, there is little good evidence on this point. However, the cross-sectional picture is not as negative as it has been painted.

We found some evidence that men and women experience burden and distress in their middle generation roles. We would characterize these effects as scattered and weak, especially for men. Men are more likely than women to combine full-time work with active support for parents and children. But women are more likely to be actively providing help to parents or adult children. Therefore, it is interesting that the more frequent negative effects are also for women. The literature on caregiving stress has focused largely on *adult daughters*, and it is certainly true that the majority of intensive caregiving is provided by wives or daughters or mothers. Nevertheless, in the normal range of intergenerational relationships, it is an overstatement to describe these roles as stressful. We emphasize:

First, that the most consistent negative impact for women is the increased family burden experienced by married women. But this is counterbalanced by increased satisfaction for married women.

Second, that combining roles is not especially problematic. Role combinations mostly have no effect on well-being, beyond the effect of each individual role, and the few effects that we have identified (here and elsewhere) include both positive and negative outcomes for well-being.

It should be kept in mind that our measures of helping are limited to tasks relating to the household. We did not measure financial assistance, which drains the giver's own financial resources, or emotional support, which may sometimes be psychologically exhausting to the provider. While emotional support is subjective and particularly hard to measure, it would be useful to attempt to determine the effect of these additional forms of assistance on psychological well-being.

We do not wish to minimize the high levels of stress that must be involved in full-time care for a frail elderly parent. Many people experience high levels of stress from such care. There may also be subtle differences in the experience of stress and burden by gender, with women experiencing more guilt and emotional involvement (Robinson and Thurnher 1979; Brody 1985; Stoller and Pugliesi 1989). But we *would* suggest that it may not be the configuration of roles but this one highly stressful responsibility that is difficult to manage.

# 6
# The Family in Social Networks

*Family ties invigorate social relations within the neighborhood. They generally inhibit use of formal or paid services to accomplish routine tasks. For older people, help from either a spouse or a child substitutes for use of public aging services. Thus we conclude that ties between parents and their adult children are at the core of their social networks, durable in the face of other social changes.*

■ Previous chapters have stressed the vitality of family relationships, describing their altruistic and reciprocal character, showing their durability despite competing responsibilities, and demonstrating that family ties have positive as well as negative effects on well-being. In various ways we have been developing the point that the family is "alive and well." This is also the conclusion of those who have studied the larger social networks in which the family is embedded. Barry Wellman's (1979) pioneering study of the "intimate relationships" of East Yorkers, for example, found that family members comprised about half of the persons listed by respondents who were asked about the six "people outside your home that you feel closest to." Further, Wellman found that East Yorkers feel closer to kin than to unrelated intimates, and that parents and children are more likely than other intimates to provide regular or emergency help.

In this chapter we examine more closely how family ties fit together with other aspects of people's social networks, not only the relative frequency or strength of various sources of support but also the effect that one has on the other. We deal with two specific dimensions of social networks: the local neighborhood and formal services (which could include both private and public assistance).

The neighborhood is especially interesting in light of the historic relationship between community and kinship in social theory. Kinship was central to the "urban village" life that sociologists believe was common in the industrial city of the nineteenth and early twentieth centuries. And both of these traditional social forms have been described as receding under the advance of modernization. We will show that the

126

two remain closely linked in a modern metropolis and that "family neighbors"—that is, people who are both close family and live in the same neighborhood—are still at the core of many Americans' social networks.

Formal services are important, on the other hand, because they are so often depicted as having supplanted informal supports. This is the view clearly enunciated by Preston (1984), as cited in Chapter 1: the family is losing its support function for children and older persons, and is being replaced by government. As we will acknowledge, much of the gerontological literature now ascribes a much stronger continuing role to family support systems, but there are large gaps in our understanding of how informal and formal supports interact. What is the relative balance between the two, and are they best seen as mutually reinforcing sources of help or as alternatives?

### Family and Neighborhood

In a theoretical tradition rooted in Louis Wirth's (1938) vision of "urbanism as a way of life," the neighborhood is regarded as having diminishing importance in people's social lives. The anonymity of the modern metropolis is thought to have freed people from ties previously imposed by the local community. Its heterogeneity allows them to choose social partners based on common interests wherever they may be found: through the workplace, or voluntary associations, or as friends of friends. Distance is becoming a weaker constraint on interaction in industrial society: people can cover a wider territory in their daily routines, they can maintain contact at greater distances through telecommunications, and they are more likely to change their place of residence. The resulting social networks not bounded by geography have been described as "community liberated," in Wellman's (1979) terms (see also Fischer 1982).

Yet there are many reasons to expect the residential neighborhood to continue to focus people's social interaction. Spatial proximity makes it convenient to spend time with others in the neighborhood and creates common interests. Neighbors have the same access to jobs and shopping, they have the same exposure to crime and receive the same protection from the police, their children typically attend the same schools, they suffer the same earthquakes. Neighborhoods are often socially homogeneous, certainly more so than the metropolis as a whole. Thus neighbors typically share bonds of class, race and ethnicity, religion, and even kinship. The resulting mixture of instrumental connections, social homogeneity, and sentiment can be a powerful basis for collective action (Logan and Molotch 1987).

What is the relation between neighboring and kinship? It is well established that a large portion of family social interaction is highly localized. Though there has been a trend away from coresidence by older parents and their adult children (see Chapter 2), a substantial proportion of parents live near at least one of their children. As Shanas (1979, p. 6) notes, "they now live next door, down the street, or a few blocks away." National surveys have found that between 15 percent (Moss 1985, based on 1969 data) and 25 percent (Lawton and Silverstein 1992, based on 1987 data) of adults with living parents reside within one mile of a parent. This is in addition to those who coreside with parents. As many as 18 percent of parents aged sixty-five and over lived with a child in 1984, and of those not living with a child, 40 percent lived within ten minutes of at least one child (Crimmins and Ingegneri 1990; see also Cantor 1979 and tables 4.4 and 4.5 above).

Further, research on intergenerational relations has demonstrated "the overwhelming importance of distance as a determinant of parent-child interaction" (Crimmins and Ingegneri 1990, p. 10). In one study, for example, the share of parents with daily face-to-face contact with a noncoresident adult child was 51.5 percent for those living in the same neighborhood, dropping to only 11.4 percent at a distance of between two and ten miles (Moss 1985). Rossi and Rossi (1990) report zero-order correlations between frequency of visiting and distance as great as −.80. In regression models predicting frequency of intergenerational contact, distance is typically the single most important predictor, accounting for as much as half of the explained variance (DeWit et al. 1988; Crimmins and Ingegneri 1990; Lawton and Silverstein 1992; Wolf et al. 1983).

These considerations imply that "family neighbors" may play a pivotal role in social interaction within the neighborhood. One recent study of neighboring networks (Campbell and Lee 1992) found that having kin living nearby significantly increased the duration, frequency, and closeness of ties with neighbors. But just as there is debate over whether neighboring of any form is still prominent in social networks, there is also doubt about the continued importance of the family in neighboring. In his review of the literature, for example, Wellman (1990) downplays this role. Though he acknowledges that people often have one or two intimate relatives in their neighborhood, he concludes that the pattern in which "many kin—extended as well as immediate—live nearby, visit often, and rely heavily on each other for support" is uncommon. "[M]ost local ties are with neighbors and not kin, and it is neighbors and friends who provide most support and companionship" (1990, p.

207). Most urban sociologists seem to regard family neighbors as a carry-over from traditional urban working-class or minority neighborhoods, such as those of inner London described by Young and Willmott (1957). Similarly family sociologists, while recognizing that some kin networks are still rooted in neighborhoods, have emphasized the emergence of a new kind of family. For example, Litwak's (1960, p. 385) concept of the "modified extended family" is distinguished from "past extended families in that it does not require geographic propinquity" to function.

This linkage between kinship and community was also a source of debate in the Chicago school of urban sociology. In the line of thought represented by Louis Wirth, as noted above, urbanization was believed both to undermine community ties and to weaken bonds of kinship. Another group of Chicago sociologists, including William Thomas, Robert Park, and Ernest Burgess, put forward what Kasarda and Janowitz (1974) describe as a "systemic model" of local solidarity. In this model, "the local community is viewed as a complex system of friendship and kinship networks," as well as "formal and informal associational ties *rooted in family life* and on-going socialization processes" (Kasarda and Janowitz 1974, p. 329, our emphasis).

Such contrasting views were the basis for these authors' classic study of community attachment. Following Wirth, they hypothesized that greater urban size and density would be associated with smaller local networks of both family and friends, and consequently with weaker community attachment. Following the systemic model, they expected that length of residence would be the key factor, as time leads naturally to larger local networks and stronger attachment.

Most subsequent research on neighboring has not distinguished between kin and friends, including all interaction in the local area as "neighboring." These studies have, however, followed the lead of Kasarda and Janowitz in exploring the Chicago school's contrasting theoretical perspectives, adding other pertinent variables to the model. Some variables, in our reading of the literature, mostly represent neighboring as a residual form of social interaction, associated with *constraints* on extralocal contacts or lack of resources to build extralocal associations. Others reflect positive commitments or *investments* made in the neighborhood, more in line with the systemic theory. Although our research is focused primarily on the role of the family in neighborhood interaction, our analytical models include the key variables discussed in this literature, many of which are familiar from analyses in previous chapters.

We contribute to these debates in two ways. First, we identify the relative weight of family neighbors, nonfamily neighbors, family outside the neighborhood, and friends outside the neighborhood in people's routine social interactions. The category of family neighbors has not been studied in this way in the past. Research on intergenerational relations has distinguished between family members at different distances, but has not compared family and nonfamily interaction within the neighborhood. Studies of general social networks provide information on both family and nonfamily network members, but usually do not distinguish between geographically proximate and distant kin. Urban researchers typically count neighbors as a single category regardless of kinship.

Second, we explore the mediating role of family neighbors in affecting how differences in people's personal characteristics (such as their social class background) result in differences in their neighborhood interaction. This general scheme is illustrated in figure 6.1. Our models assume that the number of family neighbors and the number of other neighbors known by the respondent should themselves be understood as sources, or causes, of neighborhood interaction. This assumption is most plausible for family neighbors. Residential patterns bringing families together or separating them (e.g., moves in response to marriage, schooling, or employment) are likely to be causally prior to the level of social interaction among family members, although there may also be a tendency for residential immobility among people with strong local family networks. It is also reasonable to presume that interaction with other neighbors begins with meeting them, and that the more neighbors

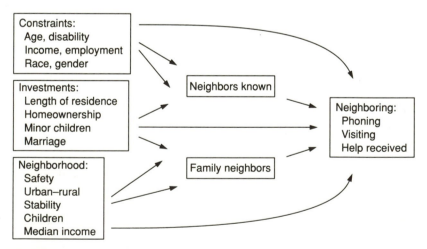

**FIGURE 6.1** Illustrative Model Predicting Neighboring via Number of Neighbors and Family Neighbors

one gets to know by name, the more likely one is to spend time with some of them. (To some extent, of course, one might argue that social integration within a neighborhood, perhaps associated with family networks, might keep people within the area. And one may get to know more neighbors by name as a byproduct of spending time with some of them.) Laying out the causal structure in this way allows us to estimate the relative effects of family neighbors and nonfamily neighbors on total social interaction in the neighborhood. We will demonstrate that a number of other variables thought to affect neighboring do so only indirectly, especially through their effects on the presence of family neighbors.

*Measures of Interaction and Help*

In previous chapters we have made use of measures of interaction and help between parents and children. Help from other relatives, friends, and neighbors was covered in the Albany survey in the same battery of questions about "how things are done" as was used for parents and children. Respondents were also asked how many other relatives they "see or hear from regularly" who live in the metropolitan area, how often they visit "with any of these relatives" or talk to them on the telephone. Regarding neighbors, they were asked "How many neighbors do you know well enough to greet by name," and how often they visit or talk on the telephone with any of their neighbors. Finally, they were asked "About how many friends do you have who live in the Albany-Schenectady-Troy area, but not in your neighborhood," and how often they visit or talk on the telephone with "any of them."

Because its distribution is highly skewed, the number of neighbors is logged when it is included as a dependent or independent variable in regression models. Children and parents include relatives by marriage. They are further categorized according to their place of residence. Coresiding family members are not counted. They are certainly "within the neighborhood," but they are not "neighbors" in the usual meaning of the term. Those living "within walking distance" are considered to be "family neighbors." (An alternative classification, based on living "within five minutes distance," would include a slightly larger number of persons but otherwise lead to no different conclusions. We use the more restrictive definition of "walking distance" here.)

Limiting consideration of other categories of network members to people within the region probably has little effect on our subsequent estimates of helping relationships because the kinds of help studied here generally require physical presence. But it does reduce the estimates of contact with friends and other relatives (see table 6.1), especially phon-

**TABLE 6.1**

Composition of People's Support Networks: Mean Values for Persons Age 40 and Above (N = 1,200)

|  | Number | Phone calls per month | Visits per month | Minutes of help per week |
|---|---|---|---|---|
| Family neighbors | .3 | 2.9 | 3.4 | 25 |
| Family beyond neighborhood | 2.5 | 14.9 | 8.8 | 50 |
| Other relatives | 8.2 | 5.0 | 2.6 | 14 |
| Friends | 21.6 | 6.5 | 3.1 | 24 |
| Neighbors | 12.6 | 3.8 | 3.8 | 4 |

ing, which is much less affected by proximity than are visiting and helping.

Information on contact with other relatives, neighbors, and friends was asked for the category as a whole, rather than for each relative, neighbor, or friend separately. Asking about these latter persons as a category may lead to an underestimate of phoning and visiting with them, compared to a procedure in which numerous individuals would be identified by name and asked about individually. This potential problem does *not* affect the indicator of help received. Help information was calculated for each individual helper (regardless of relationship to the respondent), summed across categories of helper, and expressed in minutes per week (in table 6.1). This variable is highly skewed, and its logged form is used in our regression equation.

All of these variables are measured for individual respondents. Some sociologists have argued that there may also be contextual effects on neighboring. For example, regardless of how long an individual has lived in a neighborhood, his or her ties to other neighbors may be stronger if the neighborhood as a whole has a more settled population (Sampson 1991). Campbell and Lee (1992) find that people know more of their neighbors in neighborhoods with higher average income levels and more children. We include these three neighborhood-level variables, which are based on information for the block group in which respondents lived as reported in the 1990 Census of Population and Housing: residential stability (the proportion of residents in 1990 who had lived in the block group for more than ten years), median household income, and neighborhood children (proportion of families with children under eighteen years of age). Other contextual variables were examined in preliminary analyses, but yielded no significant effects.

The variables of size and density are represented here as an urban-rural dimension: this is a pair of dummy variables representing rural and suburban locations, with central city locations treated as the omitted category. Rural residents in our sample live in small settlements at some distance from other villages or neighborhoods. People in urban areas have greater opportunities for interaction outside of the neighborhood, because of shorter distances and better transportation networks. They may also (as in some depictions of elderly shut-ins in inner cities) choose not to spend much time in the neighborhood outside of their own homes, due to fear of crime (Fischer 1982; Sampson 1991). To test this hypothesis, we include another contextual variable drawn from the survey. "Perceived safety" is a four-point scale in response to the question, "How safe do you feel being out alone in your neighborhood?"

*Neighborhood and Family in Social Networks*
Family neighbors are fairly common in our sample; their frequency (taking into account the age composition of the sample) is consistent with national estimates. In our sample 15 percent of respondents have an adult child and 7 percent have a parent living within the neighborhood (more precisely, "within walking distance"). These figures include people with no living (or no noncoresident) parents or children. Of those with at least one noncoresident adult child, 21 percent have a child in the neighborhood, and of those with at least one living and noncoresident parent, 15 percent have a parent in the neighborhood.

These family neighbors play a major part in social networks. In table 6.1 we classify all network members into categories that we shall refer to as family neighbors (parents and children in the neighborhood), neighbors (nonrelatives in the neighborhood), other family (parents and children beyond the neighborhood), relatives (additional kin within the metropolitan region regardless of where they live), and friends (nonrelatives living within the metropolitan area but outside the neighborhood). It would be preferable to be able to identify other close relatives, such as siblings, who live within the neighborhood, but we have no information on their place of residence. Therefore our category of "family neighbors" understates the actual importance of close relatives who live nearby. We report the average number of persons, the average number of visits (in each other's homes or elsewhere) and telephone conversations per month, and the average number of minutes of help per week received from persons in each category.

Note first of all that the average number of friends (21.6) is much higher than any other kind of network member, followed by neighbors (12.6) and relatives (8.2). (The number of neighbors is near the average of 14.7 reported by Campbell and Lee [1992] for Nashville.) The average number of nearby parents and children is only .3, with 2.5 parents and children beyond the neighborhood. In sheer numbers, family neighbors are the smallest fraction of people's social networks.

Telephone contact is strongly oriented toward family outside the neighborhood (14.9 calls per month). Friends account for the next highest number (6.5), followed by relatives (5.0), neighbors (3.8), and family neighbors (2.9). Visiting is also most frequently with family outside the neighborhood (8.8 per month). But here the effects of proximity seem to come into play, as neighbors (3.8) and family neighbors (3.4) account for more visits than friends (3.1) or other relatives (2.6).

Finally, routine help with daily activities is once again most likely to be received from family outside the neighborhood (fifty minutes per week). Family neighbors provide the next largest share (twenty-five minutes), followed by friends (twenty-four minutes) and relatives (fourteen minutes). Neighbors—much more significant in numbers and frequency of social interaction—provide an averge of only four minutes of help per week.

Further insight into the composition of support networks is provided in table 6.2, which reports the proportion of respondents who report receiving help on a regular basis from each of these sources. Help is further categorized into grocery shopping, meal preparation, doing laundry, transportation and errands, yard work and house repairs, housecleaning, personal care or care when sick, and (for those who have younger children) babysitting. The most common categories of help are personal care, yard work and repairs, and transportation and errands. In every category, the most common source of help is family neighbors, followed by (or equaled by) parents and children who live outside the neighborhood. Respondents were much less likely to name another rela-

**TABLE 6.2**
Proportion of Respondents Receiving Help on Specific Tasks

|  | Family neighbors | Other family | Source of help Other relatives | Friends | Neighbors |
|---|---|---|---|---|---|
| Grocery shopping | .06 | .06 | .03 | .01 | .01 |
| Meal preparation | .03 | .03 | .01 | .01 | .00 |
| Laundry | .04 | .03 | .01 | .00 | .00 |
| Transportation and errands | .10 | .09 | .05 | .04 | .01 |
| Yard work and repairs | .13 | .11 | .05 | .02 | .02 |
| Housecleaning | .04 | .04 | .02 | .00 | .00 |
| Personal care | .16 | .15 | .05 | .04 | .02 |
| Babysitting | .03 | .02 | .01 | .01 | .00 |

tive for any of these tasks, and were least likely to name a person whom they identified simply as a friend or neighbor.

These results are pertinent to the "community liberated" observation that modern social networks are heterogeneous and bounded neither by proximity nor by kinship. Although we don't have information here about trends over time, it appears that "friends" do play a significant role in social networks, with large numbers of friends accounting for a substantial share of telephone contact and more modest shares of visiting and helping. "Neighbors" are less important than friends, being smaller in number and (if we combine telephoning and visiting) participating less frequently in social interaction and helping.

Yet the difference between friends and neighbors is dwarfed by the dominant role of parents and children. Though fewer than friends in number, these family members provide the lion's share of contact and help to our respondents. Further, demonstrating the joint effects of kinship and proximity, *family neighbors* contribute contact and help vastly out of proportion to their numbers. This contrast is depicted in the pie charts of figure 6.2. Recall that the majority of respondents had no parent or child in the neighborhood, yet family neighbors account for approximately one-sixth of all visits and over 20 percent of the routine help received.

### Who Has More Neighbors?

The means and standard deviations of variables analyzed in this chapter are provided in Appendix C, table C.6.1. Figure 6.3 lists the variables that have significant effects, arranged in order of the size of their standardized coefficients (betas). The full results of multiple regression equations in which the number of neighbors and the number of family neighbors are predicted by various personal and neighborhood characteristics are presented in Appendix C, table C.6.2.

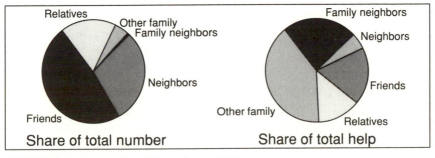

**FIGURE 6.2** Composition of People's Social Networks

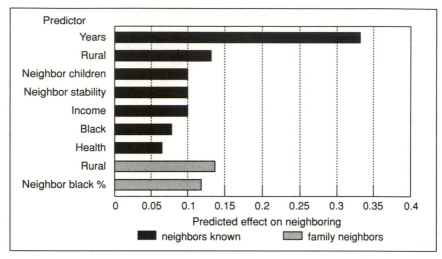

**FIGURE 6.3** Who Has More Neighbors?

Length of residence in the neighborhood is by far the best predictor of the number of neighbors known. Length of residence is also a strong predictor (though not as powerful in this case) of number of family neighbors. These effects are supportive of the systemic view of community (and are the same as reported by Kasarda and Janowitz [1974]): people who remain longer in a neighborhood develop larger local networks, and they are more likely to live in proximity to their parents and adult children.

On the other hand, we also find significantly larger neighborhood networks—both family and nonfamily—for people in rural areas, compared to central cities. This result is unaffected by our inclusion of other neighborhood variables in these equations. Here our finding is more consistent with the Wirthian view.

Age has a significant negative effect on number of family neighbors but not on number of nonfamily neighbors known. We believe that the effect of age on family neighbors reflects normal life-cycle transitions: people are more likely to move away from the parental home as they grow older, and their parents are more likely to have died.

One family characteristic has a small effect, though it is not quite significant at the .05 level. People with minor children living in their home know more of their neighbors. This finding is consistent with the hypothesis that having children at home intensifies people's investment in the neighborhood.

The effects of income and race are more difficult to interpret. Whites and higher income people are less likely to have family neighbors, which supports expectations based on their (presumed) greater residential mobility and opportunities for extra-local and extra-familial contacts. But they know more nonfamily neighbors. This result suggests that—at least with regard to differences by social status—these two sorts of neighborhood contacts have different origins. Living in the same neighborhood as a parent or child may be more directly and concretely affected by the constraints experienced by less affluent and minority persons. These constraints are external to the person rather than choices or preferences associated with their status. Perhaps, then, it is family neighbors, and neighboring associated with kinship, that have supported sociologists' image of the solidary ethnic or working-class neighborhood. But although higher status people may well be more residentially mobile, they nevertheless know more of their (nonkin) neighbors.

Aside from urban-rural differences, there are further differences among neighborhoods based on their residential stability, racial composition, and presence of children. These contextual effects are independent of the effects of these same variables measured at the level of individuals. Two of these are in the expected direction. Our respondents who live in neighborhoods where a higher proportion of residents have a tenure of at least ten years (i.e., in more stable neighborhoods) know more of their neighbors. Thus, *both* the longer one lives in the neighborhood *and* the longer one's neighbors stay in the neighborhood, the more local ties are maintained. Also, those who live in neighborhoods with more black residents, independent of their own race, have more family neighbors.

Surprisingly, respondents in neighborhoods with more children know fewer of their neighbors by name, even though having young children at home increases the size of the neighbor network. We cannot offer a simple interpretation of this result. We have not identified any other neighborhood characteristic for which age composition may be serving as a proxy—its effects are robust regardless of other variables (such as neighborhood stability or income level) included in the model. Perhaps the age composition of our sample has some relevance. Because all of our respondents are at least age forty, the presence of large numbers of children in the neighborhood may indicate a generational gap between respondents and other residents. One test of this interpretation is whether the proportion of older residents (such as the proportion aged sixty-five and above) has a positive effect on neighboring; but it does not.

Other variables that have been identified in the literature—gender, marital status, physical disability, employment, homeownership, and perceived safety—have marginal effects at most. People who perceive their neighborhood as safe, homeowners, and people with young children at home know slightly more neighbors. Married persons are likely to have more family neighbors than unmarried persons, but in additional analyses we found that this small effect is due to the larger number of family members (including parents-in-law and adult children) for married persons.

## Predicting Interaction in the Neighborhood

We proceed now to see what variables affect social interaction and help from neighbors (including both family and nonfamily neighbors). We are especially interested in the effects of the number of family neighbors and other neighbors. As stated above, we view these as intermediary variables through which other personal and contextual characteristics may affect neighboring. Figure 6.4 depicts the relative strength of those predictors that are statistically significant. (The complete regression equations are reproduced in Appendix C, table C.6.3.)

The number of family neighbors turns out to be by far the primary determinant of phoning, visiting, and helping within the neighborhood. The standardized coefficients for number of family neighbors are in the range of .440 to .568, much larger than the coefficients of other variables. The number of other neighbors known also has standardized coefficients above .100 for phoning and visiting, although (not surprising in

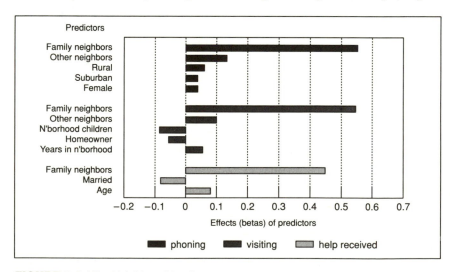

**FIGURE 6.4** Who Neighbors More?

light of the rarity of help from nonfamily neighbors) it does not significantly affect help received.

There are few other effective predictors in these models. There is a gender difference in telephone contact within the neighborhood. Because there is no gender effect on visiting or help received, we interpret this finding as an indicator of the gender-typing of telephoning (see Chapter 3) rather than (as suggested in the neighboring literature) a reflection of social or time constraints on women. Phone contact is also more frequent in suburban and rural than in central city neighborhoods.

With respect to visiting, there is a positive effect of length of residence, which was expected. Other coefficients are surprising. First, homeowners visit their neighbors less frequently, which seems to contradict the finding that they know more of their neighbors. Second, persons in neighborhoods with more children visit less often, again contradicting the theory that children promote neighboring.

Finally, two other variables have significant effects on help received. Married people receive less help from within the neighborhood. Since spouses are the single most common source of help, marital status is an indicator not of investment in the neighborhood but of availability of a helper. Older people receive more help, which is the first indication in these analyses that the neighborhood has a special significance for the elderly.

It is striking that several predictors that have strong effects on neighbors known and on number of family neighbors have no effect, mixed effects, or weaker effects on measures of social interaction. For many variables, their strongest effects are indirect, mostly through number of family neighbors as an intervening variable.

## Neighbors and Family: An Interpretation

Family neighbors represent two kinds of traditional social ties, those based on kinship and those based on proximity. Both of these have been described by influential theorists as being in a long-term decline. Their survival as key elements of social networks leads us to question such observations—a point we have made repeatedly with respect to families, and which we now extend to neighborhoods.

We find that the majority of people over forty have no parents or adult children living in their neighborhood, and even when they do, their number is very limited. Yet a sizeable minority do have at least one such nearby family member, and a substantial share of all social interaction with nonhousehold members—in the range of 15–25 percent—is with family neighbors. Most important, these local parents and children play a key role in neighboring. In our sample nearly half of the average person's *neighborhood* telephone and visiting contacts are with parents and children, and people are much more likely to receive help with routine tasks from family neighbors than from other neighbors. Further, the best predictor of all three forms of neighborhood interaction is the number of family neighbors; the number of other neighbors known is important but subsidiary to this central factor. More than we would have expected from the sociological literature, local community networks remain founded on kinship ties, even today.

The discovery of the centrality of family neighbors in neighboring encourages us to examine the family's role in other aspects of social networks. We turn now to the effect of family ties on people's use of formal and paid services.

## The Family and Formal Services

Although formal and paid services are not part of people's social networks in the same way as family, friends, and neighbors, they are nevertheless an important means of getting routine tasks accomplished. Based on responses to our basic set of questions about how routine tasks are accomplished, about a third of our respondents (34.2 percent) make regular use of a service provider, either a paid helper or a public organization, to help them with such activities as shopping, cleaning, and yard maintenance. What distinguishes those who do from those who do not seek outside help?

Following the logic of our earlier analyses of intergenerational help, we begin with measures of people's needs. Needs indicators include age and health (ability to do things on your own). Employment—as a competitor for scarce time—may create a greater need for help. In addition to needs, we take into account some measures of people's willingness or predisposition to accept help and of factors that make it easier or harder to obtain it (see Andersen 1968; Wan and Odell 1981; and Wolinsky et al. 1983 for further discussion of such factors). Many of the variables that we have used in previous analyses can be encompassed under these rubrics. Income is relevant as an indicator of ability to purchase private services. Gender may be a predisposing factor, as we have noted previously that women appear more willing to accept help than men. Geographic location is relevant as an indicator of availability of services, with both paid and public services more readily at hand in urban centers than in suburban or rural areas.

To these factors we wish to introduce measures of people's informal social networks: their marital status, their living arrangement, and whether they receive help from family members, neighbors, and friends. Does a strong informal social network diminish or increase people's reliance on formal and paid services? Which parts of the social network are more important—the family household, the extended family beyond the household, or nonfamily friends and neighbors? A majority of our sample are married (and almost all of these live with their spouse). Among the single, widowed, or divorced, the most important distinction is between those who live with another person (typically a child or other relative) and those who live alone. Therefore we treat people in three categories: married, not married but living with another person, and living alone. The receipt of help from each other source is a simple dichotomy.

Estimation of a model for service use incorporating these predictors is straightforward. Because service use is measured as a dichotomy, logistic regression is the preferred method of multivariate analysis. In a logistic regression, coefficients represent the effect of a unit change in the independent variable on the natural logarithm of the odds (the "log odds") of using a particular formal service. This model specification is appropriate where the dependent variable is a dichotomy. As we noted in Chapter 2, in relation to the logistic regression models predicting coresidence, the antilogarithm of a logit coefficient can be transformed into an effect on the probability of service use, and at several points in the text below we report this more interpretable measure of the magnitude of the effect. This transformation depends on the value of other predictors; in our comparisons, we assume the case of a respondent who would otherwise have the average probability of service use and report the increase in that probability that is predicted. It is best used only as a general guide to the size of effects.

Results of logistic regression analysis are reported in Appendix C, table C.6.4. We find that several aspects of the informal support system have negative effects on using outside services: marriage, living with another person, receiving help from parents or adult children, and receiving help from other relatives. These are as expected. We also find that persons with higher income but worse health, women (compared to men), and residents of urban areas (compared to rural and suburban areas) are more likely to use outside services.

What is surprising is not the direction of these effects but their magnitude. To show this, we must make some computations based on the logit equation. The simplest approach is to work with the case of a person with a .342 probability (the average probability) of using a formal service. We can then calculate, holding other variables equal, what would be the increase or decrease in this probability for a person with a higher value on a particular predictor. For most variables (dichotomies) it is clear how to make this calculation. For two variables we must decide how much of an increase to assume: for income, we take an increase of $10,000 and for health we take an increase of one point on our five-point scale. Either of these would be a substantial change.

Table 6.3 shows the results of these calculations, comparing a person with the "average" probability of using a formal service (.342) to the probability for a comparable person who has the higher-coded value on a single predictor. Only two variables have positive effects. Being a woman rather than a man increases the probability from .342 to .455. Having $10,000 more income increases the probability more modestly, to .388. Other variables have negative effects, decreasing the probability to as little as .105 for a married person, .184 for an unmarried person living with others, .209 for someone who receives help from relatives, and .247 for someone receiving help from a parent or adult child. The informal network has very substantial effects. Of course these predicted values are somewhat arbitrary, depending on the initial value that we assumed. But they represent very well the relative order of magnitude of effects on service use. And they reveal that people with a strong informal support network, particularly from one's household and close family, are much less likely to rely on formal services.

## The Informal Network and Services for the Elderly

If the family plays such a prominent role in everyday activities across the whole age range of our respondents (that is, forty and above), we might well expect to find similar impacts for older persons (we will focus now on those who are sixty and above). Of course, we have already shown (Chapter 2) that parents are net providers of family help, rather than receivers, until they are quite old. At the same time, we would expect that *when parents do need help*, they are more likely to turn

**TABLE 6.3**
Predicted Probabilities of Using Formal Services

| Compared to a person with the average probability of .342, if respondent were: | |
| --- | --- |
| A woman | .455 |
| Earning $10,000 more | .388 |
| In better health | .293 |
| Receiving help from parent/child | .247 |
| Living in a rural area | .215 |
| Receiving help from relatives | .209 |
| Living in a suburban area | .186 |
| Living with others | .184 |
| Married | .105 |

to their family, including children, than to formal service providers. This hypothesis is consistent with the entire gerontological literature about the use of formal services, and especially with Cantor's "hierarchical compensatory" model, which emphasizes public programs rather than paid help. Cantor (1979, p. 453; see also Hess and Waring 1978; Cicirelli 1983a; Shanas 1979) attributes the usual pattern of reliance on the family to predominant preferences in the older generation: "In the value system of the present generation of elderly, kin is generally seen as the most appropriate support giver followed by significant others and lastly by formal organizations." But when children are unavailable, "the support function begins to be shared by other relatives, friends, neighbors, and even, in some cases, formal organizations" (Cantor 1979, p. 460). As a result, according to Stoller and Earl (1983), one's spouse and adult children are the most likely source of assistance for older persons who receive help in any aspect of daily living. Help from friends or neighbors is less common, but is more likely to occur for unmarried persons and persons whose children and other relatives live more than an hour away. Formal assistance is least likely (reported in less than 6 percent of the cases).

Such results seem to contradict popular accounts that have stressed the growing reliance of the elderly on public programs, attributing this shift in part to the supposed abandonment of the elderly by their adult children. Among policy analysts, concerned with reducing public expenditures, there is great interest in how to enhance informal care—particularly family care. But whatever the relative balance between the amount of formal care and the use of informal help, most discussions of this question assume that informal and formal support substitute for each other and are therefore inversely related. Thus Coe et al. (1984) report that elders' use of formal health services was greatest among those who were "abandoned" by either the family or neighbor network (that is, people who perceived a low level of involvement with the network and who desired more), a finding that is perfectly consistent with Stoller and Earl's research—except that Stoller and Earl find few people "abandoned" by their families.

A very different position is taken by those who suggest that people's informal networks may act as a bridge between the older person and formal services, bringing the person into contact with public service providers and thus facilitating formal care (Sussman 1976). If so, persons with a stronger informal network might actually make more use of the formal system (this is the conclusion for use of formal health care services in Chappell 1987; and George 1987). From this perspective, informal support is seen as a possible enabler for formal assistance.

When will the informal network serve as a bridge to public programs? Ward, Sherman, and LaGory (1984) suggest that close relatives such as spouses and children tend simply to substitute their own help for formal services. By contrast, they believe that friends and neighbors are more apt to perform the bridging function hypothesized by Sussman (1976). "Friends and especially neighbors (because of their proximity) are often in a particularly good position to become aware of the needs of older individuals," they conclude. But "over the long term they are more likely to make referrals to other sources of assistance" than to provide help themselves (Ward et al.1984, p. 222; see also Wagner and Keast 1981).

There is yet another complication in gerontological theory: the hierarchy of potential caregivers may depend upon the particular tasks that need to be provided. This has been called the "task specific" model. Litwak (1985) argues that formal service providers are least suited to unsupervised and unskilled in-home care, where the motivation and proximity of a spouse or other close relative are especially advantageous. For other needs, particularly where specialized training or facilities are required, formal services may be much more appropriate (see also Dono et al. 1979). Therefore, for some kinds of services the availability of informal assistance might not much affect formal service use.

Are older people with more help from their family (or friends, or neighbors) less likely to use public services? Conversely, are people without a strong informal network more likely to rely on public assistance? Or does the informal network tend to enable people to identify and exploit those services that are available to them? We believe that the direction of the relationship between formal service use and receipt of informal help is a valid test of whether informal support tends to substitute for or provide a bridge to formal support. According to either model of substitution effects (the hierarchical compensatory or task specific model), there should be negative associations between informal and formal support. In the bridging model, these coefficients are expected to be positive. In the hierarchical compensatory model, preferences for help from close kin are expected to be reflected in stronger coefficients for help from spouse and children than for help from other informal sources. By contrast, according to the task specific model, the relative importance of various sources of informal support should vary according to the kind of formal service that is analyzed.

*Measures of Service Use*

The Albany survey inquired about respondents' use of several kinds of senior services. The most widely used is the multipurpose senior center: 18.8 percent of our respondents aged sixty and above stated that they belong to or participate in senior centers. Other questions referred to specific sorts of services that are commonly available in this and other metropolitan areas, and respondents were asked "Have you used this service for yourself in the past year?" Some of these services are typically provided at senior centers and similar locations away from the older person's home. For example, 6.3 percent reported eating "meals served at a group dining site." Our canvassing of service providers confirms that in most cases the group dining site is a senior citizen center, and there is a moderate positive association (r = .35) between center participation and use of congregate meals. Other services of this type (though generally not restricted to older persons and not necessarily offered at a senior center) are much less likely to be used: legal advice at reduced rates (3.1 percent), help in finding work (2.7 percent), help in finding housing (1.4 percent), and financial or personal counseling (2.2 percent). We will refer to these services collectively as "community-based services," and altogether about one out of four seniors (25.5 percent) reported using at least one of these.

Another kind of service is provided to people in their own homes, sometimes as a substitute for institutionalization. "Meals on wheels" is the most commonly used of these (reported by 4.2 percent of our respondents). Others include personal care such as bathing or shampooing (2.5 percent), help with housekeeping chores (2.5 percent), special door-to-door transportation services (2.5 percent), telephone check-in calls (1.3 percent), social visits by volunteers (2.3 percent), and transportation to and from grocery stores (1.6 percent). We inquired also about adult daycare, but found no respondents in our sample whose families made use of this service. Finally, we asked a series of questions about how the respondent "gets things done" in the household (e.g., cooking and cleaning). Of all respondents, 2.0 percent mentioned assistance from a nonprofit or public organization on these tasks. Altogether a total of 12.1 percent of respondents reported use of at least one "home-based" service.

Three dependent variables are modeled here: the use of senior centers or congregate meals, other community-based services, and home-based services. The service use measures are dichotomized because of their extreme skewness. Of the 12.1 percent of persons who used any home-based service, for example, more than two-thirds (8.3 percent) used only one. The same is true of the two community-based service indices. In exploratory analyses not reported here, we found no significant differences between those who used only one and those who used more than one service, so little information is lost by dichotomization.

*Predictors of Senior Service Use*

Studies of senior services have considered a wide variety of predictors of the use of such services. As noted in our discussion of formal services above, these include their *need* for the service, as well as factors that *enable* or *predispose* them to use it. Past research offers contradictory evidence on the effects of most of these indicators (these findings are reviewed in detail in Logan and Spitze 1994).

Our predictors of senior service use follow this same general scheme and include all of the indicators in Appendix C, table C.6.4. Two additional indicators of predisposition are used (these are among the set of attitudes introduced in Chapter 1). "Entitlement" is extent of agreement (on a four-point scale) with the statement that "Old age pensioners have a right to be taken care of in a dignified way even if younger people must contribute their taxes to make this possible." "Age identification" is a dummy variable for response to the question "Do you describe yourself as young, middle-aged, old, or what?" It is coded 1 for persons who described themselves as old, elderly, or aged; 0 for other responses, most of which were "middle-aged." We hypothesize that those who consider older persons entitled to public support and those who identify themselves as old are likely to be more predisposed to use formal senior services. Another new predisposition indicator is sociability. Sociability is measured as the total of respondents' memberships other than senior centers, including civic groups, charity organizations, cooperatives, fraternal lodges, veterans organizations, political clubs, unions, neighborhood associations, community centers, professional organizations, social clubs, sports teams or clubs, and religious groups.

We also introduce some enabling factors that are specific to studying senior service use. One is the respondent's own mobility. Because over 90 percent of respondents still drive an automobile, and because public transportation is widely available (through buses or special van systems), we do not use indicators of availability of transportation. Rather, we asked respondents, "How many trips have you taken outside your home in the last seven days?" Those who have left their homes more often are considered *functionally* more mobile (therefore more likely to use community-based services and less likely to use home-based services).

Another new enabling factor is the availability of services. Analysis of the geography of service delivery is a unique feature of this study. In addition to the personal interviews used throughout this book, this analysis makes use of one additional sort of information. Interviews were conducted during 1988 and 1989 with ninety-nine service providers in the three counties. These included all of the nutrition programs and day activities that could be identified through the Area Agency on Aging of each county. Some voluntary organizations and clubs, such as church groups with a predominantly older membership, were not included. Private for-profit service providers were also not considered. These interviews included numerous questions about service provision, including types of services offered, hours of operation, eligibility requirements, staffing, and areas served. We developed a coding scheme for availability of services for residents in each of the census block groups in which interviews were conducted (for details, see Logan and Spitze 1994). Availability of three kinds of services was evaluated: home-delivered meals, congregate meals, and day activity programs. For home-delivered meals the highest ranking is for people in areas where two meals per day are provided, with some provision for weekend service. For congregate meals the highest ranking is for people who live within three blocks of a meal site that serves meals at least five days per week. And for day activity programs the highest ranking is for areas within seven miles of a center that is open six or seven days per week. Other services, typically arranged on an individual basis with clients, could not be coded in a similar way. We include availability of congregate meals and day activity programs as predictors of the use of these community-based services. Availability of home-delivered meals is included as a predictor of home-based services. Because we were unable to develop a systematic code for other community-based services, no availability measure is included in the prediction equation for those services.

*Results for Senior Service Use*

Following the usual logic leads to the following hypotheses. First, formal service use should be positively associated with age and minority racial/ethnic status and negatively associated with income and health (these are typically considered indicators of needs). Second, service use should be positively associated with acceptance of one's aging and dependency and with belief in entitlement to public support, and it should be greater for women, and (at least for some services) be higher among more socially active people (we see these as measures of predispositions). Third, service use should be higher when it is more available and more accessible in terms of its location and clients' own mobility (enabling factors).

To these factors we add the characteristics of people's informal networks and their use of paid assistance. Once again our principal question is what role people's family ties play in their daily lives. Note that the majority of older persons have active informal networks. Almost half

(47 percent) are married and live with their spouse, and another 15 percent are unmarried but live with someone else. In these cases, household tasks are typically shared. A large fraction of respondents, 29 percent, receive help from adult children on a regular basis, while smaller percentages receive help from others (10 percent from other relatives, 8 percent from neighbors, and 7 percent from friends). Nearly half (40 percent) make regular use of paid services. Thus, a much smaller number of older persons use senior public services of any kind than rely on their informal network or paid services.

It is also revealing to see how various sources of help are combined. To reduce the possible number of combinations, we make several simplifications here (although in the multivariate analysis every form of help is treated separately). We consider unmarried and married persons separately. We treat "living with another person" as a form of family help (because in most cases it involves a family member), and combine it with receipt of help from adult children and receipt of help from other relatives. We also combine help from friends and from neighbors as nonfamily help. And we disregard paid help for the moment. Table 6.4 presents the number of persons in each of various combinations of these situations: receiving no help, or receiving help from family, and nonfamily, and public services.

A majority of those who receive senior services of some kind (nearly a third of the total) are unmarried persons. Those who receive no help

**TABLE 6.4**
Percentage of Older Persons (Age 60 and Above) Receiving Help from Various Combinations of Sources

|  | Unmarried | Married | Total |
|---|---|---|---|
| Receive no help | 12% | 41% | 26% |
| Receive family help only | 34 | 35 | 35 |
| Receive nonfamily help only | 3 | 0 | 2 |
| Receive family + nonfamily help only | 8 | 1 | 4 |
| Receive senior services only | 12 | 13 | 12 |
| Receive senior services + other help | 30 | 9 | 20 |
| Total who receive senior services alone or in combination with other sources | 42% | 22% | 32% |
| Number of cases | 293 | 261 | 554 |

(about a quarter of the total) are concentrated among married persons. (We note, though, that marriage is not much related to receipt of help from family or nonfamily informal sources.) This finding is consistent with the important role that spouses play in meeting each other's needs.

More directly relevant to our analysis here, family help is much more common than use of senior services. And senior services are most often (by a ratio of nearly two to one) found in combination with some form of informal help (in most cases, with family help). This shows that senior service users are not by and large "abandoned" by their family and friends. However, this tabulation does not reveal whether the coincidence of formal and informal assistance is due to a causal link between them (such as the bridging hypothesis suggests) or to possibly greater needs or predispositions of some older persons for help from any source. That requires a multivariate analysis, which is our next step.

Means and standard deviations for the sample of older respondents are presented in Appendix C, table C.6.5. Table 6.5 illustrates the direc-

**TABLE 6.5**
Predicted Probabilities of Using Three Kinds of Senior Services

| | Home-based services | Senior center/ congregate meals | Other community-based services |
|---|---|---|---|
| Compared to an average probability of: | .121 | .202 | .105 |
| **If a person were:** | | | |
| a married person | .057 | * | .046 |
| living with others (not a spouse) | .227 | .128 | * |
| receiving help from children | * | .104 | .049 |
| receiving help from friends | * | * | .258 |
| five years older | .158 | .231 | * |
| in worse health | * | .140 | * |
| $10,000 higher income | * | .134 | * |
| black | * | * | .383 |
| employed part-time | * | * | .266 |
| involved in another social activity | * | .278 | * |
| a woman | * | .318 | * |
| with an "old" age identity | .229 | * | * |
| believing in old-age entitlements | * | * | .195 |
| better served by home-delivered meals | .148 | * | * |

Note: Based on the logistic regression model in Appendix C, table C.6.4.
* Indicates that the variable has no effect on use of this service.

tion and relative size of the significant coefficients in logistic regression equations (see Appendix C, table C.6.6 for the full results predicting whether persons aged sixty and above are users of any home-based service, senior centers or congregate meals, and any other community-based service). We include here several variables that are significant at .05 or better based on one-tailed tests, a less conservative standard than we have used previously. In most cases, the one-tailed test is appropriate because the direction of the relationship was correctly predicted. It is useful to point out these instances because several involve the informal network variables that are the main focus of interest.

We begin with the informal network variables. Several findings are supportive of the hierarchical compensatory model for community-based services. Having a spouse reduces predicted use of home-based services (from the average level of .121, the predicted probability would drop to .057 for a married person). It equally reduces use of other community-based services. Living with others (compared to living alone) and receiving help from children both substantially reduce use of senior centers and congregate meals. Receiving help from children also reduces the predicted probability of using other community-based services (from .105 to .049). Once again, these are large effects of the informal network. Surprisingly, the fairly common use of paid help has no effect on use of senior services, one way or the other.

The most important anomaly in this portion of the models is that receiving help from friends *greatly increases* the predicted probability of using other community-based services. For a person who would otherwise have the average probability of .105, help from a friend increases the probability to .258—an effect strong enough to outweigh the negative impact of being married. The combination of negative effects for the most intimate family members (spouse and children) and positive effects for more distant connections (friends) is exactly in line with the contrasting effects of strong and weak ties hypothesized by Ward, Sherman, and LaGory (1984).

The pattern of results demonstrates the importance of distinguishing among types of formal services. Our indicators of needs and predispositions have disparate effects on the three kinds of formal services. Use of home-based services is positively associated with being older and having an "old" age identity. Use of other community-based services is associated with being black or belief in old-age entitlements (also with part-time employment, for which we cannot provide an interpretation). These relationships are mostly in the expected directions. Use of senior centers and congregate meals, on the other hand, seems in some ways more like a form of social engagement than a "service"—it is less likely for people in poorer health, more likely for persons involved in other activities, and more likely for women. There is clearly an element of conviviality in this activity. It is only the effects of age (older people are more likely) and income (affluent people are less likely) that seem consistent with an interpretation in terms of "needs for assistance."

Unexpectedly, none of the enabling factors in this study has any independent effect on use of community-based services. This finding may allay concerns about the location, hours of operation, and provision of special transportation for such services. Apparently, at least to the degree that such characteristics vary in the Albany area, they do not affect service use for the average older person. There is, however, a small significant effect of availability (availability of home-delivered meals, $p < .05$ in a one-tailed test) on use of home-based services. This is the service least bounded to a particular service site (hence, *potentially* the most flexible in delivery across the region). In principle, therefore, it is the service for which geographic disparities should have least importance. But at the same time, it is the kind of service over which users have the least control: they can receive it only if the service comes to them.

We call special attention to the weak and mixed effects of enabling factors related to availability. As increasing consideration is given to the provision of community services for older persons, concerns have been expressed about their accessibility throughout the metropolis (Golant et al. 1989). Our study is unusual in its use of independent measures of the actual availability of specific services for people in a given neighborhood, providing a sound basis for testing these concerns. But inequalities in availability do not affect people's utilization of community-based services such as day activity and congregate meal programs.

In expecting substantial effects of availability, we implicitly accepted a certain view of persons who might use these services: that they are relatively immobile and more affected by environmental barriers than are younger people. It seems more consistent with our results in this chapter, and more consistent with the image of the older generation developed in Chapters 1 and 2, to conceive of older persons as active and capable of searching out services they desire to use. Thus, where the problem is one of an older person's getting to a service site, people are reasonably able to solve this problem on an individual basis. A lower level of service availability—such as a greater distance to a site or fewer days of operation—may affect the frequency or difficulty of use, but does not affect whether the service is *ever* used.

By contrast, we find that receipt of home-based services is related to availability (in this case, the measure is availability of home-delivered meals). Note that these services are directed toward persons who better fit our initial assumptions: not only are these recipients older and more frail, but they are also more likely to think of themselves as old. And perhaps more important, these are services that depend on the distribution system, not on the mobility of the user. A service that is not available cannot be used.

## The Family in Social Networks

Our central question in this chapter has been the role of the family in people's broader social networks. How are family relationships linked to other aspects of their social lives and support systems? In the two main parts of the chapter we have asked this question in different ways. In the first section, on neighboring, we essentially asked what share of neighborhood social interaction is with family members who live nearby, and our conclusion is that this share is large indeed. In the second, on formal services, we asked whether having an active family support system affects reliance on formal services, and we found strong evidence that it reduces their use.

These questions have rarely been asked in this way in the past. Marital status, to be sure, has routinely been introduced in studies of neighboring and formal service use. But researchers have shied away from thinking in terms of the family network as a whole, including parents and children and other relatives outside the household. To some degree this may be due to the paucity of information about this network—most surveys include few questions about such family members. But more likely the lack of information reflects disinterest, and this disinterest stems both from the assumption that the family has been losing its social functions and from a preference for other theoretical questions. To illustrate this point, we note that marital status has typically been interpreted not as a central feature of a person's social network (as we have used it here) but as an indicator of some other concept—in the urban literature as an indicator of investment in the neighborhood, and in the service literature as an indicator of needs for assistance.

We find that even beyond marriage the family continues to be important. Of course we cannot begin to say whether this importance is greater or lesser than it was for previous generations, but only that, by comparison with other predictors, it exerts very strong effects. It is central even in two areas of social relations where it has been widely thought to be weakening, in the neighborhood and in care of the elderly.

# 7
# Extending the Family

*The older family is important in itself and also as part of the larger "family matrix" that includes young children, their parents, and their grandparents. Other researchers have demonstrated the potential contributions of the older generation to the well-being of young children. We find that ties between the middle and older generations are strong and durable under conditions of demographic change. We suggest that discussions of crisis in the modern family should take into account the whole life course of the family.*

■ Probably no day passes without a reminder in the mass media that the family is in trouble. Americans have come to accept this view without question. Commentators and politicians bemoan the crisis of the family and the failure of family values without having to explain what they are talking about. These understandings have become part of our common folklore at the close of the twentieth century, part of what we take for granted as an issue of our time. Of course there is a crisis, and it sells newspapers and garners votes.

Social scientists have been more cautious about the prospects for the family, but academic writing echoes the concerns found in the media. These issues are highly politicized. For example, in their discussion of single-parent families, McLanahan and Booth (1989, p. 569) argue that "the position taken by analysts on this issue is shaped by their values regarding women's traditional family roles and whether they view single motherhood as a cause or consequence of economic insecurity." At the extreme, analysts who see the traditional two-parent family as a primary civilizing influence, "view women's employment and the subsequent decline in the nuclear family as disasters for society" (McLanahan and Booth 1989, p. 571).

As we acknowledged at the very beginning, we also started with the presumption that the family as a core set of social relations was headed for trouble. Our focus has been exclusively on parent-child relations in their adult stage, the years when "children" have come of age. This is an important period in the family life cycle because it encompasses so many critical events in the lives of many members of the older genera-

153

tion: the peak of working years, grandparenthood, retirement, widowhood, disability, death. It now includes the larger part of the family life cycle: one is typically a dependent minor child for only eighteen or twenty years (or at the outside, twenty-five years), but potential relations with parents take up as much as thirty or forty or even fifty years of one's adult life.

We identified several sources of apprehension about the resilience of these intergenerational ties, especially as these trends are played out in the future:

- the aging of the population, accompanied by a sharpening consciousness of generational conflicts as a growing older generation demands that its needs be met;
- the shrinking of average family sizes, associated with rising standards and costs of living, that reduces children's chances of being able to share the duty of caring for aging parents;
- the growth of external demands on young parents, particularly women who are increasingly involved in employment outside the home, cutting their involvement with parents;
- the rising rate of divorce, depleting the financial and time resources of younger adults, and making them both more reliant on parents and less able to provide help to them;
- the special burden on women as the traditional kinkeepers in the American family, caught more often in the tangle of conflicting family roles, especially between their own parents and minor children;
- and finally, and more broadly, the replacement of traditional social networks, both family and local community, by secondary relationships and public institutions.

The underlying population trends listed here have been continuing for decades, and they show little sign of reversal. The question is how they are affecting intergenerational relations. One by one, chapter after chapter, we have laid out the theoretical assumptions on which each expectation is based, reviewed the empirical literature, and offered our own new evidence. And in every case, the reality, as best we can determine it, is different from expectations.

Despite speculation to the contrary, we find that the subjective boundaries between generations are not at all clear. In terms of value orientations—in expectations about family relationships, as well as about public programs and policies—people in the older generation express greater concern for the younger generation than for their own self-interest. Older people with fewer children are less involved in intergenerational exchanges (though in partial compensation, children with fewer siblings are more involved with parents). But in fact most exchanges, until parents reach very old ages, flow from the parent to the child. Thus the trend toward smaller families actually relieves parents from children's demands for assistance. Neither employment nor divorce has a negative impact on an employed or divorced daughter's relations with parents. Though women clearly still have disproportionate responsibility for household labor, child care, and some forms of kinkeeping, there are important dimensions of intergenerational ties that do not exhibit gender differences. It is indeed the case that many middle-aged people simultaneously have the responsibilities of being a parent and being a child (as well as a spouse and a paid worker), but few devote more than three hours per week to both their parents and their adult children. And if either women or men experience difficulty with juggling multiple roles, this effect is not measurable in terms of reported burden, stress, or life satisfaction.

We have been surprised to find fewer gender differences than we expected, not only in intergenerational relations but also in such issues as age identity. Others, including Rossi and Rossi (1990), have argued that gender is a major organizing factor in intergenerational relations. They conclude that "gender of parent and child is a highly salient axis of family life and intergenerational relations. On topic after topic, we have found that ties among women were stronger, more frequent, more reciprocal, and less contingent on circumstances than those of men. Women's ties to women, as mothers, daughters, sisters, or grandmothers, provide social and emotional connecting links among members of a family and lineage" (p. 495).

Our findings regarding gender are less clearcut. We think these seeming discrepancies can be explained in several ways. First, we do find some differences between men and women. Most prominently, there are clearcut gender differences in frequency of telephoning, the most common form of interaction between parents and adult children.

Second, there are some commonly gender-identified activities that we did not tap, such as kinkeeping and arranging family visits. Much of this may occur during telephone contacts. We think it is possible that some of the gendered patterns in kin contact are more subtle than can be measured in a structured interview survey, and some would require different kinds of questions. Just as surveys about household labor for years measured task performance without tapping task responsibility and management (e.g., Mederer 1993), studies of intergenerational relations need to measure both frequency of contact and who arranges contact.

Further, we think part of the difference between our own conclusions and those of others depends on one's emphasis. For example, Rossi and Rossi find, as we do, that there is no significant difference between frequency of visiting with sons and daughters in multivariate analysis (though there *is* a difference in telephone contact). They also find that daughters help with certain tasks—specifically household chores—more than sons do. However, even among sons, 48 percent help mothers and 36 percent help fathers with household chores (compared to 59 percent and 48 percent of daughters). Obviously there is a difference here, but it is also striking that between one-third and one-half of sons are providing this kind of help. Patterns for "fixing or making something for you" show the opposite pattern, with sons helping more than daughters. We measured help in slightly different categories, and also found that some tasks are gender-typed. But when we measured total weekly hours of help (as suggested by Rossi and Rossi 1990, p. 507) we found much smaller gender differences. There are strong differences in types of help, but weak differences in the overall total.

Finally, it is probably worth repeating that much of the literature on gender and aging families focuses on intensive caregiving situations. We did not study people in these kinds of situations in very large numbers, and such caregivers are predominantly female.

## Centrality of Family Ties

Our analyses are remarkable for the apparent resilience of parent-child ties in later life. Even more noteworthy is the importance of these ties compared to other parts of people's social networks. Whether measured as contact, visiting, help given, or help received, these family ties are at the very core of people's networks outside the home. And the most traditional of them—family neighbors, that is, parents or children living within the same neighborhood—retain a special weight in social relationships. Rather than being displaced by secondary associations, by friends or coworkers living at a distance or by paid helpers or public services, we find that family ties—when they are present—are people's preferred source of routine assistance. Others play distinctly subordinate roles. These conclusions are parallel to those of Rossi and Rossi regarding normative obligations. They describe a pattern of normative social relations as a set of concentric circles, with parent and child in the center.

No doubt the family is being stretched today, as could only be expected under conditions of growing social inequality and poverty, weakening job security, and reduced public assistance. Even the most affluent households bear the emotional scars of divorce, the strains of remarriage, and the pressures of long working hours. Family patterns including high incidence of female-headed households, resulting from divorce and out-of-wedlock childbirth, have extended well beyond the confines of the inner city and the minority community. Yet there are reasons to believe that the family is also being regenerated, and the task of sociologists is not only to identify the failures of the old family but also to perceive the emergence of the new one. Vital institutions don't just cease to function; they may be battered and punished by change, but people must and do find ways to adapt to their conditions. It is not a Pollyana but a realist who, like Stacey (1991, p. 16), looks for the ways in which people "have been creatively remaking American family life." Stacey describes the current period as one where little is taken for granted about family form and people struggle to adapt existing institutions to new needs. No single family structure has emerged to replace the modern family: this is "a transitional and contested period of family history, a period after the modern family order, but before what we cannot foretell" (1991, p. 18).

Our own view is that less is changing than meets the eye. Any interpretation reflects the particular blinders of the theorist. Our interpretation may reflect the emphases of the gerontological literature in which we have worked together for nearly ten years. Let us be clear about what we mean. Sociologists are now more inclined than ever before to study family issues in the context of people's whole life histories, from childhood to retirement and widowhood (Elder 1985). Yet the core of family studies has been, and perhaps still is, that phase of family life that runs from marriage to nest leaving: the family, the nuclear family or the modern family, is a childbearing and childraising institution. Social gerontologists, grounded in a medical and social work tradition and specializing in the problems of older people, have been separated from this theoretical core. The linkage between aging and family studies was established by the recognition that adult children were often the primary caregivers for the frail elderly. But the framing of the issues at that time—the concern about whether these caregivers would continue to be available because of divorce, women's employment, etc.—simply reflected the questions that family theorists were already asking about the younger family. The crisis of the younger family became a crisis in support for older family members.

## Extending the Family

Thus our tendency has been to study the younger family only insofar as it is mirrored in intergenerational relations in the older family. The corresponding bias of most family researchers has been to assume that the extended family died out long ago, and that only the younger nuclear family has survived. For example, a single-minded focus on the young family is found in the recent essay on the decline of the family by David Popenoe (1993) cited in our Preface. Though he recognizes that family change is not necessarily family decline, he regards recent changes as "both unique and alarming." This is because, in his view, "it is not the extended family that is breaking up but the nuclear family. The nuclear family can be thought of as the last vestige of the traditional family unit; all other adult members have been stripped away, leaving but two—the husband and the wife. The nuclear unit—man, woman, and child—is called that for good reason: It is the fundamental and most basic unit of the family. Breaking up the nucleus of anything is a serious matter. . . . Adults for their own good purposes, most recently self-fulfillment, have stripped the family down to its nucleus. But any further reduction—either in functions or in number of its members—will likely have adverse consequences for children, and thus for generations to come" (Popenoe 1993, pp. 539–40).

We do not dispute the importance of this younger nuclear family. The family of parents and minor children is the site of many key activities. It is first of all the setting where most child-raising issues arise. It is where divorce has its greatest incidence and perhaps its greatest impact. And it is arguably where the greatest gender-related tensions are found, particularly because the tasks of economic support, homemaking, and child-rearing are typically most stressful for young parents. Perhaps for these same reasons it is the least secure component of the American family.

But it is not the whole family. On the contrary, as others have argued persuasively (Rossi and Rossi 1990), the nuclear family is a lifelong and multigenerational event. It is a network of two sorts of relationships of central importance in people's lives: with their parents, lasting until their parents' death (when, in many cases, they themselves are well into middle age), and with their own children, usually extending through their own lifetime. We all acknowledge this point, when confronted by it, but family sociologists have focused particularly on the childhood years.

The research literature on young families and on grandparenting demonstrates the relevance for children of relationships with older kin. The well-known ethnographic accounts of resilient kin and neighbor networks of poor single mothers by Stack (1974) offer at least the possibility that there are workable alternatives to the two-parent family, even in the worst conditions. There is evidence that intergenerational ties do play a strong role in coping with difficult family situations. Only a small minority of the grandparents studied by Cherlin and Furstenberg (1986) were "involved" in a parent-like relationship with grandchildren, but others were viewed by the authors as "sources of support in reserve. This latent support may never be activated; but, like a good insurance policy, it is important nevertheless" (p. 206). They predict that demographic trends including the increase in divorce will work to make this support more salient in the future.

The great majority of teenage mothers live in a larger family environment (Voydanoff and Donnelly 1990), typically in the grandmother's home, and this may occur even when the mother is married. This is particularly true for black teen mothers (married or unmarried), who are twice as likely to live with other adult kin than are white teen mothers (Hogan et al. 1990; see also Taylor et al. 1993). White mothers, though less likely to coreside with kin, are more likely to receive other forms of assistance (Hofferth 1984).

Coresidence may create problems for grandparents, who may feel burdened by and conflicted with the contradictory norms of noninterference and obligation to help if needed, but grandchildren and their mothers may benefit from these arrangements (Aldous 1995). Generally, mothers who live with kin benefit from higher levels of assistance in child care, psychological support, and help in returning to school or work (Hogan et al. 1990). And the payoff of this intergenerational presence is evident in the performance of the children: the negative effects of having been born to a teenage mother are partly offset by the presence of other adults in the household (Voydanoff and Donnelly 1990, p. 90). McLanahan and Sandefur (1994) note that studies of younger families have found that "being raised by a mother and grandmother is just as good as being raised by two parents, at least in terms of children's psychological well-being" (p. 74; see also Cherlin and Furstenberg 1986). Their own study of teenage grandchildren found no positive effect.

Adopting a multigenerational view of the family leads in a different direction than the reports of its decline. A recent essay by Matilda White Riley and John Riley (1993) offers an alternate perspective. Riley and Riley argue that the "simple kinship structure" of a young nuclear family that only sometimes included a surviving older generation has already been supplanted by an "expanded" structure. Because people live longer, the number of generations surviving jointly has increased. As a result, "linkages among family members have been prolonged. Thus parents and their offspring now survive jointly for so many years that a mother and her daughter are only briefly in the traditional relationship of parent and little children; during the several remaining decades of their lives they have become status equals" (1993, p. 163).

This expanded family, extended in generations and in duration, points the way toward an even more flexible type of kinship structure, a "latent matrix" of kin connections. Riley and Riley (1993, p. 169) point to four features of this new family:

"First, numerous social and cultural changes—especially cohort increases in longevity—are yielding a large and complex network of kin relationships. Second, these many relationships are flexible . . . increasingly matters of choice rather than obligation. A plethora of options is potentially at hand. Third, these relationships are not constrained by age or generation; people of any age, within or across generations, may opt to support, love, or confide in one another. Fourth, many of these kinship bonds remain latent until called upon. They form a safety net of significant connections to choose from in case of need."

The "latent matrix" loses "the sharp boundaries set by generation or age or geographical proximity . . . the boundaries of the family network have been widened to encompass many diverse relationships, including several degrees of stepkin and in-laws, single-parent families, adopted and other 'relatives' chosen from outside the family." (1993, p. 174). Further, it adds the element of greater choice rather than obligation to family relationships—even for motherhood itself.

## The Future of the Family

So we can't equate the future of the family with the future of the nuclear family, or the "modern" nuclear family, as Stacey calls it. It is the family as a latent matrix or multigenerational network that has to be evaluated, the family that endures throughout adulthood and that only sometimes is characterized by living together. This is a family structure in which people are relatively independent and self-sufficient, but nonetheless they maintain core relationships.

In this family form (the "extended" family, by which we mean the nuclear family extended through time and generations), we certainly find consequences of the changing nuclear family, though in most respects we do not share a sense of crisis. Perhaps the most often discussed set of family issues is associated with divorce and single-parent families. The harshest impacts here are probably on children in their younger years, most commonly including poverty and weakened or absent ties to their fathers. Our own research bears only on intergenerational relations at a later stage in the life cycle. Goldscheider (1990; see also Bumpass 1990) argues that there are special risks for people, especially men, who will become old in the next century, due to their weak ties to children (already visible in their relationships to these children today). But it is hard to predict the future impact of the single-parent or blended families of today.

We cannot be sure of the degree to which the multigenerational family network can substitute for the two-parent nuclear family that became our cultural model in the 1950s. Commentators have often pointed out that divorce and remarriage simultaneously undermine a child's links to one parent while expanding the universe of potential kin in the form of stepparents, stepsiblings, and stepgrandparents. But as Furstenberg and Cherlin (1991, pp. 91–95) point out, little is known about the long-term consequences of exchanging one very close tie for a wider network of weaker ties (see also Bumpass 1990). This is largely uncharted territory. The evidence so far, however, is that intergenerational ties in adulthood remain strong in spite of the social currents that have been expected to disrupt them. These ties are a firm foundation for the family of the future.

# *Appendix A:* The Albany Survey

The analyses reported in this monograph are based on a personal interview survey conducted in the Albany-Schenectady-Troy, New York, metropolitan area during a six-month period from September 1988 through Febrary 1989. Twelve hundred persons ages forty and over were interviewed in the three-county area. In this appendix we discuss a number of issues relating to choice of study site, sampling and interview procedures, sample composition, and measurement. The original survey questionnaire is also reproduced in Appendix B as a reference for readers who are interested in details of question wording and placement, and also for those who may wish to reanalyze these data.

The choice of a single metropolitan area over a national sample of primary sampling units was in part due to cost considerations. However, it also stemmed from our interest in differences in availability of formal support services across small geographical areas. This allowed us to analyze the behavior of our respondents in relation both to aggregate-level attributes of their block groups and to information on formal services derived from interviews with directors of agencies in the three countries.

We chose the Albany area in particular partly due to its convenience for us—not an insignificant factor when one considers the importance of maintaining frequent contact with the surveying organization and some degree of familiarity with the study area so as to ensure that the sampling design is executed properly. However, the Capital District shares many population and economic characteristics of moderate-sized metropolitan areas in the Northeast and North Central United States. These include a declining manufacturing base, relative decline and recent partial rejuvenation of central city neighborhoods, substantial suburbanization encompassing several industrial satellite towns, and relatively recent but rapid expansion of services for a growing elderly population. Among the area's suburbs are older and recently growing neighborhoods, dormitory suburbs and employment centers, affluent and poor communities. Thus, although no single area can fairly represent the diversity of situations across the country, the Capital District represents a common situation.

Sampling was done in two stages. Using 1980 census data, we sampled block groups in the three-county area with probabilities proportionate to size. Of the 607 block groups in the area, 120 were selected. The decision to select 120 primary sampling units and ten respondents within each (based on advice from

163

sampling expert Seymour Sudman of the Survey Research Center, University of Illinois) was made in an attempt to maximize both efficiency, through clustering, and variation in locational attributes. Within each block group, the staff of the survey organization (described below) listed blocks, then selected one randomly. Within each selected block, an interviewer was given a random starting corner and was instructed to approach each household at a given interval from there on. If a block was exhausted, interviewers went to an adjacent block within the block group. At a selected household, interviewers determind whether one or more adults was aged forty or over and requested an interview with the one with the most recent birthday. They went back up to four times if no one answered or the eligible respondent was not home. (In a few cases, they went back up to seven times.) Clearly, since one adult per household was interviewed no matter how many eligible adults lived there, ours is a household sample rather than an individual one. This decision was made in part because many of our interests related to interhousehold connections. To interview more than one adult per household would have wastefully duplicated information on these linkages.

The interview ranged from fifteen minutes to two hours and forty minutes (one outlier lasted five and a half hours) with a median time of sixty minutes. Interviews were conducted by Policy Research Associates, a Delmar, New York, firm whose president is a sociologist with a great deal of experience with federally funded research. The organization hired one full-time and one part-time interview supervisor and twenty-five main interviewers for the conduct of this project. (An additional eight interviewers did a total of twenty interviews.) The majority of the interviewers were women, as is usual in the survey research field, although seven were men. Two interviewers were African American, and one was Asian American. Interviews were trained for a period of three days.

Respondents were quite cooperative, given the amount of their time we were requesting. The overall cooperation rate was 67.25 percent, varying slightly across the three counties. At the end of the interview schedule, the interviewers were asked to rate respondent attitude, understanding of questions, and understanding of English. Eighty-nine percent were rated as having a good attitude, and only 2 percent were rated as poor. Ninety-six percent had a good understanding of English, while 85 percent seemed to have a good understanding of the questions.

We chose to interview respondents ages forty and above for several reasons. We were interested in how older people accomplish daily tasks and wanted to find out about help exchange and contact with adult children from both the parent's and child's perspective. We were also interested in attitudes toward a number of issues, such as family assistance, age consciousness, and related political attitudes, that we would expect to vary over the life course. Having an even broader age range would have given us more useful attitudinal data and information from the point of view of younger adult children, but would have decreased the numbers in other subgroups. Thus, we view this age cutoff as a reasonable compromise.

To assess the usefulness of our sample, we make two kinds of comparisons. First, we compare our survey respondents to those in the Albany tricounty area who are ages forty and above (table A.1). This comparison is based on the 1980 census Public Use Microdata Sample, and of course is useful only to the extent that the population remained stable during 1980–88. In table A.1, we find our sample to include fewer married persons and men than did the 1980 population census. These figures are due in part to our sampling design, which dictated that only one adult per household was interviewed no matter how many eligible adults lived there. Other census comparisons, including education and income, show a closer correspondence between the two samples.

Second, we compare our sample, on key measures of intergenerational ties, to the National Survey of Families and Households respondents who are ages forty and above. Is the Albany sample similar to a national sample on key indicators of linkages with parents and adult children? If so, we would argue that our data can provide insight on these issues with implications beyond the local area. In table A.2, we find that our sample is strikingly similar to the NSFH respondents in the same age range, for presence of children and of biological parents. We also compare patterns of contact, although these comparisons may be affected by differences in measures. Mean monthly contacts for the most frequently seen child (we have no summary measure for frequency of seeing any child), and for seeing any parent, are also quite similar. We conclude that analysis of data on our respondents can provide useful information likely to be generalizable beyond the Albany area.

**TABLE A.1**
Comparison of Albany Sample Respondents with Albany Tricounty 1980 Census
Data for Persons Aged 40 and Above

|                                | Albany survey | 1980 Census |
| ------------------------------ | ------------- | ----------- |
| currently married              | 56.8%         | 66.4%       |
| widowed                        | 21.3%         | 17.9%       |
| male                           | 36.5%         | 43.5%       |
| male, of persons ages 70+      | 30.5%         | 34.6%       |
| black                          | 5.4%          | 3.2%        |
| 40–49                          | 30.6%         | 24.3%       |
| 50–59                          | 23.0%         | 28.5%       |
| 60–69                          | 25.8%         | 24.3%       |
| 70+                            | 20.6%         | 22.9%       |
| mean years of education        | 12.8          | 13.4        |
| mean income last year          | $34,134       | $29,112[a]  |

a Inflated to 1987 figures.

**TABLE A.2**
Comparison of Albany Sample Respondents with National Survey of Families
and Households, Respondents Aged 40 and Above

|                                                  | Albany survey | NSFH  |
| ------------------------------------------------ | ------------- | ----- |
| any children at home                             | 41.0%         | 41.8% |
| any children ages 19+ at home                    | 24.2%         | 24.5% |
| mean # of children                               | 2.68          | 2.79  |
| mean monthly contacts with child most frequently seen | 9.87     | 8.22  |
| mother alive                                     | 36.0%         | 36.9% |
| father alive                                     | 18.4%         | 17.9% |
| any parent alive                                 | 41.7%         | 42.5% |
| mean monthly contacts with either or both parents | 5.40         | 4.26  |

# *Appendix B:* Questionnaire

We have discussed questionnaire items that have been combined into scales in the relevant chapters. The following is a list of general categories of items used in each chapter, along with questionnaire numbers for easy cross-reference.

| *Type of item* | *Question Numbers* | *Chapters in use* |
|---|---|---|
| Demographics on R | Q 1–8, Q 118–30 | all |
| Information on children including closeness, interaction | Q 13–32 | all |
| Information on parents including closeness, interaction | Q 33–49 | all |
| Other relatives, neighbors, friends | Q 51–62 | Ch. 6 |
| Division of household tasks; help from others outside household | Q 63–73 | Ch. 2, 3, 4, 6 |
| Help to nonhouseholders | Q 74 | Ch. 2–5 |
| Feelings of family burden | Q 75k | Ch. 5 |
| Services used | Q 76 | Ch. 6 |
| Health, well-being, mobility | Q 77–92, Q 116–17 | Ch. 1, 5 |
| Sociability | Q 76, Q 93–94 | Ch. 6 |
| Political attitudes | Q 99–102 | Ch. 6 |
| Age identification | Q 108–15 | Ch. 1, 6 |
| Attitudes toward family relations and public support of the elderly | Q 107 | Ch. 1, 3, 4, 6 |
| Filial responsibility items | Q 107 C,M,R,S | |
| Gender-based filial responsibility items | Q 107 A,G | |

1. First, I'd like to ask you some questions about you and your family. Are you currently working full-time, part-time, retired, keeping house, or what?

GO TO Q.2

Working full-time .................................................. 1
Working part-time ................................................. 2
Has job, but not working due to
    temporary illness, strike, vacation, etc.......... 3
Unemployed, laidoff, looking for work .............. 4
Retired, on permanent disability ...................... 5
Keeping house ..................................................... 6
In school .............................................................. 7

a. How many hours do you usually work each week?    |__|__

2. How many years ago did you begin (THIS STATUS)?    |__|__

3. What were you doing immediately before this - working full-time, part-time, retired, keeping house or what? ☐    _____

4. What kind of work are you doing now (have you done most of your working life)?   That is, what is (was) the job called?    _____

a. What are (were) your main duties on the job?    _____

b. In what type of business or industry is(was) this?  That is, what product is(was) made or what service is(was) given?    _____

5. Are you ....

GO TO Q.13

married, ............................................................. 1
divorced, ........................................................... 2
separated, ......................................................... 3
living apart, ....................................................... 4
widowed, or ...................................................... 5
never married? ................................................. 6

6. How long have you been (THIS STATUS)?  RECORD YEARS    |__|__

7. IF NOT CURRENTLY DIVORCED:
Have you ever been divorced?    no ................... 0    yes................... 1

8. IF NOT CURRENTLY WIDOWED:
Have you ever been widowed?    no ................... 0    yes ................... 1

IF NOT CURRENTLY MARRIED, GO TO Q.13

9. Is your (husband/wife) currently working full-time, part-time, retired, keeping house, or what?  IF CODED 4-7, GO TO Q.10 ☐    _____

a. How many hours does s/he usually work each week?    |__|__

10. How many years ago did s/he begin (THIS STATUS)?    |__|__

11. What was s/he doing immediately before this - working full-time, part-time, retired, keeping house, or what? ☐    _____

12. What kind of work is s/he doing now (has s/he done most of his/her working life)? That is, what is (was) the job called?    _____

a. What are (were) his/her main duties on the job?    _____

b. In what type of business or industry is (was) this; that is, what product is(was) made or what service is(was) given?    _____

13. Do you have any living children or stepchildren? (no=0,     never........................................................................ 0
yes=1) IF YES: Please tell me the first names and ages of    once a day or more............................................. 1
all your living children, including stepchildren, starting with   2-6 days a week .................................................. 2
the oldest. PUT NAMES ON CHART.              once a week ....................................................... 3
                                             at least once a month ...................................... 4
IF NO CHILDREN, GO TO Q.33                    6-11 times a year............................................. 5
                                             2-5 times a year................................................ 6
                                             once a year or less........................................... 7

     a. How old is _____?

     b. Is that a male or a female? (male=1; female=2)

14. Is any of these children a step-child? IF YES: Which ones? (no=0, yes=1)

     a. Was there ever a time you didn't have custody of any of your children? IF YES: Which ones? (no=0, yes=1)

Now I'm going to ask you about each of your children:

15. How is _____'s physical health at the present time?       very poor,. ........................................................... 1
     Would you say....                                       poor,.. ................................................................... 2
                                             fair,. ...................................................................... 3
                                             good, or. ............................................................... 4
                                             excellent?. ........................................................... 5

16. Where does _____ live?        GO TO Q.22       in the same house or building as R................. 1
                                               within walking distance.................................... 2
                                               in the same town, not walking distance...........3
                                                in the Albany-Schenectady-Troy area.............. 4
                                                outside Albany-Schenectady-Troy area...........5

17. Using your usual means of transportation, how long does it take to get to _____'s?

     a. Time unit                                        MINUTES........................................................... 1
                                               HOURS .............................................................. 2
                                               DAYS ................................................................. 3

PRESENT CARD A

18. How often do you visit with _____ in your home or his/her's or somewhere else? ☐

19. How often do you talk to _____ on the telephone? ☐

20. How often do you send or give letters, cards, or presents to _____ (or _____'s family)? ☐

21. How often do you receive letters, cards or presents from _____ (or _____'s family)? ☐

TAKE BACK CARD A

22. Taking everything into consideration, how <u>close</u> do you      not very close,.................................................... 1
     feel is your relationship with _____? Would you say.....     somewhat close, ............................................... 2
                                                very close, or..................................................... 3
                                                extremely close? ............................................... 4

IF NO CHILDREN AGE 15+, GO TO Q.33

CHILDREN

| 13. | 0 1 | 0 1 | 0 1 | 0 1 | 0 1 | 0 1 | 0 1 | 0 1 | 0 1 |
|---|---|---|---|---|---|---|---|---|---|
|  | 101 | 201 | 301 | 401 | 501 | 601 | 701 | 801 | 901 |

| a. |  |  |  |  |  |  |  |  |  |
|---|---|---|---|---|---|---|---|---|---|
| b. | 1 2 | 1 2 | 1 2 | 1 2 | 1 2 | 1 2 | 1 2 | 1 2 | 1 2 |
| 14. | 0 1 | 0 1 | 0 1 | 0 1 | 0 1 | 0 1 | 0 1 | 0 1 | 0 1 |
| a. | 0 1 | 0 1 | 0 1 | 0 1 | 0 1 | 0 1 | 0 1 | 0 1 | 0 1 |

| 15. | 1 2 3 4 5 | 1 2 3 4 5 | 1 2 3 4 5 | 1 2 3 4 5 | 1 2 3 4 5 | 1 2 3 4 5 | 1 2 3 4 5 | 1 2 3 4 5 | 1 2 3 4 5 |
|---|---|---|---|---|---|---|---|---|---|
| 16. | 1 2 3 4 5 | 1 2 3 4 5 | 1 2 3 4 5 | 1 2 3 4 5 | 1 2 3 4 5 | 1 2 3 4 5 | 1 2 3 4 5 | 1 2 3 4 5 | 1 2 3 4 5 |
| 17. |  |  |  |  |  |  |  |  |  |
| a. | 1 2 3 | 1 2 3 | 1 2 3 | 1 2 3 | 1 2 3 | 1 2 3 | 1 2 3 | 1 2 3 | 1 2 3 |

| 18. |  |  |  |  |  |  |  |  |  |
|---|---|---|---|---|---|---|---|---|---|
| 19. |  |  |  |  |  |  |  |  |  |
| 20. |  |  |  |  |  |  |  |  |  |
| 21. |  |  |  |  |  |  |  |  |  |

| 22. | 1 2 3 4 | 1 2 3 4 | 1 2 3 4 | 1 2 3 4 | 1 2 3 4 | 1 2 3 4 | 1 2 3 4 | 1 2 3 4 | 1 2 3 4 |
|---|---|---|---|---|---|---|---|---|---|

RECORD NAMES ON CHART FOR CHILDREN 15+

23. Is _____

married, ............................................................. 1
divorced, ........................................................... 2
separated, .......................................................... 3
living apart ........................................................ 4
widowed, or ....................................................... 5

GO TO Q.26        never married? ................................................. 6

24. How long has s/he been (THIS STATUS)?  RECORD YEARS

IF CHILD CURRENTLY DIVORCED, GO TO Q.26.

25. Has _____ ever been divorced?  (no = 0, yes = 1)

26. Does _____ have any children?  (no = 00 - IF YES: How many?)        IF NO, GO TO Q.27.

a. Are any of them over age 21?  (no = 00 - IF YES:  How many?)

b. Are any of them under age 12?  (no = 00 - IF YES:  How many?)

IF CHILD NEVER MARRIED, GO TO d.

c. Are any of these children from a previous marriage?  (no = 0, yes = 1)  IF NO, GO TO Q.27

d. Who has custody of the children?

R's child .............................................................. 1
child's ex-spouse............................................... 2
joint custody...................................................... 3
other (specify _____ ) ........................................ 4

27. Is _____ currently working full-time, part-time, retired,
keeping house, or what?

Working full-time ............................................... 1
Working part-time ............................................. 2
Has job, but not working due to temporary
  illness, strike, vacation, etc. ........................ 3
Unemployed, laidoff, looking for work ........... 4
Retired, on permanent disability ..................... 5
Keeping house ................................................... 6
In school ............................................................ 7

28. How many years ago did s/he begin (THIS STATUS)?

29. What was _____ doing immediately before this - working full-time, part-time, retired, keeping house, or what? ☐

IF CHILD NOT CURRENTLY MARRIED, GO TO Q.33.

30. Is _____'s (wife/husband) currently working full-time, part-time, retired, keeping house, or what? ☐

31. How many years ago did s/he begin (THIS STATUS)?

32. What was s/he doing immediately before this - working full-time, part-time, retired, keeping house, or what? ☐

CHILDREN 15+

| | 101 | 201 | 301 | 401 | 501 | 601 | 701 | 801 | 901 |
|---|---|---|---|---|---|---|---|---|---|
| 23. | 1 2 3 4 5 6 | 1 2 3 4 5 6 | 1 2 3 4 5 6 | 1 2 3 4 5 6 | 1 2 3 4 5 6 | 1 2 3 4 5 6 | 1 2 3 4 5 6 | 1 2 3 4 5 6 | 1 2 3 4 5 6 |
| 24. | | | | | | | | | |
| 25. | 0 1 | 0 1 | 0 1 | 0 1 | 0 1 | 0 1 | 0 1 | 0 1 | 0 1 |
| 26. | | | | | | | | | |
| a. | | | | | | | | | |
| b. | | | | | | | | | |
| c. | 0 1 | 0 1 | 0 1 | 0 1 | 0 1 | 0 1 | 0 1 | 0 1 | 0 1 |
| d. | 1 2 3 4 | 1 2 3 4 | 1 2 3 4 | 1 2 3 4 | 1 2 3 4 | 1 2 3 4 | 1 2 3 4 | 1 2 3 4 | 1 2 3 4 |
| 27. | 1 2 3 4 5 6 7 | 1 2 3 4 5 6 7 | 1 2 3 4 5 6 7 | 1 2 3 4 5 6 7 | 1 2 3 4 5 6 7 | 1 2 3 4 5 6 7 | 1 2 3 4 5 6 7 | 1 2 3 4 5 6 7 | 1 2 3 4 5 6 7 |
| 28. | | | | | | | | | |
| 29. | | | | | | | | | |
| 30. | | | | | | | | | |
| 31. | | | | | | | | | |
| 32. | | | | | | | | | |

33. Is either of your (spouse's) biological parents living?  IF YES:  What are their names?  IF NO, GO TO Q.34

(no = 0, yes = 1)

IF BOTH PARENTS LIVING:

a. Do they live together in the same residence?  (no = 0, yes = 1)

b. Are they currently married to each other, divorced,      never married ....................................................0
separated, or never married?      married ............................................................1
      divorced............................................................2
      separated..........................................................3

34. Do you (Does your spouse) have any step-parents?  IF YES:  What are their names?  IF NO, GO TO Q.35

a. Do your (Do your spouse's) mother and step-father / father and step-mother live together in the same residence?
(no = 0, yes = 1) - IF YES, GO TO Q.35

b. Are they currently married to each other, separated, or      married ............................................................1
divorced?      divorced............................................................2
      separated..........................................................3

35. How long has your (spouse's) mother/father been [(re)married, divorced, separated, widowed]?  RECORD YEARS

GO BACK AND ASK ABOUT SPOUSE'S PARENTS.  IF NO PARENTS/IN-LAWS LIVING, GO TO Q.49

36. How old is _____ ?

37. Is _____ currently working full-time, part-time, retired,      Working full-time ..............................................1
keeping house, or what?      Working part-time .............................................2
      Has job, but not working due to temporary
        illness, strike, vacation, etc...........................3
      Unemployed, laid off, looking for work............4
      GO TO Q.38      Retired, permanent disability...........................5
      Keeping house .................................................6
      In school...........................................................7

a. How many hours a week does _____ work?

38. How many years ago did _____ begin (THIS STATUS)?

39. How is _____ 's health at the present time?  Would you      very poor, ........................................................1
say ...      poor, ...............................................................2
      fair, .................................................................3
      good, or..........................................................4
      excellent? .......................................................5

ASK FOR BIO-PARENTS / BIO-IN-LAWS ONLY, IF PARENTS LIVE TOGETHER, ASK AS ONE UNIT:

40. How many living daughters including stepdaughters do(es) _____ have?  IF NONE, GO TO Q.41

a. How many of them live in the same house or building as _____ ?

b. How many of them live within one hours drive of _____ ?

33.

| | 0 1 | 0 1 | 0 1 | 0 1 | | 0 1 | 0 1 | 0 1 | 0 1 |
| | 003 | 004 | 006 | 007 | | 010 | 011 | 013 | 014 |
| | BIOLOGICAL | | STEP– | | | BIOLOGICAL | | STEP– | |

*PARENTS*

| | M | F | M | F |
|---|---|---|---|---|

*IN-LAWS*

| | M | F | M | F |
|---|---|---|---|---|

a.  0  1                          0  1

b.
```
0                              0
1                              1
2                              2
3                              3
```

34.

a.  0  1    0  1                0  1    0  1

b.
```
1    1                         1    1
2    2                         2    2
3    3                         3    3
```

35.

36.

37.
```
1    1    1    1               1    1    1    1
2    2    2    2               2    2    2    2

3    3    3    3               3    3    3    3
4    4    4    4               4    4    4    4
5    5    5    5               5    5    5    5
6    6    6    6               6    6    6    6
7    7    7    7               7    7    7    7
```

a.

38.

39.
```
1    1    1    1               1    1    1    1
2    2    2    2               2    2    2    2
3    3    3    3               3    3    3    3
4    4    4    4               4    4    4    4
5    5    5    5               5    5    5    5
```

40.

a.

b.

41. How many living sons including step-sons do(es) _____ have? IF NONE, GO TO Q.42

   a. How many of them live in the same house or building as _____?

   b. How many of them live within one hour's drive of _____?

42. Where do(es) _____ live?          GO TO Q.48          in the same building as R................................ 1
                                                           within walking distance................................ 2
                                                           in same town, not walking distance ................ 3
                                                           in Albany-Schenectady-Troy area.................... 4
                                                           outside Albany-Schenectady-Troy area........... 5

43. Using your usual means of transportation, how long does it take to get to _____'s?

   a. Time unit                                            MINUTES........................................................ 1
                                                           HOURS .......................................................... 2
                                                           DAYS ............................................................. 3

PRESENT CARD A

44. How often do you visit with _____ in your home or          never...................................................................0
    his/hers/theirs or somewhere else? ☐                       once a day or more............................................ 1
                                                                2-6 days a week ................................................ 2
                                                                once a week ..................................................... 3
                                                                at least once a month ....................................... 4
                                                                6-11 times a year.............................................. 5
                                                                2-5 times a year................................................ 6
                                                                once a year or less............................................ 7

45. How often do you talk to _____ on the telephone? ☐

46. How often do you send or give letters, cards or presents to _____? ☐

47. How often do you receive letters, cards, or presents from _____? ☐

ASK FOR EACH INDIVIDUAL:

48. Taking everything into consideration, how close do you          not very close...................................................... 1
    feel is your relationship with _____? Would you say...          somewhat close ................................................. 2
                                                                    very close .......................................................... 3
                                                                    extremely close .................................................. 4

IF R HAS NEVER BEEN MARRIED, DIVORCED OR WIDOWED, GO TO Q.50

49. Do you have any parents-in-law from a previous marriage      GO TO Q.50          no...................0
    who are still living?                                                            yes.................1

   a. How often do you visit with them in your home or theirs or somewhere else? ☐          _____

   b. How often do you talk to them on the telephone? ☐          _____

| | 003 | 004 | 006 | 007 | | 010 | 011 | 013 | 014 |
|---|---|---|---|---|---|---|---|---|---|
| | BIOLOGICAL | | STEP- | | | BIOLOGICAL | | STEP- | |
| PARENTS | M | F | M | F | IN-LAWS | M | F | M | F |
| 41. | | | | | | | | | |
| a. | | | | | | | | | |
| b. | | | | | | | | | |
| 42. | 1 2 3 4 5 | 1 2 3 4 5 | 1 2 3 4 5 | 1 2 3 4 5 | | 1 2 3 4 5 | 1 2 3 4 5 | 1 2 3 4 5 | 1 2 3 4 5 |
| 43. | \| | \| | \| | \| | | \| | \| | \| | \| |
| a. | 1 2 3 | 1 2 3 | 1 2 3 | 1 2 3 | | 1 2 3 | 1 2 3 | 1 2 3 | 1 2 3 |
| 44. | 0 1 2 3 4 5 6 7 | 0 1 2 3 4 5 6 7 | 0 1 2 3 4 5 6 7 | 0 1 2 3 4 5 6 7 | | 0 1 2 3 4 5 6 7 | 0 1 2 3 4 5 6 7 | 0 1 2 3 4 5 6 7 | 0 1 2 3 4 5 6 7 |
| 45. | | | | | | | | | |
| 46. | | | | | | | | | |
| 47. | | | | | | | | | |
| 48. | 1 2 3 4 | 1 2 3 4 | 1 2 3 4 | 1 2 3 4 | | 1 2 3 4 | 1 2 3 4 | 1 2 3 4 | 1 2 3 4 |

50. Do any other persons live in this household that haven't been mentioned?

GO TO Q.51

no....................0
yes..................1

a. What is each person's age, gender, and relationship to you?

RELATIONSHIP    AGE    M    F

| RELATIONSHIP CODES: |
|---|
| sibling....................................019 |
| friend.....................................020 |
| lodger....................................021 |
| cohabitant/lover....................022 |
| ~~other relative~~.................~~023~~ |
| other (SPECIFY_____)...~~024~~ |

| 0 | | | ___ | 1 | 2 |
| 0 | | | ___ | 1 | 2 |
| 0 | | | ___ | 1 | 2 |
| 0 | | | ___ | 1 | 2 |
| 0 | | | ___ | 1 | 2 |

51. Do you have any relatives (other than your children / parents / and those in your household) living in the Albany-Schenectady-Troy area?

GO TO Q.52
IF YES: How many?

no...............00

___

a. How many do you see or hear from regularly?

___

b. How often do you visit with any of these relatives in your home or theirs or somewhere else? ☐

| never.........................................................0 |
|---|
| once a day or more....................................1 |
| 2-6 days a week ........................................2 |
| once a week ..............................................3 |
| at least once a month ...............................4 |
| 6-11 times a year.......................................5 |
| 2-5 times a year.........................................6 |
| once a year or less....................................7 |

c. How often do you talk to any of these relatives on the telephone? ☐

_____

52. Now I would like to ask you some questions about your neighborhood. How long have you lived at this address?

GO TO Q.53

| less than one year.........................................1 |
|---|
| 1 to less than 2 years....................................2 |
| 2 to less than 5 years....................................3 |
| 5 to less than 10 years..................................4 |
| 10 to less than 20 years................................5 |
| 20 years or more...........................................6 |

a. How long have you lived in this neighborhood?

| less than one year.........................................1 |
|---|
| 1 to less than 2 years....................................2 |
| 2 to less than 5 years....................................3 |
| 5 to less than 10 years..................................4 |
| 10 to less than 20 years................................5 |
| 20 years or more...........................................6 |

53. Do you own or rent this residence?

| own................................................................1 |
|---|
| rent...............................................................2 |
| other (explain_____) .................................3 |

54. How many neighbors do you know well enough to greet by name?

___

55. How many neighbors do you think you could rely on for help in emergencies?

___

56. How often do you visit with any of your neighbors in your home or theirs or somewhere else? ☐

_____

57. How often do you talk to any of your neighbors on the telephone? ☐                    _____

58. How well do you think the people in this neighborhood
know each other?  Would you say.....

very well............................................................ 1
quite well.......................................................... 2
fairly well.......................................................... 3
not so well ....................................................... 4
not at all .......................................................... 5

59. Which of the following statements would best describe the
relationship you have with your nearest neighbors?

We visit in each other's homes ......................... 1
We frequently chat if we happen to see
each other ...................................................... 2
We occasionally chat if we happen to see
each other ...................................................... 3
We hardly know each other............................... 4

60. Think about the person who most recently moved into
your neighborhood.  About how much time went by before
you visited them or invited them over for a social visit?
Would you say...

within the first day or two,............................... 1
first week, .......................................................... 2
first month, ....................................................... 3
first 2-3 months, ............................................. 4
a year, or ......................................................... 5
longer or never?.............................................. 6

61. How safe do you feel being out alone in your
neighborhood?  Do you feel ....

safe all of the time, ......................................... 1
safe most of the time,...................................... 2
unsafe most of the time, or............................. 3
unsafe all of the time? .................................... 4
safe during day, not at night
(VOLUNTEERED)............................... 5

62. Now I would like to ask some questions about your friends
who do not live in this neighborhood.  About how many
friends do you have who live in the Albany-Schenectady-
Troy area, but not in your neighborhood?                    _|_

a. How often do you visit with any of them in your home or theirs or somewhere else? ☐                    _____

b. How often do you talk to any of them on the telephone? ☐                    _____

63. I would now like to ask you some questions on how you manage some everyday activities. For each of the following activities, please tell me who does it. Do you do it yourself, does your spouse do it, a friend, someone you pay, or what? AFTER R'S INITIAL RESPONSE, ASK: Does anyone else help? UP TO 3 TIMES.

| | |
|---|---|
| once a day or more | 1 |
| 2-6 days a week | 2 |
| once a week | 3 |
| at least once a month | 4 |
| 6-11 times a year | 5 |
| 2-5 times a year | 6 |
| once a year or less | 7 |
| only in emergencies (VOLUNTEERED) | 8 |

x1    x2    x3

Who does the grocery shopping?

a. How often do/es _____ do this?

64. Who cooks meals?

a. How often do/es _____ do this?

65. Who does the laundry?

a. How often do/es _____ do this?

66. Who provides transportation for local errands, appointments, etc.?

a. How often do/es _____ do this?

67. Who does home repairs, yardwork, or similar chores?

a. How often do/es _____ do this?

68. Who cleans your house?

a. How often do/es _____ do this?

69. Who takes care of you when you're sick or need personal care?

70. Who would take care of you if you were incapacitated by illness for a week or more?

71. IF R HAS CHILDREN UNDER 12: Besides you or your spouse, who takes care of your young children?

a. How often do/es _____ do this?

ASK FOR ALL PERSONS AND ORGANIZATIONS MENTIONED IN Q.63-71 EXCEPT R

72. In an average week, taking all of these jobs together, how many hours would you say ____ spends doing these kinds things for your household?

| 96+ hours | 96 |
| rarely or emergency | 97 |
| don't know | 98 |

| | NAME | CODE | HRS. | | NAME | CODE | HRS. |
|---|---|---|---|---|---|---|---|
| 1. | | | | 5. | | | |
| 2. | | | | 6. | | | |
| 3. | | | | 7. | | | |
| 4. | | | | 8. | | | |

ASK FOR ALL INDIVIDUALS EXCEPT R, SPOUSE, CHILDREN, PARENTS, PAID HELP, AND ORGANIZATIONS

73. Now I'd like to ask you some questions about some of the individuals we have just mentioned.

CODE

| # | # | # | # | # | # |
|---|---|---|---|---|---|

a. CODE GENDER (male = 1, female = 2)

| 1 2 | 1 2 | 1 2 | 1 2 | 1 2 | 1 2 |
|---|---|---|---|---|---|

b. How old is ____?

c. Where does ____ live?

GO TO e

| | in the same house or building as R | 1 |
| | within walking distance | 2 |
| | in same town, not walking distance | 3 |
| | in Albany-Schenectady-Troy area | 4 |
| | outside Albany-Schenectady-Troy area | 5 |

| 1 | 1 | 1 | 1 | 1 | 1 |
|---|---|---|---|---|---|
| 2 | 2 | 2 | 2 | 2 | 2 |
| 3 | 3 | 3 | 3 | 3 | 3 |
| 4 | 4 | 4 | 4 | 4 | 4 |
| 5 | 5 | 5 | 5 | 5 | 5 |

d. Using your usual means of transportation, how long does it take to get to ____'s?

| | Minutes | 1 |
| | Hours | 2 |
| | Days | 3 |

| 1 | 1 | 1 | 1 | 1 | 1 |
|---|---|---|---|---|---|
| 2 | 2 | 2 | 2 | 2 | 2 |
| 3 | 3 | 3 | 3 | 3 | 3 |

e. Is ____ married | 1 |
| divorced | 2 |
| separated, | 3 |
| living apart, | 4 |
| widowed, or | 5 |
| never married? | 6 |

| 1 | 1 | 1 | 1 | 1 | 1 |
|---|---|---|---|---|---|
| 2 | 2 | 2 | 2 | 2 | 2 |
| 3 | 3 | 3 | 3 | 3 | 3 |
| 4 | 4 | 4 | 4 | 4 | 4 |
| 5 | 5 | 5 | 5 | 5 | 5 |
| 6 | 6 | 6 | 6 | 6 | 6 |

f. Is ____ currently working full-time, part-time, retired, keeping house, or what?

| | Working full-time | 1 |
| | Working part-time | 2 |
| | Has job, not working due to temporary illness, strike, vacation, etc. | 3 |
| | Unemployed, laidoff, looking for work | 4 |
| | Retired, on permanent disability | 5 |
| | Keeping House | 6 |
| | In school | 7 |

| 1 | 1 | 1 | 1 | 1 | 1 |
|---|---|---|---|---|---|
| 2 | 2 | 2 | 2 | 2 | 2 |
| 3 | 3 | 3 | 3 | 3 | 3 |
| 4 | 4 | 4 | 4 | 4 | 4 |
| 5 | 5 | 5 | 5 | 5 | 5 |
| 6 | 6 | 6 | 6 | 6 | 6 |
| 7 | 7 | 7 | 7 | 7 | 7 |

74. Now let's think about some of the people in your family. Does it ever happen that you help them manage some everyday activities?

no.......................................... 0
IF YES, ASK: How often?
once a day or more ............. 1
2-6 days a week.................... 2
once a week......................... 3
at least once a month.......... 4
6-11 times a year................. 5
2-5 times a year................... 6
once a year or less.............. 7
only in emergencies
   (VOLUNTEERED).............. 8

SEE Q.16

| 0 1 | 0 1 | 0 1 | 0 1 | 0 1 | 0 1 | 0 1 | 0 1 | 0 1 |

ADULT CHILDREN LIVING ELSEWHERE

CODE ALL COLUMNS (no = 0, yes = 1)

What about _____? Do you ever help him/her or his/her family with ...

| | 101 | 201 | 301 | 401 | 501 | 601 | 701 | 801 | 901 |
|---|---|---|---|---|---|---|---|---|---|
| a. housekeeping, cleaning, or cooking? | | | | | | | | | |
| b. shopping or providing transportation? | | | | | | | | | |
| c. heavy chores around the house, yardwork, repairs, etc.? | | | | | | | | | |
| d. personal care or care when sick? | | | | | | | | | |
| e. IF CHILD HAS CHILDREN: babysitting? | | | | | | | | | |

TAKE BACK CARD A

f. LIST ALL MENTIONED ABOVE. Taking all kinds of help together, in an average week, how many hours would you say you spend helping _____ in one way or another?

(no = 0, yes = 1)

g. Do you ever give money or large gifts to _____?

| 0 1 | 0 1 | 0 1 | 0 1 | 0 1 | 0 1 | 0 1 | 0 1 | 0 1 |

h. Has _____ ever moved out of his/her home to stay with you?

| 0 1 | 0 1 | 0 1 | 0 1 | 0 1 | 0 1 | 0 1 | 0 1 | 0 1 |

i. Have you ever moved out of your home to stay with _____?

| 0 1 | 0 1 | 0 1 | 0 1 | 0 1 | 0 1 | 0 1 | 0 1 | 0 1 |

SEE Q.72

SEE Q.33, 34

| 0 1 | 0 1 | 0 1 | 0 1 | 0 1 |

GRANDCHILDREN WHO HELP R

| 0 1 | 0 1 | 0 1 | 0 1 |

PARENTS

| 0 1 | 0 1 | 0 1 | 0 1 |

IN-LAWS

| M | F | M | F |
|---|---|---|---|
| BIO- | | STEP- | |
| 003 | 004 | 006 | 007 |

| M | F | M | F |
|---|---|---|---|
| BIO- | | STEP- | |
| 010 | 011 | 013 | 014 |

| 0 1 | 0 1 | 0 1 | 0 1 | 0 1 |
|-----|-----|-----|-----|-----|
| 0 1 | 0 1 | 0 1 | 0 1 | 0 1 |
| 0 1 | 0 1 | 0 1 | 0 1 | 0 1 |

| 0 1 | 0 1 | 0 1 | 0 1 |
|-----|-----|-----|-----|
| 0 1 | 0 1 | 0 1 | 0 1 |
| 0 1 | 0 1 | 0 1 | 0 1 |

| 0 1 | 0 1 | 0 1 | 0 1 |
|-----|-----|-----|-----|
| 0 1 | 0 1 | 0 1 | 0 1 |
| 0 1 | 0 1 | 0 1 | 0 1 |

PRESENT CARD B

75. How do you feel about the time you spend helping family members? For each of the following statements, please indicate whether you strongly agree, agree, disagree, or strongly disagree.

| | | Strongly Agree | Agree | Disagree | Strongly Disagree | NA |
|---|---|---|---|---|---|---|
| SPOUSE | a. My (husband/wife) should do more of the housework around here | 1 | 2 | 3 | 4 | 5 |
| | b. My (husband/wife) should do more to help with our children | 1 | 2 | 3 | 4 | 5 |
| CHILDREN | c. (My/our) children expect (me/us) to do too much for them | 1 | 2 | 3 | 4 | 5 |
| | d. My parents expect (me/us) to do too much for them | 1 | 2 | 3 | 4 | 5 |
| PARENTS | e. My (husband/wife) should do more to help me with my parents | 1 | 2 | 3 | 4 | 5 |
| | f. My brothers and sisters don't do their share to help with our parents | 1 | 2 | 3 | 4 | 5 |
| | g. My parents-in-law expect (me/us) to do too much for them | 1 | 2 | 3 | 4 | 5 |
| IN-LAWS | h. My (husband/wife) should do more to help (his/her) own parents | 1 | 2 | 3 | 4 | 5 |
| | i. My (husband's/wife's) brothers and sisters don't do their share to help with (his/her) parents | 1 | 2 | 3 | 4 | 5 |
| | j. I do more than my share of the housework around here | 1 | 2 | 3 | 4 | 5 |
| | k. I sometimes feel overburdened by my family's demands on me. | 1 | 2 | 3 | 4 | 5 |

TAKE BACK CARD B

76. Now I am going to read you a list of services which are sometimes available from public agencies or non-profit organizations. I'd like to know if they are available to people who live in this area.

|  | Is this service available to people who live in this area? | | | IF YES: Have you used this service for yourself in the past year? | |
|---|---|---|---|---|---|
|  | NO | YES | DK | NO | YES |
| a. Legal advice at reduced rates or no charge | 0 | 1 | 8 | 0 | 1 |
| b. Information on services for senior citizens | 0 | 1 | 8 | 0 | 1 |
| c. Help in finding work | 0 | 1 | 8 | 0 | 1 |
| d. Help in finding housing | 0 | 1 | 8 | 0 | 1 |
| e. Meals served at a group dining site | 0 | 1 | 8 | 0 | 1 |
| f. Childcare services | 0 | 1 | 8 | 0 | 1 |
| g. Hot meals brought to your home | 0 | 1 | 8 | 0 | 1 |
| h. Help with personal care such as bathing or shampooing | 0 | 1 | 8 | 0 | 1 |
| i. Temporary help with housekeeping chores such as cooking, house-cleaning, and shopping | 0 | 1 | 8 | 0 | 1 |
| j. Door-to-door transportation for mobility impaired | 0 | 1 | 8 | 0 | 1 |
| k. After school programs for children of working parents | 0 | 1 | 8 | 0 | 1 |
| l. Daily phone calls to check if you're OK? | 0 | 1 | 8 | 0 | 1 |
| m. Friendly visits by volunteers | 0 | 1 | 8 | 0 | 1 |
| n. Adult daycare for people who need supervision | 0 | 1 | 8 | 0 | 1 |
| o. Transportation to or from grocery stores | 0 | 1 | 8 | 0 | 1 |
| p. Counseling on financial, management, or personal problems | 0 | 1 | 8 | 0 | 1 |

77. How is your physical health at the present time? Would you say ....

very poor, ............................................................ 1
poor, ................................................................... 2
fair ...................................................................... 3
good, or ............................................................. 4
excellent? .......................................................... 5

78. Do you have any chronic physical problems that prevent you from doing things you would otherwise do?

GO TO Q.79          no .................... 0
                    yes .................... 1

a. What is that?

_____

79. How much does your health stand in the way of you doing the things you want to do? Would you say...

not at all, ........................................................... 1
a little, or ........................................................... 2
a great deal? ...................................................... 3

80. In the past six months, about how many times have you been to the doctors?

81. In the past six months, how many days were you so sick that you were unable to carry out your usual activities?

none ..................................................................... 0
a week or less ..................................................... 1
more than a week but less than 1 month .......... 2
1-3 months ......................................................... 3
4-6 months ......................................................... 4

82. In the past six months, how many days were you in a hospital or nursing home for physical health problems?

83. Do you regularly participate in any vigorous physical activity such as walking, jogging, gardening, or swimming?

no .................... 0
yes .................... 1

84. Taking all things together, how would you say things are these days? Would you say you are....

very happy, ......................................................... 1
pretty happy, or .................................................. 2
not too happy? .................................................... 3

IF NOT CURRENTLY MARRIED, GO TO Q.89

NOT MARRIED = 0     MARRIED = 1

85. How is your (husband's/wife's) physical health at the present time? Would you say ....

very poor, ........................................................... 1
poor, ................................................................... 2
fair, ..................................................................... 3
good, or .............................................................. 4
excellent? ........................................................... 5

86. Does s/he have any chronic physical problems that prevent him/her from doing things s/he would otherwise do?

GO TO Q.87          no .................... 0
                    yes .................... 1

a. What is that?

_____

87. All things considered, how happy are you with your marriage? Would you say...

very happy, ......................................................... 1
somewhat happy, ................................................ 2
not very happy, or .............................................. 3
not happy at all? ................................................. 4

88. Has the thought of getting a divorce from your (husband/wife) ever crossed your mind?

no .................... 0
yes .................... 1

89. Now I would like to ask you about some activities of daily living. As I read each item, please tell me if you can usually do it by yourself <u>without</u> difficulty, by yourself with <u>some</u> difficulty, or if you <u>cannot</u> do it without the help of another person.

|  | without difficulty | some difficulty | need help |
|---|---|---|---|
| What about _____? Can you usually do that... | | | |
| a. going outdoors | 3 | 2 | 1 |
| b. walking up and down stairs | 3 | 2 | 1 |
| c. getting around the house/apartment/room | 3 | 2 | 1 |
| d. cleaning and other household chores | 3 | 2 | 1 |

90. How many trips have you taken outside your home in the last 7 days?  IF NONE, GO TO Q.91          |__|__

a. How many different places did you go?          |__|__

91. How long would it take someone to walk to the nearest bus stop, if any?  RECORD MINUTES          |__|__
     IF NO BUS STOP, CODE 00 AND GO TO Q.92

PRESENT CARD A

a. How often do you use the bus? ☐

| | |
|---|---|
| never | 0 |
| once a day or more | 1 |
| 2-6 days a week | 2 |
| once a week | 3 |
| at least once a month | 4 |
| 6-11 times a year | 5 |
| 2-5 times a year | 6 |
| once a year or less | 7 |

92. Do you have a drivers license?          GO TO Q.93          no....................0
                                                                yes..................1

a. Do you have a car available to drive yourself?          GO TO Q.93          no....................0
                                                                              yes..................1

b. How often do you drive yourself somewhere? ☐          _____

93. Now I'd like to ask you some questions about groups and          no....................0
    organizations. Are you a part of a religious organization          yes..................1
    such as a church or temple?

94. How often do you attend religious services? ☐          _____

IF NO CHILDREN AGE 18+, CODE 2 AND GO TO Q.96          _____

IF Q.93 AND 94 CODED 0, GO TO Q.96

95. Do any of your adult children attend or belong to the          no....................0
    same church, temple, or organization?          yes..................1

96. Here is a list of various types of organizations. Do you presently belong to or participate in any of these types of organizations? IF YES: How often do you spend time in activities connected with this group? ☐

| | |
|---|---|
| never | 0 |
| once a day or more | 1 |
| 2-6 days a week | 2 |
| once a week | 3 |
| at least once a month | 4 |
| 6-11 times a year | 5 |
| 2-5 times a year | 6 |
| once a year or less | 7 |

PRESENT CARD C

| | NO | YES | HOW OFTEN |
|---|---|---|---|
| a. business or civic groups | 0 | 1 | _____ |
| b. charity or welfare organizations | 0 | 1 | _____ |
| c. cooperatives (farming,consumer,childcare,etc.) | 0 | 1 | _____ |
| d. fraternal lodges or veterans' organizations | 0 | 1 | _____ |
| e. special interest groups (issue-oriented or lobbies), political clubs or organizations | 0 | 1 | _____ |
| f. labor unions | 0 | 1 | _____ |
| g. neighborhood associations | 0 | 1 | _____ |
| h. PTA or other school related groups | 0 | 1 | _____ |
| i. community center | 0 | 1 | _____ |
| j. professional associations or groups | 0 | 1 | _____ |
| k. social clubs, card playing, music,or hobby groups | 0 | 1 | _____ |
| l. sports teams or clubs | 0 | 1 | _____ |
| m. youth groups (Scout leader, Little League,etc.) | 0 | 1 | _____ |
| n. religious groups | 0 | 1 | _____ |
| o. senior citizen center | 0 | 1 | _____ |
| p. other (SPECIFY _____ ) | 0 | 1 | _____ |

TAKE BACK CARD A AND C

97. Now we would like to ask you some questions about some political matters. What political party do you most often vote for or do you feel the most sympathy for?

| | |
|---|---|
| Republican | 1 |
| Democrat | 2 |
| other | 3 |
| vote evenly for both | 4 |

98. Did you vote in the 1984 Presidential election?

GO TO Q.99

| | |
|---|---|
| no | 0 |
| yes | 1 |

a. Did you vote for the Republican or the Democratic candidate?

| | |
|---|---|
| Republican | 1 |
| Democratic | 2 |
| neither | 3 |

99. On most domestic political issues, do you think of yourself as more of a conservative, a liberal, or a middle-of-the-roader?

conservative ...................................................... 1
middle-of-the-road ............................................ 2
liberal ................................................................. 3
depends on issue (VOLUNTEERED) ................ 4

100. On the whole, do you think the government has cut back too much on domestic programs or not cut back enough?

cut back too much ............................................ 1
not cut back enough ......................................... 2
just right (VOLUNTEERED) ............................. 3

101. We are faced with many problems in this country, none of which can be solved easily or inexpensively. I'm going to name some of these problems, and for each one I'd like you to tell me whether you think the government is spending too much money on it, too little money, or about the right amount. First (ITEM A)... are we spending too much, too little, or about the right amount on (ITEM)?

a. Health
Too much ............. 1
Too little ............... 2
About right .......... 3

b. Education
Too much ............. 1
Too little ............... 2
About right .......... 3

c. Assistance to Minorities
Too much ............. 1
Too little ............... 2
About right .......... 3

d. National Defense
Too much ............. 1
Too little ............... 2
About right .......... 3

e. Assistance to Poor People
Too much ............. 1
Too little ............... 2
About right .......... 3

f. Assistance to Elderly
Too much ............. 1
Too little ............... 2
About right .......... 3

102. I'd like to turn now to some questions about problems in your neighborhood. As you think about the future of this neighborhood, would you prefer to keep it just as it is, keep it pretty much as it is, or would some major changes would be helpful?

keep it just as it is ............................................ 1
keep it pretty much as it is ............................... 2
some major changes would be helpful ........... 3

|                                                        | No | Yes |
|--------------------------------------------------------|----|-----|
| 103. Over the last year, have any of the following issues affecting this neighborhood ever come up in discussions with family, friends, or neighbors? | | |
| a. Schools | 0 | 1 |
| b. Parks, playgrounds, etc. | 0 | 1 |
| c. Condition of the housing | 0 | 1 |
| d. Reputation of the area | 0 | 1 |
| e. Police protection | 0 | 1 |
| f. Fire protection | 0 | 1 |
| g. Streets and sidewalks | 0 | 1 |
| h. Cleanliness of the area | 0 | 1 |
| i. Garbage collection | 0 | 1 |
| j. Traffic congestion and parking | 0 | 1 |
| k. Noise level | 0 | 1 |
| l. Personal safety | 0 | 1 |
| m. Housing costs, rents, property taxes | 0 | 1 |
| n. Services of landlords | 0 | 1 |
| o. Impact of commercial, industrial, or institutional activities on residential land use | 0 | 1 |
| p. Residential land use changes, such as new housing construction | 0 | 1 |

| PRESENT CARD B |

104. In the past year, has there been any important issue
facing this neighborhood?

GO TO Q.106                no..................0
                           yes.................1

a. What is that issue?

_____

105. To what degree would the following groups agree or disagree with your point of view on this issue?

| What about _____? | Strongly Agree | Agree | Both/Mixed Neutral (VOLUNTEERED) | Disagree | Strongly Disagree |
|--------------------|----------------|-------|----------------------------------|----------|-------------------|
| a. Local officials or agencies | 1 | 2 | 3 | 4 | 5 |
| b. State or federal officials or agencies | 1 | 2 | 3 | 4 | 5 |
| c. Builders or real estate developers | 1 | 2 | 3 | 4 | 5 |
| d. Business community | 1 | 2 | 3 | 4 | 5 |
| e. Other residents of the area | 1 | 2 | 3 | 4 | 5 |
| f. Neighborhood association or other voluntary groups | 1 | 2 | 3 | 4 | 5 |

106. Some people think it would be better if everyone lived in
neighborhoods where all people had the same kind of
racial background while others think it would be better if
each neighborhood included people from different racial
backgrounds. Which do you prefer, the same or different?

Same................................................................1
Different ...........................................................2
It depends (VOLUNTEERED) ...........................3

107. Now I would like to read some statements. Would you
please tell me whether you strongly agree, agree, disagree,
or strongly disagree with each statement.

| | strongly agree | agree | disagree | strongly disagree | DK |
|---|---|---|---|---|---|
| a. Taking care of elderly parents is as much a son's responsibility as a daughter's. | 1 | 2 | 3 | 4 | 8 |
| b. I don't like to get help from other people unless I can help them too. | 1 | 2 | 3 | 4 | 8 |
| c. Parents should not expect to move in with their adult children even if they are having health problems. | 1 | 2 | 3 | 4 | 8 |
| d. Nowadays adult children do not take as much care of their elderly parents as they did in past generations. | 1 | 2 | 3 | 4 | 8 |
| e. Retired people are happiest in the company of people who are their own age. | 1 | 2 | 3 | 4 | 8 |
| f. The help people give their elderly relatives should be considered a repayment for the help they received earlier in life. | 1 | 2 | 3 | 4 | 8 |
| g. Adult sons should be expected to do the same kinds of household chores as adult daughters for their elderly parents. | 1 | 2 | 3 | 4 | 8 |
| h. Old age pensioners have a right to be taken care of in a dignified way even if younger people must contribute their taxes to make this possible. | 1 | 2 | 3 | 4 | 8 |
| i. A woman who works outside the home can be just as good a mother as one who does not. | 1 | 2 | 3 | 4 | 8 |
| j. The older person gets a fair break in benefits from our society. | 1 | 2 | 3 | 4 | 8 |
| k. Programs should be developed which allow older people to continue living at home rather than in a nursing home. | 1 | 2 | 3 | 4 | 8 |
| l. People should help their parents-in-law as much as they help their own parents. | 1 | 2 | 3 | 4 | 8 |
| m. Adult children should stay in touch with their parents on a regular basis. | 1 | 2 | 3 | 4 | 8 |
| n. If people get into financial trouble, they should be able to depend on their parents for help. | 1 | 2 | 3 | 4 | 8 |
| o. Anyone over 65 should be entitled to health care at an affordable cost. | 1 | 2 | 3 | 4 | 8 |
| p. Adult children should not expect to move back in with their parents even if they are having health problems. | 1 | 2 | 3 | 4 | 8 |

| | strongly agree | agree | disagree | strongly disagree | DK |
|---|---|---|---|---|---|
| q. Even if it meant an increase in taxes, this area should be provided with a public transportation program for the elderly. | 1 | 2 | 3 | 4 | 8 |
| r. Children should live close to their parents whenever possible. | 1 | 2 | 3 | 4 | 8 |
| s. Children should be in touch with their parents at least weekly. | 1 | 2 | 3 | 4 | 8 |
| t. Children should be able to expect babysitting help from their parents. | 1 | 2 | 3 | 4 | 8 |
| u. A married woman should be able to have a job even if it is not always convenient for her family. | 1 | 2 | 3 | 4 | 8 |
| v. Married couples who do not want children are being too self-centered. | 1 | 2 | 3 | 4 | 8 |

[TAKE BACK CARD B.]

108. Comparing yourself to most people your age, would you say you feel...

older, ................................................ 1
younger, or ........................................ 2
the same? ......................................... 3

109. Do you describe yourself as young, middle-aged, old, or what?

young ................................................. 1
middle-aged ...................................... 2
old ..................................................... 3
elderly ............................................... 4
aged ................................................. 5
young-old .......................................... 6
other (SPECIFY _____) ..................... 7

110. What ages would you include in this category?

＿＿＿ – ＿＿＿

111. Whom do you like to spend time with the most, people who are ....

older than you, ................................. 1
the same age as you, or ................... 2
younger than you? ............................ 3
mixed ages (VOLUNTEERED) ........... 4
I don't care (VOLUNTEERED) ........... 5

[PRESENT CARD D]

112. Using the categories on this card, at what age is a person most respected?

Youth (to age 30) ............................. 1
Early middle age (31-50) .................. 2
Later middle age (51-64) .................. 3
Older age (65 and over) ................... 4

113. At what age does a person have the most influence? [ ]        ＿＿＿

114. At what age is a person least respected? [ ]        ＿＿＿

115. At what age does a person have least influence? [ ]        ＿＿＿

[TAKE BACK CARD D]

116. We have talked about various parts of your life. Now I would like to ask you how satisfied are you with your life as a whole these days? If you had to pick a number from 1 to 7, with 1 being very dissatisfied and 7 being very satisfied, which number would come closest to how you feel?

_____

117. Please tell me whether or not the following statements are true.

| | NO | YES | |
|---|---|---|---|
| a. Things keep getting worse as I get older. | 0 | 1 | |
| b. I have as much pep as I did last year. | 0 | 1 | 2 More pep (VOLUNTEERED) |
| c. Little things bother me more this year. | 0 | 1 | |
| d. As I get older I feel less useful. | 0 | 1 | |
| e. I sometimes worry so much that I can't sleep. | 0 | 1 | |
| f. I get upset easily. | 0 | 1 | |
| g. I am as happy now as I was when I was younger. | 0 | 1 | 2 Happier (VOLUNTEERED) |
| h. I am afraid of a lot of things. | 0 | 1 | |
| i. I get mad more than I used to. | 0 | 1 | |
| j. I take things hard. | 0 | 1 | |

118. I would like to ask you just a few more questions to finish the interview. We need this information for statistical purposes. From what countries did your ancestors come? CIRCLE FIRST THREE COUNTRIES MENTIONED.

| | | | |
|---|---|---|---|
| Africa .................... 01 | | Japan ..................... 21 | Puerto Rico.......... 31 |
| American Indian/ | Denmark................. 11 | Korea...................... 22 | Russia (USSR)...... 32 |
| Native American... 02 | England/Wales ....... 12 | Lithuania ................ 23 | Scotland (or |
| Austria .................. 03 | Finland................... 13 | Mexico ................... 24 | Scottish Irish) ..... 33 |
| Belgium ................. 04 | France ................... 14 | Netherlands | Spain..................... 34 |
| Canada (French).... 05 | Germany................. 15 | (Dutch/Holland) ....25 | Sweden.................. 35 |
| Canada (other)....... 06 | Hungary.................. 16 | Norway................... 26 | Switzerland............ 36 |
| Central or South........ | India....................... 17 | Pakistan ................ 27 | West Indies........... 37 |
| America ................ 07 | Ireland ................... 18 | Phillipines.............. 28 | Yugoslavia............ 38 |
| China .................... 08 | | Poland.................... 29 | Other (specify) ..... 39 |
| Cuba..................... 09 | Italy........................ 20 | Portugal ................. 30 | _____ |

IF MORE THAN ONE COUNTRY:

a. Which one of these countries do you feel closer to? USE CODES FROM Q.118. IF NEITHER, CODE 00.

more than one country ..................................... 40

119. How important is your ethnic background to you? Would you say it is ....

very important, ..................................... 1
somewhat important, or........................ 2
not important?...................................... 3

120. Was either of your parents born outside the United States?

no.......................................................... 0
mother only ........................................... 1
father only............................................. 2
both....................................................... 3

121. What is your religious preference? Is it ....

Protestant, ............................................ 1
Catholic, ............................................... 2
Jewish, .................................................. 3

GO TO Q.122

some other religion (SPECIFY _____ ), or 4
no religion?............................................ 5

a. What specific denomination is that, if any?

Baptist.................................................................1
Methodist...........................................................2
Lutheran .............................................................3
Presbyterian ......................................................4
Episcopalian.......................................................5
Other (SPECIFY _____)........................6
No denomination given/nondenominational.... 7

122. In what year were you born?                          |_|_|_|

123. IF MARRIED: In what year was your spouse born?      |_|_|_|

PRESENT CARD E

124. In the past year, have you or other family members in your household received income from any of these sources?

|  | NO | YES | DK |
|---|---|---|---|
| a. Own business, operating a farm | 0 | 1 | 8 |
| b. Rental income, interest or dividends from savings, stocks, bonds, or income from estates or trusts | 0 | 1 | 8 |
| c. Social Security (old age or survivors benefits) | 0 | 1 | 8 |
| d. Alimony and/or child support | 0 | 1 | 8 |
| e. Unemployment compensation, disability payments such as Veteran's compensation or pension, Workman's compensation, or Social Security disability | 0 | 1 | 8 |
| f. Retirement pensions | 0 | 1 | 8 |
| g. AFDC, food stamps, a Title V program | 0 | 1 | 8 |

TAKE BACK CARD E AND PRESENT CARD F

125. In the past year have you received financial help from any of the following sources? IF YES: Which ones?

no................000

_____   |_|_|_|
_____   |_|_|_|
_____   |_|_|_|

TAKE BACK CARD F

_____   |_|_|_|

126. What is the highest grade or year of school you have completed?

none...............................................................00
ASK a — elementary....................01 02 03 04 05 06 07 08
high school......................................09 10 11 12
college or postsecondary................13 14 15 16
ASK b   some graduate school ....................................17
graduate or professional degree...................18

a. Do you have a high school diploma or G.E.D.?

no...................0
yes.................1

b. Do you have a college or professional degree?

no...................0

IF YES: What degree?            _____

IF NOT CURRENTLY MARRIED, GO TO Q.128

127. What is the highest grade or year of school your spouse has completed?

            Ask a

            Ask b

none.................................................................. 00
elementary.................... 01 02 03 04 05 06 07 08
high school......................................09 10 11 12
college or postsecondary................. 13 14 15 16
some graduate school ....................................17
graduate or professional degree.....................18

a. Does s/he have a high school diploma or G.E.D.?

no .................... 0
yes.................. 1

b. Does s/he have a college or professional degree?

no .................... 0

IF YES: What degree?   _____

128. CODE RACE, IF UNCERTAIN, ASK: What race to you consider yourself - White, Black, Asian, Hispanic, or what?

White................................................................ 1
Black................................................................ 2
Asian origin...................................................... 3
Hispanic........................................................... 4
Other (specify_____) ........................5

129. RECORD SEX OF RESPONDENT

male ................ 1
female ............ 2

PRESENT CARD G

130. Please look at the card and give me the letter of the income group that describes your total family income before taxes last year.  This figure should include all forms of income--wages, salaries, interest, dividends, child support, and all other incomes.

A. None.......................................................... 00
B. Less than $3,000....................................... 01
C. $3,000 to $3,999........................................ 02
D. $4,000 to $4,999 ....................................... 03
E. $5,000 to $5,999........................................ 04
F. $6,000 to $7,999........................................ 05
G. $8,000 to $9,999........................................ 06
H. $10,000 to $11,999..................................... 07
I. $12,000 to $14,999...................................... 08
J. $15,000 to $19,999...................................... 09
K. $20,000 to $24,999 .................................... 10
L. $25,000 to $29,999..................................... 11
M. $30,000 to $34,999 .................................... 12
N. $35,000 to $39,999 .................................... 13
O. $40,000 to $49,999..................................... 14
P. $50,000 to $59,999 .................................... 15
Q. $60,000 to $74,999..................................... 16
R. $75,000 and over ....................................... 17

IF "DON'T KNOW" OR REFUSED, ASK:

a. Was it......

More than 17,000 or.......................................... 1
Less than 17,000? ........................................... 2

TAKE BACK CARD G

131. I'd like to verify your name and address. Is it _____? What is your phone number?

Name_____          Phone_____

Address_____

_____

_____

132. In about three years we may wish to contact you again to see if your opinions on these topics have changed. In the event you were to move, could you please tell me the name, address and phone number of two people who would always know your whereabouts.

Name_____          Name_____

Address_____          Address_____

_____          _____

Phone_____          Phone_____

THANK YOU FOR YOUR COOPERATION.

Were there problems in scheduling that would be helpful to
    know next time? If so, what were they? _____

I.D. #  ☐☐|_|_|_|_|☐☐|_|

1. Length of Interview:_____ hr. _____ min.

2. Date: _____ month _____ day 19 ____

3. Were any other members of the household present during     GO TO 4.            no....................0
   the interview?                                                                 yes..................1

   a. Did any of them take part in the interview or did the                       no....................0
      respondent seek advice or opinions from any of them in                      yes..................1
      answering some of the questions?

4. In general, what was the respondent's attitude toward the     good ...............................1
   interview?                                                     fair................................2
                                                                  poor................................3

5. What was the respondent's understanding of the               good ...............................1
   questions?                                                     fair................................2
                                                                  poor................................3

6. What kind of housing unit does the respondent live in?       trailer..............................00
                                                                 single-family detached house.........01
                                                                 two-family, duplex...................02
                                                                 3 or more unit apartment
                       CODE 97 FOR 97+                           (fill in number of units..........._____)

7. How well did the respondent seem to understand and           speaks and comprehends fluently.....1
   speak English?                                                minor problems in speaking/understanding....2
                                                                 appeared to have great difficulty.....3

8. Did the respondent make any general remarks about the interview during or after it? If yes, what were they?

_____

_____

_____

_____

INTERVIEWER: Name _____ I.D. # ___|___

# Appendix C: Tables

**TABLE C.1.1**

Age Identification by Age and Gender of Respondent (N = 1,139)

|  | Chronological age | | | | |
|  | 40–49 | 50–59 | 60–69 | 70–79 | 80+ |
|---|---|---|---|---|---|
| **Men** | | | | | |
| Young | 41% | 18% | 9% | 4% | 0% |
| Middle | 57 | 75 | 68 | 44 | 31 |
| Young-old | 0 | 2 | 4 | 4 | 6 |
| Old | 2 | 5 | 18 | 49 | 63 |
| Number of cases | 148 | 101 | 98 | 57 | 16 |
| **Women** | | | | | |
| Young | 42% | 17% | 10% | 8% | 0% |
| Middle | 55 | 80 | 66 | 49 | 22 |
| Young-old | 1 | 1 | 6 | 8 | 12 |
| Old | 3 | 3 | 18 | 35 | 66 |
| Number of cases | 206 | 161 | 201 | 110 | 41 |

**TABLE C.1.2**

Means and Standard Deviations for Analysis of Age Identity, Family Obligation, and Senior Public Program Support

|  | All cases | | Aged 60+ | |
| --- | --- | --- | --- | --- |
| Family obligation scale | .08 | 2.94 | − .83 | 2.45 |
| Public policy scale | .05 | 3.36 | − .86 | 3.05 |
| Age identity (elderly) | * | * | .34 | .47 |
| Age preference | * | * | .36 | .48 |
| Center membership | * | * | .19 | .39 |
| Nearest child | * | * | 62.07 | 305.65 |
| Closeness to child | * | * | 2.76 | 1.83 |
| Liberal ideology | 1.88 | .67 | 1.83 | .66 |
| Favor public spending | .03 | 2.20 | − .19 | 2.27 |
| Ages 50–59 | .23 | .42 | * | * |
| Ages 60–69 | .25 | .44 | .56 | .50 |
| Ages 70–79 | .15 | .36 | .33 | .47 |
| Ages 80 and above | .05 | .22 | * | * |
| Health | 3.97 | .86 | 3.19 | .41 |
| Female | .63 | .48 | .67 | .47 |
| Black | .06 | .23 | .03 | .18 |
| Income | $29,481 | $22,386 | $20,412 | $18,372 |
| Income missing | .12 | .32 | .16 | .37 |
| Married | .58 | .49 | .49 | .50 |
| Have children | .85 | .36 | * | * |
| Number of living children | 2.65 | 1.93 | 2.63 | 2.00 |
| Full-time employment | .52 | .50 | .20 | .40 |
| Retired | .32 | .47 | * | * |
| Both parents deceased | .58 | .49 | * | * |
| Number of living parents | 1.03 | 1.22 | .26 | .55 |
| Rural | .12 | .32 | .10 | .30 |
| Suburban | .22 | .41 | .19 | .39 |
| N |  | 1,187 |  | 537 |

*    Not used for this sample.

**TABLE C.1.3**
Logistic Regression Equations Predicting Age Identification

| | Middle-Aged vs. Young | | Old vs. Middle-Aged | |
| --- | --- | --- | --- | --- |
| | b | SE | b | SE |
| Age | .074*** | .012 | .115*** | .013 |
| Health | −.590*** | .138 | −.352* | .159 |
| Gender | −.132 | .175 | −.281 | .225 |
| Black | .780* | .412 | .642 | .434 |
| Income ($1,000s) | .006 | .005 | .005 | .006 |
| Income missing | −.137 | .323 | −.184 | .308 |
| **Roles** | | | | |
| Married | −.005 | .202 | −.608** | .240 |
| Have children | .574** | .244 | .227 | .285 |
| Retired | −.149 | .281 | .367 | .230 |
| Both parents deceased | .256 | .199 | −.241 | .287 |
| Intercept | −2.279 | .671 | −8.021 | .941 |
| N | 927 | | 870 | |
| Model chi-square | 136.7 | | 229.2 | |
| Degrees of freedom | 10, 916 | | 10, 859 | |

Note: Unstandardized regression coefficients, with standard errors.
* $p < .05$.     **$p < .01$.     ***$p < .001$.

**TABLE C.1.4**

Predictors of Sense of Family Obligation and Support for Public Programs for Older Persons

| | Family obligation | | Public programs | |
|---|---|---|---|---|
| | Age only | Full model | Age only | Full model |
| Age 50–59 | −1.411***(.221) | −1.061 (.242) | −.860***(.256) | −.529* (.274) |
| Age 60–69 | −2.294***(.214) | −1.798***(.282) | −1.901***(.248) | −1.610***(.320) |
| Age 70–79 | −2.274***(.253) | −1.841***(.342) | −2.505***(.293) | −2.011***(.388) |
| Age 80+ | −2.926***(.369) | −2.396***(.450) | −2.180***(.427) | −1.493** (.511) |
| Income ($1,000s) | | .001 (.005) | | −.006 (.006) |
| Income missing | | −.418 (.289) | | −.670* (.328) |
| Black | | .676 (.366) | | .801* (.416) |
| Female | | .197 (.175) | | .613** (.199) |
| Health | | .064 (.105) | | .071 (.119) |
| Full-time employment | | .031 (.217) | | .276 (.246) |
| Married | | −.094 (.197) | | .128 (.223) |
| Number of living parents | | .134 (.093) | | −.085 (.106) |
| Number of living children | | −.128** (.044) | | −.034 (.049) |
| Rural | | 1.057***(.257) | | .485 (.292) |
| Suburban | | .482* (.204) | | .372 (.231) |
| Liberal ideology | | −.205 (.125) | | .482***(.142) |
| Favor public spending | | −.005 (.038) | | .317***(.043) |
| Constant | 1.414***(.144) | 1.181* (.549) | 1.180***(.167) | −.604 (.622) |
| Adjusted R² | .120 | .134 | .080 | .147 |

Note: Unstandardized regression coefficients, with standard errors in parentheses.

\* p < .05.    \*\*p < .01.      \*\*\* p < .001.

**TABLE C.1.5**

Effects of Additional Measures of Age Consciousness and Isolation for Persons Aged 60 and Above

|  | Family obligation | | Public programs | |
|---|---|---|---|---|
| Age 60–69 | .550 | (.403) | −.352 | (.485) |
| Age 70–79 | .481 | (.386) | −.738 | (.465) |
| Income ($1,000s) | .005 | (.007) | .006 | (.009) |
| Income missing | .141 | (.342) | −.060 | (.411) |
| Black | 1.516* | (.617) | 1.155 | (.742) |
| Female | .158 | (.247) | .998*** | (.298) |
| Health | .017 | (.138) | .050 | (.166) |
| Full-time employment | −.277 | (.289) | −.244 | (.348) |
| Married | .133 | (.265) | .594 | (.319) |
| Number of parents | .278 | (.214) | −.198 | (.257) |
| Number of children | −.185** | (.066) | −.057 | (.080) |
| Rural | .337 | (.370) | .061 | (.445) |
| Suburban | .145 | (.279) | .146 | (.335) |
| Liberal ideology | −.105 | (.167) | .690*** | (.201) |
| Favor public spending | .036 | (.050) | .284*** | (.060) |
| Age identity | −.267 | (.246) | −.292 | (.296) |
| Age preference | .260 | (.231) | .123 | (.278) |
| Center membership | .277 | (.287) | −.056 | (.345) |
| Nearest child | −.0003 | (.0003) | .0004 | (.0004) |
| Closeness to child | −.157 | (.102) | −.003 | (.122) |
| Constant | −.719 | (.726) | −2.666** | (.873) |
| Adjusted $R^2$ | .033 | | .095 | |

*Note:* Unstandardized regression coefficients, with standard errors in parentheses.

\* $p < .05$.    \*\*$p < .01$.    \*\*\*$p < .001$.

**TABLE C.2.1**

Help Between Respondent Parents and a Randomly Selected Noncoresident
Adult Child Age 21 and Over, by Respondent Age

| | Respondent age | | | | | | | |
| | 40–44 | 45–49 | 50–54 | 55–59 | 60–64 | 65–69 | 70–74 | 75+ |
|---|---|---|---|---|---|---|---|---|
| **Help to parent** | | | | | | | | |
| Housekeeping | 0% | 3% | 4% | 3% | 4% | 2% | 5% | 7% |
| Shop, errands | 0% | 3% | 4% | 5% | 3% | 6% | 6% | 23% |
| Repairs, yard | 7% | 1% | 10% | 5% | 9% | 8% | 5% | 12% |
| Any type of help | 7% | 5% | 14% | 9% | 14% | 11% | 14% | 35% |
| Mean hrs/week | .05 | .25 | .39 | .50 | .87 | .41 | .70 | 1.24 |
| **Help to child** | | | | | | | | |
| Housekeeping | 20% | 20% | 14% | 11% | 9% | 17% | 16% | 7% |
| Shop, errands | 27% | 16% | 17% | 18% | 14% | 10% | 19% | 5% |
| Repairs, yard | 2% | 7% | 6% | 13% | 10% | 8% | 8% | 3% |
| Babysit | 15% | 11% | 35% | 27% | 30% | 21% | 9% | 7% |
| Any type of help | 46% | 34% | 51% | 46% | 45% | 38% | 36% | 18% |
| Mean hrs/week | 1.29 | 1.13 | 1.73 | 1.80 | 2.33 | .61 | 1.09 | .41 |
| N | 41 | 70 | 112 | 107 | 134 | 124 | 76 | 106 |

**TABLE C.2.2**

Percentage of Respondent Parents Who Have Any Noncoresident Adult Children, and Measures of Help between Them and All Noncoresident Adult Children Age 21 and Over, by Respondent Age

| | Respondent age | | | | | | | |
|---|---|---|---|---|---|---|---|---|
| | 40–44 | 45–49 | 50–54 | 55–59 | 60–64 | 65–69 | 70–74 | 75 + |
| Have noncoresident adult children | 19% | 50% | 76% | 87% | 89% | 83% | 78% | 73% |
| **Help to parent** | | | | | | | | |
| Housekeeping | 0% | 4% | 5% | 8% | 8% | 7% | 8% | 12% |
| Shop, errands | 0% | 5% | 8% | 14% | 8% | 15% | 10% | 44% |
| Repairs, yard | 10% | 3% | 15% | 13% | 20% | 15% | 12% | 16% |
| Any type of help | 10% | 12% | 23% | 25% | 28% | 23% | 24% | 53% |
| Mean hrs/week | .67 | .57 | 1.43 | 1.09 | 2.22 | 1.36 | 2.24 | 3.01 |
| **Help to children** | | | | | | | | |
| Housekeeping | 19% | 27% | 24% | 15% | 22% | 26% | 23% | 12% |
| Shop, errands | 38% | 28% | 31% | 24% | 27% | 20% | 28% | 8% |
| Repairs, yard | 5% | 10% | 12% | 22% | 16% | 15% | 13% | 5% |
| Babysit | 24% | 23% | 50% | 48% | 53% | 43% | 29% | 13% |
| Any type of help | 60% | 52% | 68% | 67% | 65% | 58% | 54% | 30% |
| Mean hrs/week | 3.00 | 3.38 | 4.38 | 4.35 | 4.14 | 2.75 | 2.15 | 1.31 |
| N | 42 | 73 | 113 | 110 | 139 | 126 | 78 | 107 |

**TABLE C.2.3**

Help between Respondent Parents and a Randomly Selected Noncoresident
Adult Child Age 21 and Over, by Respondent Age and Gender

| | | Respondent (parent) age | |
| --- | --- | --- | --- |
| | 40–59 | 60–74 | 75+ |
| **Mother-daughter pairs** | | | |
| Daughters helping | 6% | 13% | 44% |
| Mean hrs/week | .39 | .40 | 2.24 |
| Mothers helping | 53% | 44% | 25% |
| Mean hrs/week | 2.06 | 1.49 | .19 |
| N | 109 | 121 | 32 |
| **Mother-son pairs** | | | |
| Sons helping | 12% | 18% | 39% |
| Mean hrs/week | .44 | .79 | 1.09 |
| Mothers helping | 44% | 35% | 9% |
| Mean hrs/week | 1.61 | 1.74 | .56 |
| N | 112 | 109 | 44 |
| **Father-daughter pairs** | | | |
| Daughters helping | 12% | 8% | 14% |
| Mean hrs/week | .28 | 1.42 | .85 |
| Fathers helping | 41% | 38% | 14% |
| Mean hrs/week | .80 | 1.06 | .29 |
| N | 56 | 52 | 14 |
| **Father-son pairs** | | | |
| Sons helping | 9% | 7% | 24% |
| Mean hrs/week | .19 | .26 | .24 |
| Fathers helping | 39% | 44% | 29% |
| Mean hrs/week | 1.33 | .93 | .53 |
| N | 57 | 57 | 17 |

**TABLE C.2.4**
Percentage of Parents with Any Coresident Adult Children Age 21 and Over of Those with Any Adult Children

|                                        | Parent age |       |       |       |
| -------------------------------------- | ---------- | ----- | ----- | ----- |
|                                        | 40s        | 50s   | 60s   | 70+   |
| **Total**                              | 35%        | 36%   | 29%   | 15%   |
| **By parent gender and marital status** |           |       |       |       |
| Unmarried father*                      | 9%         | 18%   | 38%   | 16%   |
| Married father                         | 35         | 36    | 27    | 14    |
| Unmarried mother*                      | 26         | 41    | 25    | 15    |
| Married mother                         | 43         | 36    | 31    | 15    |
| N                                      | 138        | 237   | 273   | 190   |

*Note:* Overall, 29 percent of parents have coresident adult children.

*    Includes divorced, separated, widowed, and never married parents.

**TABLE C.2.5**
Percentage of Randomly Selected Adult Children Age 21 and Over Coresiding with Parents

|  | Parent age | | | |
|---|---|---|---|---|
|  | 40s | 50s | 60s | 70+ |
| **Total** | 23% | 17% | 13% | 8% |
| **By parent and child gender** | | | | |
| Son-father | 16% | 21% | 19% | 6% |
| Son-mother | 30 | 17 | 13 | 11 |
| Daughter-father | 32 | 11 | 14 | 7 |
| Daughter-mother | 14 | 18 | 9 | 7 |
| **By parent gender and marital status** | | | | |
| Unmarried father | 0% | 12% | 23% | 16% |
| Married father | 33 | 17 | 15 | 2 |
| Unmarried mother | 16 | 20 | 7 | 11 |
| Married mother | 26 | 16 | 15 | 6 |
| **By child gender and marital status** | | | | |
| Unmarried son | 33% | 34% | 34% | 31% |
| Married son | 0 | 0 | 2 | 3 |
| Unmarried daughter | 33 | 26 | 33 | 16 |
| Married daughter | 0 | 3 | 0 | 2 |
| N | 138 | 237 | 273 | 190 |

**TABLE C.2.6**
Means and Standard Deviations of Variables Used in Analysis of Coresidence with Randomly Selected Adult Child

| | Parent < 60 | | Parent 60+ | |
| | Mean | s.d. | Mean | s.d. |
|---|---|---|---|---|
| Son-father pair | .17 | .37 | .17 | .37 |
| Son-mother pair | .33 | .47 | .36 | .48 |
| Daughter-father pair | .18 | .39 | .16 | .37 |
| Child married | .39 | .49 | .67 | .47 |
| Child health | 4.48 | .64 | 4.27 | .67 |
| Child employed full-time | .74 | .44 | .74 | .44 |
| Child employed part-time | .06 | .23 | .11 | .31 |
| Child # children < 21 | .67 | 1.05 | 1.27 | 1.41 |
| Child ever noncustodial | .10 | .31 | .03 | .18 |
| Child is stepchild | .09 | .28 | .05 | .22 |
| Child # unmarried siblings | 2.10 | 1.45 | 1.10 | 1.30 |
| Parent married | .70 | .46 | .56 | .50 |
| Parent health | 4.09 | .84 | 3.81 | .82 |
| Parent employed full-time | .64 | .48 | .13 | .33 |
| Parent employed part-time | .10 | .30 | .09 | .29 |
| Parent income ($1,000s) | 37.07 | 22.82 | 20.80 | 18.45 |
| Parent black | .07 | .26 | .03 | .18 |
| Parent age | 51.03 | 5.19 | 69.20 | 7.17 |
| Rural residence | .16 | .36 | .10 | .30 |
| Suburban residence | .23 | .42 | .19 | .40 |
| N | 368 | | 444 | |

**TABLE C.2.7**

Logistic Regression of Coresidence with Any Adult Child

|  | Parent < 60 | | Parent 60+ | |
|  | b | SE | b | SE |
|---|---|---|---|---|
| Parent married | .717* | .291 | .242 | .311 |
| Parent gender | .383 | .267 | .043 | .306 |
| Parent health | .181 | .155 | .275 | .180 |
| Parent employed full-time | .342 | .297 | .100 | .418 |
| Parent employed part-time | −.087 | .453 | −.034 | .468 |
| Parent income | −.015* | .068 | −.010 | −.010 |
| Parent black | −.506 | .505 | −1.508 | .901 |
| Parent age | −.005 | .023 | −.027 | .022 |
| Rural residence | −.012 | .337 | −.150 | .459 |
| Suburban residence | .507 | .281 | .292 | .325 |
| # unmarried adult children | .427*** | .101 | .995*** | .130 |
| Intercept | −1.749 | 1.654 | −.247 | 2.131 |
| N | 368 | | 444 | |
| Model chi-square | 33.47 | | 106.89 | |
| Degrees of freedom | 12 | | 12 | |

\*   $p < .05.$        \*\*$p < .01.$        \*\*\*$p < .001.$

**TABLE C.2.8**
Logistic Regression of Coresidence with a Randomly Selected Adult Child

| | Parent < 60 | | Parent 60+ | |
| | b | SE | b | SE |
|---|---|---|---|---|
| Son-father pair | − .299 | .498 | .229 | .571 |
| Son-mother pair | .106 | .395 | .744 | .468 |
| Daughter-father pair | − .138 | .513 | .243 | .602 |
| | | | | |
| Child married | − 3.254*** | .783 | − 2.615*** | .559 |
| Child health | − .011 | .281 | − .221 | .269 |
| Child employed full-time | .337 | .423 | .317 | .550 |
| Child employed part-time | .982 | .808 | 1.705* | .848 |
| Child # children < 21 | − .623* | .297 | − .464* | .213 |
| Child ever noncustodial | − 7.481 | 14.164 | .549 | .015 |
| Child is stepchild | − 1.107 | .853 | − 1.464 | 1.081 |
| Child # unmarried siblings | − .154 | .144 | .345* | .152 |
| | | | | |
| Parent married | .692 | .407 | .053 | .439 |
| Parent health | − .020 | .237 | .170 | .250 |
| Parent employed full-time | .704 | .438 | − .077 | .601 |
| Parent employed part-time | .336 | .673 | .614 | .616 |
| Parent income | − .007 | .010 | .012 | .013 |
| Parent black | − .151 | .673 | − .491 | .996 |
| Parent age | − .041 | .034 | .037 | .029 |
| Rural residence | .241 | .453 | .167 | .667 |
| Suburban residence | .579 | .384 | − .069 | .511 |
| | | | | |
| Intercept | 1.049 | 2.471 | − 4.174 | 3.024 |
| N | 364 | | 438 | |
| Model chi-square | 108.66 | | 103.66 | |
| Degrees of freedom | 21 | | 21 | |

\* p < .05.  \*\*p < .01.  \*\*\*p < .001.

**TABLE C.3.1**

Means and Standard Deviations for All Variables, Respondents and all
Noncoresident Adult Children 21 Years and Older (N = 745)

|                          | Mean     | s.d.     |
|--------------------------|----------|----------|
| Visits per month         | 15.77    | 20.24    |
| Phone calls per month    | 27.22    | 26.56    |
| Help hours/week to parent| 1.57     | 5.83     |
| Help hours/week to child | 3.24     | 7.58     |
| **Respondent**           |          |          |
| Unmarried father[a]      | .07      | .26      |
| Married mother           | .36      | .48      |
| Married father           | .27      | .44      |
| Age                      | 61.33    | 10.89    |
| Health                   | 3.93     | .84      |
| Family income            | $27,937  | $21,901  |
| Income missing           | .11      | .32      |
| Employed full-time[a]    | .35      | .48      |
| Employed part-time       | .10      | .30      |
| Black                    | .06      | .23      |
| Rural[a]                 | .13      | .34      |
| Suburban                 | .20      | .40      |
| # noncores. adult children | 2.68   | 1.52     |

a   Omitted category: unmarried woman; not employed; city resident.

**TABLE C.3.2**

Regression Coefficients Predicting Visiting, Phone Calls, and Help for Respondents and All Noncoresident Adult Children 21 Years and Older (N = 745)

| | Visit | Phone | Help parent | Help child |
|---|---|---|---|---|
| Unmarried man[a] | −3.051*** | −11.484*** | −1.954* | −2.675* |
| | (2.850) | (3.510) | (.882) | (1.160) |
| Married woman | 1.947 | .705 | −.861 | −.104 |
| | (1.834) | (2.260) | (.568) | (.747) |
| Married man | 3.244 | 1.486 | −.956 | −.205 |
| | (1.941) | (2.391) | (.601) | (.790) |
| Age | .064 | .169 | .069** | −.082* |
| | (.082) | (.101) | (.025) | (.033) |
| Health | .118 | −1.013 | −.604* | .406 |
| | (.880) | (1.084) | (.272) | (.358) |
| Family income ($1,000s) | −.124** | −.032 | −.016 | −.029 |
| | (.043) | (.053) | (.013) | (.053) |
| Employed full-time[a] | 3.083 | 2.196 | 1.370* | −.333 |
| | (1.922) | (2.368) | (.595) | (.782) |
| Employed part-time | 2.904 | 1.950 | .908 | −.175 |
| | (2.425) | (2.988) | (.751) | (.987) |
| Black | 1.432 | −6.740 | 1.980* | .731 |
| | (3.139) | (3.868) | (.972) | (1.278) |
| Rural[a] | 2.564 | −.295 | 1.241* | −.795 |
| | (2.092) | (2.578) | (.648) | (.852) |
| Suburban | −.334 | −.661 | −.373 | −.799 |
| | (1.752) | (2.158) | (.542) | (.713) |
| # noncores. adult children | 5.502*** | 8.966*** | .370** | .575** |
| | (.451) | (.556) | (.140) | (.184) |
| Constant | −4.085 | 4.109 | −2.726 | 6.059 |
| | (7.944) | (9.751) | (2.450) | (3.222) |
| $R^2$ | .17 | .27 | .04 | .02 |

Note: Unstandardized coefficients, with standard errors in parentheses.

a   Omitted category: Unmarried woman; not employed; city resident

*   $p < .05$.       ** $p < .01$.       *** $p < .001$.

**TABLE C.3.3**

Alternative Measures of Adult-Child Structure: Regression Coefficients (Unstandardized) Predicting Visits, Phone Calls, and Help to Parent and Children for Respondents and All Noncoresiding Children 21 Years and Older (N = 705)

|  | Visit | Phone | Help to Parent | Help to Child |
|---|---|---|---|---|
| # noncoresident adult children | 5.502*** | 8.966*** | .370** | .575** |
| # noncoresident adult daughters | 6.022*** | 11.350*** | .304 | .655** |
| # noncoresident adult sons | 5.027*** | 6.785*** | .430* | .502 |
| One son only[a] | −7.054* | −13.574*** | .160 | −1.126 |
| One daughter only | −5.970** | −9.596** | .042 | −2.166* |
| 2+ sons | −2.932 | −3.423 | .362 | −.521 |
| 2+ daughters | 3.007 | 10.511** | 1.727* | .314 |
| 3+ mixed gender | 10.738*** | 18.021*** | 1.144 | .874 |

*Note:* All equations include control variables as in table C.3.2.

a    Structure measures refer to noncoresident adult children only; omitted category is one noncoresident adult son and one noncoresident daughter.

*    p < .05.          ** p < .01.          *** p < .001.


**TABLE C.3.4**

Distribution of Contact between Respondents and Randomly Selected Child, by Child Gender

|  | Visit | | Phone | |
|---|---|---|---|---|
|  | Sons | Dtrs | Sons | Dtrs |
| Never | 5% | 3% | 7% | 3% |
| Once a year or less | 10% | 9% | 2% | 1% |
| 2–5 times a year | 18% | 13% | 4% | 4% |
| 6–11 times a year | 10% | 10% | 6% | 3% |
| At least once a month | 17% | 15% | 21% | 14% |
| Once a week | 20% | 21% | 27% | 21% |
| 2–6 days a week | 13% | 20% | 22% | 27% |
| Once a day or more | 7% | 9% | 12% | 27% |
| Total | 100% | 100% | 101% | 100% |
| N = | 397 | 385 | 396 | 385 |

*Note:* Third column total slightly higher due to rounding.

**TABLE C.3.5**

Means and Standard Deviations for Characteristics of Respondent Parents and Their Randomly Selected, Noncoresiding Adult Child

| | Sons | | Daughters | |
| --- | --- | --- | --- | --- |
| | Mean | s.d. | Mean | s.d. |
| Visits per month | 5.28 | 8.42 | 7.15 | 9.38 |
| Phone calls per month | 8.68 | 9.84 | 13.43 | 11.48 |
| Help hours/week to parent | .57 | 2.65 | .65 | 2.89 |
| Help hours/week to child | 1.45 | 5.77 | 1.37 | 4.02 |
| **Respondent** | | | | |
| Unmarried man[a] | .07 | .25 | .07 | .25 |
| Married woman | .35 | .48 | .38 | .49 |
| Married man | .28 | .45 | .25 | .44 |
| Age | 61.03 | 10.66 | 61.45 | 10.86 |
| Health | 3.92 | .87 | 4.00 | .76 |
| Distance (travel hrs.) | 3.32 | 7.65 | 2.86 | 7.38 |
| Family income | $28,308 | $22,501 | $28,713 | $21,645 |
| Income missing | .12 | .33 | .09 | .29 |
| Employed full-time[a] | .38 | .49 | .32 | .47 |
| Employed part-time | .07 | .26 | .13 | .34 |
| Black | .05 | .23 | .05 | .22 |
| Rural[a] | .10 | .31 | .16 | .37 |
| Suburban | .23 | .42 | .17 | .38 |
| **Child** | | | | |
| # siblings | 2.39 | 1.75 | 2.41 | 1.81 |
| # sisters | 1.14 | 1.06 | 1.20 | 1.22 |
| # brothers | 1.25 | 1.26 | 1.21 | 1.17 |
| Only child[a] | .10 | .29 | .10 | .30 |
| One brother only[a] | .12 | .33 | .14 | .34 |
| Two or more siblings | .65 | .48 | .63 | .48 |
| Never married[a] | .29 | .46 | .22 | .41 |
| Divorced/separated | .09 | .29 | .09 | .28 |
| Remarried | .07 | .26 | .07 | .26 |
| Widowed | .01 | .08 | .01 | .11 |
| Health | 4.41 | .62 | 4.32 | .72 |
| Employed full-time[a] | .87 | .33 | .57 | .50 |
| Employed part-time | .02 | .13 | .16 | .37 |
| # children < 21 home | 1.07 | 1.34 | 1.11 | 1.25 |
| Ever noncustodial | .08 | .28 | .06 | .23 |
| Stepchild | .06 | .23 | .09 | .29 |
| N | 349 | | 356 | |

a   Omitted category: Unmarried woman; not employed; city resident; one sister; married child; child not employed.

**TABLE C.3.6**
Regression Coefficients Predicting Visiting, Phone Calls, and Help for
Respondent-Child Pairs, Noncoresiding Daughters 21 Years and Older (N = 356)

|  | Visit | Phone | Help parent | Help child |
|---|---|---|---|---|
| **Respondent** |  |  |  |  |
| Unmarried man[a] | −.392 | −6.111* | .094 | −1.402 |
|  | (2.189) | (2.577) | (.695) | (.954) |
| Married woman | 1.862 | −1.460 | .221 | .078 |
|  | (1.344) | (1.583) | (.427) | (.586) |
| Married man | 3.442* | −.619 | .204 | −.400 |
|  | (1.385) | (1.630) | (.440) | (.604) |
| Age | .028 | .023 | .031 | −.079** |
|  | (.062) | (.073) | (.020) | (.027) |
| Health | .434 | −.437 | −.234 | −.121 |
|  | (.731) | (.861) | (.232) | (.319) |
| Distance (travel hrs.) | −.265*** | −.368*** | −.020 | −.075* |
|  | (.069) | (.081) | (.022) | (.030) |
| Family income ($1,000s) | −.018 | .027 | −.005 | −.012 |
|  | (.031) | (.037) | (.010) | (.014) |
| Employed full-time[a] | .599 | −1.151 | .895* | −.955 |
|  | (1.457) | (1.716) | (.463) | (.635) |
| Employed part-time | 1.022 | 3.140 | .746 | −1.033 |
|  | (1.562) | (1.834) | (.496) | (.681) |
| Black | 3.121 | .642 | −.263 | 2.668** |
|  | (2.355) | (2.773) | (.748) | (1.027) |
| Rural[a] | −.593 | 1.081 | .854* | −.197 |
|  | (1.372) | (1.615) | (.436) | (.598) |
| Suburban | .271 | 1.457 | .209 | .287 |
|  | (1.371) | (1.615) | (.435) | (.598) |
| **Child** |  |  |  |  |
| # siblings | −.088 | −.111 | −.121 | −.369* |
|  | (.291) | (.343) | (.092) | (.127) |
| Never married[a] | −2.524 | −3.102 | −.352 | −1.102 |
|  | (1.367) | (1.610) | (.434) | (.596) |
| Divorced/separated | .910 | 2.213 | .026 | −.771 |
|  | (1.795) | (2.113) | (.570) | (.783) |
| Remarried | .070 | −.131 | −1.030 | .146 |
|  | (1.964) | (2.312) | (.624) | (.856) |

*continued*

**TABLE C.3.6 (continued)**

| | Visit | Phone | Help parent | Help child |
|---|---|---|---|---|
| Health | −1.056 | −2.158* | −.502* | −.229 |
| | (.756) | (.890) | (.240) | (.330) |
| Employed full-time[a] | −.611 | −1.542 | .266 | .023 |
| | (1.213) | (1.428) | (.385) | (.529) |
| Employed part-time | .105 | −.283 | .104 | .703 |
| | (1.540) | (1.813) | (.489) | (.671) |
| # children < 21 home | .320 | −.157 | −.067 | .183 |
| | (.459) | (.541) | (.146) | (.200) |
| Ever noncustodial | .231 | −6.077* | .586 | −.511 |
| | (2.355) | (2.773) | (.748) | (1.027) |
| Stepchild | −1.884 | −3.489 | −.335 | −.919 |
| | (1.828) | (2.152) | (.580) | (.767) |
| Constant | 4.831 | 25.734 | 1.961 | 6.314 |
| | (6.789) | (7.993) | (2.155) | (2.960) |
| $R^2$ | .08 | .15 | .02 | .05 |

a  Omitted category: Unmarried woman; not employed; city resident; married child; child not employed; coefficients for widowed child omitted from table, based on 3 cases.
*  $p < .05$.        ** $p < .01$.        *** $p < .001$.

**TABLE C.3.7**
Regression Coefficients Predicting Visiting, Phone Calls, and Help for
Respondent-Child Pairs, Noncoresiding Sons 21 Years and Older (N = 349)

|  | Visit | Phone | Help parent | Help child |
|---|---|---|---|---|
| **Respondent** | | | | |
| Unmarried man[a] | −.114 | −1.845 | −1.123 | −1.225 |
|  | (2.046) | (2.400) | (.656) | (1.429) |
| Married woman | −1.903[b] | .106 | −.089 | .331 |
|  | (1.239) | (1.453) | (.397) | (.865) |
| Married man | −.547[b] | −.262 | −.321 | .295 |
|  | (1.320) | (1.549) | (.423) | (.922) |
| Age | −.072 | .057 | .019 | −.078 |
|  | (.061) | (.072) | (.020) | (.043) |
| Health | −.814 | −.843 | −.120 | .921* |
|  | (.583) | (.683) | (.187) | (.407) |
| Distance (travel hrs.) | −.276*** | −.303*** | −.027 | −.057 |
|  | (.060) | (.070) | (.019) | (.042) |
| Family income ($1,000s) | .007 | .055 | −.016 | −.019 |
|  | (.030) | (.034) | (.010) | (.020) |
| Employed full-time[a] | −.447 | −.244 | .583 | −.312 |
|  | (1.250) | (1.466) | (.401) | (.873) |
| Employed part-time | 1.542 | −3.656[b] | .776 | 1.948[b] |
|  | (1.836) | (2.154) | (.589) | (1.282) |
| Black | −.677 | −.953 | .131 | .770 |
|  | (2.158) | (2.530) | (.692) | (1.507) |
| Rural[a] | 2.780 | −.861 | .282 | −.569 |
|  | (1.549) | (1.816) | (.496) | (1.081) |
| Suburban | .149 | −.063 | −.252 | −.595 |
|  | (1.107) | (1.298) | (.355) | (.773) |
| **Child** | | | | |
| # siblings | −.232 | −.118 | −.208* | −.501** |
|  | (.266) | (.312) | (.085) | (.186) |
| Never married[a] | −.776 | −1.544 | −.547 | −.245 |
|  | (1.267) | (1.486) | (.406) | (.885) |
| Divorced/separated | .508 | .664 | −.916 | .808 |
|  | (1.652) | (1.937) | (.530) | (1.153) |
| Remarried | .215 | −2.950 | .403 | .026 |
|  | (1.785) | (2.093) | (.572) | (1.246) |

*continued*

**TABLE C.3.7 (continued)**

|  | Visit | Phone | Help parent | Help child |
|---|---|---|---|---|
| Health | −.022 | −.472 | .302 | −.922 |
|  | (.795) | (.934) | (.255) | (.556) |
| Employed full-time[a] | .409 | −1.346 | −.287 | −.981 |
|  | (1.560) | (1.829) | (.500) | (1.089) |
| Employed part-time | 2.382 | .690 | .042 | −2.055 |
|  | (3.787) | (4.442) | (1.214) | (2.645) |
| # children < 21 home | −.052 | .164 | −.094 | .437 |
|  | (.405) | (.475) | (.130) | (.283) |
| Ever noncustodial | −2.308 | −1.309 | −.176 | −.913 |
|  | (1.787) | (2.096) | (.573) | (1.248) |
| Stepchild | 2.612 | 1.396 | −.192 | −1.142 |
|  | (2.001) | (2.347) | (.641) | (1.397) |
| Constant | 15.057 | 13.033 | −.004 | 8.525 |
|  | (6.485) | (7.605) | (2.079) | (4.528) |
| $R^2$ | .05 | .04 | .01 | .01 |

a   Omitted category: unmarried woman; not employed; city residence; married child; child not em-
    ployed; coefficients for widowed child omitted from table, based on 2 cases.
b   Coefficient differs significantly from coefficient for daughters
*   $p < .05$.        ** $p < .01$.        *** $p < .001$.

# TABLE C.3.8

Alternative Measures of Sibling Structure and Interaction of Sibling Structure with Gender: Regression Coefficients Predicting Visits, Phone Calls, and Help to Parent for Respondents and Randomly Selected, Noncoresiding Adult Children (N = 705)

| | Visit | | Phone | | Help to parent | | Help to child | |
|---|---|---|---|---|---|---|---|---|
| | Direct effects | Interaction | Direct effects | Interaction | Direct effects | Interaction | Direct effects | Interaction |
| Gender (child) | 1.243 | .898 | 3.298*** | 4.329* | .032 | −.189* | −.357 | −.863 |
| # siblings | −.259 | −.332 | −.192 | −.107 | −.160** | −.104 | −.413*** | −.520*** |
| Gender* siblings | | .145 | | −.169 | | .058 | | .213 |
| Gender (child) | 1.241 | .895 | 3.930*** | 4.322** | .023 | −.089 | −.334 | −.900 |
| # sisters | −.249 | −.256 | −.205 | .085 | −.105 | −.163 | −.544*** | −.772*** |
| # brothers | −.266 | −.389 | −.182 | −.252 | −.208* | −.206 | −.299* | −.338 |
| Gender* sisters | | .010 | | .144 | | −.002 | | .398 |
| Gender* brothers | | .270 | | −.508 | | .102 | | .095 |
| Gender (child) | 1.247 | 2.456 | 3.910*** | 6.052** | −.018 | −.758 | −.406 | −.406 |
| Only child | 3.339* | 3.868* | .669 | 1.869 | 1.112* | 2.015* | −.199 | .563 |
| One brother only[a] | −.546 | .141 | −1.600 | .009 | −.872* | −.460 | −1.922*** | −1.795 |
| 2+ siblings | .708 | 1.435 | −1.065 | .109 | −.493 | −.131 | −1.732* | −2.021** |
| Gender* only child | | −1.091 | | −2.443 | | −1.780* | | −1.462 |
| Gender* one brother | | −1.373 | | −3.168 | | −.825 | | .118 |
| Gender* 2+ siblings | | −1.482 | | −2.390 | | −.736 | | .203 |

Note: All equations include control variables as in Table C.3.6.

a Omitted category: respondent has one sister only.

\* p < .05.    \*\* p < .01.    \*\*\* p < .001.

**TABLE C.3.9**

Frequency of Contact between Respondents and Their Parents, by Respondent Gender

|  | Visit | | Phone | |
|---|---|---|---|---|
|  | Sons | Dtrs | Sons | Dtrs |
| Never | 4% | 3% | 9% | 13% |
| Once a year or less | 11% | 12% | 1% | 2% |
| 2–5 times a year | 18% | 19% | 6% | 2% |
| 6–11 times a year | 11% | 10% | 7% | 5% |
| At least once a month | 19% | 14% | 18% | 17% |
| Once a week | 23% | 16% | 33% | 19% |
| 2–6 days a week | 11% | 19% | 15% | 19% |
| Once a day or more | 4% | 8% | 11% | 23% |
| Total | 101% | 101% | 100% | 100% |

*Note:* First two column totals slightly higher due to rounding.

**TABLE C.3.10**
Means and Standard Deviations for Respondent Children and Their Living,
Noncoresiding Biological Parents

|  | Sons | | Daughters | |
|---|---|---|---|---|
|  | Mean | s.d. | Mean | s.d. |
| Visits per month | 4.02 | 6.92 | 6.35 | 9.09 |
| Phone calls per month | 6.82 | 9.04 | 11.05 | 11.92 |
| Hours help per week | 1.29 | 2.85 | 2.12 | 4.45 |
| **Parent variables** | | | | |
| Father only[a] | .15 | .36 | .14 | .35 |
| Both parents | .31 | .47 | .28 | .44 |
| Parent age | 76.43 | 7.70 | 77.09 | 8.07 |
| Parent health | 3.46 | 1.08 | 3.29 | 1.05 |
| Distance (travel hours) | 3.47 | 6.31 | 3.54 | 6.35 |
| **Respondent variables** | | | | |
| # siblings | 2.55 | 1.84 | 2.49 | 2.13 |
| # brothers | 1.33 | 1.20 | 1.32 | 1.34 |
| # sisters | 1.22 | 1.28 | 1.17 | 1.28 |
| Only child[a] | .08 | .27 | .10 | .31 |
| One brother only | .11 | .31 | .13 | .34 |
| Two or more siblings | .68 | .47 | .64 | .48 |
| Never married[a] | .11 | .31 | .05 | .21 |
| Divorced/separated | .11 | .31 | .25 | .43 |
| Remarried | .19 | .39 | .10 | .31 |
| Widowed | .02 | .14 | .08 | .27 |
| # children < 21 home | 1.04 | 1.15 | .78 | 1.11 |
| Work full-time[a] | .84 | .37 | .55 | .50 |
| Work part-time | .03 | .16 | .18 | .38 |
| Health | 4.31 | .67 | 4.19 | .76 |
| Family income ($1,000s) | 42.87 | 20.74 | 35.87 | 22.48 |
| Family income missing | .03 | | .10 | .29 |
| Black | .04 | .20 | .05 | .23 |
| Rural[a] | .14 | .34 | .15 | .36 |
| Suburban | .23 | .42 | .27 | .44 |
| N | | 163 | | 241 |

a   Omitted categories: mother only; sister only; respondent married; respondent not employed; city
    resident.

**TABLE C.3.11**
Regression Coefficients Predicting Visits, Phone Calls, and Hours of Help from Female Respondents to Noncoresiding Biological Parents (N = 241)

|  | Visit/month | Phone/month | Help/week |
|---|---|---|---|
| **Parent variables** | | | |
| Father only[a] | −1.432 | 1.933 | .535 |
|  | (1.689) | (2.225) | (.888) |
| Both parents | .045 | .161 | −.211 |
|  | (1.351) | (1.751) | (.710) |
| Age | .199* | −.031 | .081* |
|  | (.081) | (.107) | (.043) |
| Health | .436 | 1.346 | −.277 |
|  | (.561) | (.739) | (.295) |
| Distance (travel hours) | −.378*** | −.630*** | −.118* |
|  | (.092) | (.122) | (.049) |
| **Respondent variables** | | | |
| # siblings | −.743** | −.648 | −.224 |
|  | (.282) | (.372) | (.148) |
| Never married[a] | −.635 | −2.679 | 1.154 |
|  | (2.829) | (3.729) | (1.487) |
| Divorced/separated | .218 | −.314 | 1.005 |
|  | (1.521) | (2.004) | (.800) |
| Remarried | −.485 | −5.077* | −.277 |
|  | (1.904) | (2.508) | (1.001) |
| Widowed | 3.448 | 1.945 | −.518 |
|  | (2.165) | (2.853) | (1.138) |
| # children < 21 home | −.910 | 1.634* | .271 |
|  | (.558) | (.735) | (.293) |
| Work full-time[a] | −1.052 | −1.257 | −.825 |
|  | (1.430) | (1.884) | (.752) |
| Work part-time | −.593 | −1.047 | −.103 |
|  | (1.740) | (2.292) | (1.915) |
| Health | −.612 | −1.757 | −.287 |
|  | (.870) | (1.146) | (.457) |
| Family income | −.068* | −.017 | −.018 |
|  | (.032) | (.042) | (.017) |
| Black | −1.509 | −6.188 | −1.363 |
|  | (2.688) | (3.542) | (1.413) |

*continued*

**TABLE C.3.11 (continued)**

|  | Visit/month | Phone/month | Help/week |
|---|---|---|---|
| Rural[a] | 1.309 | − 1.211 | − .248 |
|  | (1.603) | (2.111) | (.842) |
| Suburban | − .821 | − 1.750 | − .098 |
|  | (1.345) | (1.772) | (.707) |
| Constant | − .487 | 28.252 | 1.267 |
|  | (8.398) | (11.064) | (4.414) |
| Adjusted $R^2$ | .17 | .16 | .04 |

Note: Unstandardized coefficients; standard errors in parentheses.

a   Omitted categories: mother only; respondent married; respondent not employed; city residence.

\*   $p < .05$.        \*\* $p < .01$.        \*\*\* $p < .001$.

**TABLE C.3.12**
Regression Coefficients Predicting Visits, Phone Calls, and Help from Male
Respondents to Noncoresiding Biological Parents (N = 163)

| | Visit/month | Phone/month | Help/week |
|---|---|---|---|
| **Parent variables** | | | |
| Father only[a] | − 1.484 | − .324 | − .520 |
| | (1.566) | (2.071) | (.631) |
| Both parents | − 1.053 | − .921 | − .736 |
| | (1.275) | (1.687) | (.514) |
| Age | − .040[b] | .095 | − .027 |
| | (.076) | (.101) | (.031) |
| Health | − .400 | .811 | − .326 |
| | (.540) | (.714) | (.218) |
| Distance (travel hours) | − .308*** | − .436*** | − .092*** |
| | (.085) | (.112) | (.034) |
| **Respondent variables** | | | |
| # siblings | .297[b] | − .790* | .255*[b] |
| | (.298) | (.394) | (.120) |
| Never married[a] | − 4.208* | .552 | − 2.168**[b] |
| | (1.962) | (1.596) | (.791) |
| Divorced/separated | 1.192 | .952 | .089 |
| | (1.894) | (2.506) | (.764) |
| Remarried | − .924 | .667 | − .646 |
| | (1.427) | (1.887) | (.575) |
| Widowed | − 5.022 | − 6.617 | .561 |
| | (4.225) | (5.589) | (1.703) |
| # children < 21 home | − .194 | − .606[b] | − .156 |
| | (.542) | (.717) | (.218) |
| Work full-time[a] | .035 | − .805 | − 1.551* |
| | (1.801) | (2.382) | (.726) |
| Work part-time | − 5.184 | − 6.092 | − 2.203 |
| | (3.694) | (4.886) | (1.489) |
| Health | − .696 | 1.142 | − .855* |
| | (.865) | (1.144) | (.349) |
| Family income | − .063 | − .140** | − .010 |
| | (.034) | (.045) | (.014) |
| Black | − .516 | 2.475 | − 1.902 |
| | (2.771) | (3.665) | (1.117) |

*continued*

**TABLE C.3.12 (continued)**

|              | Visit/month | Phone/month | Help/week |
| ------------ | ----------- | ----------- | --------- |
| Rural[a]     | 3.164*      | −.641       | −.294     |
|              | (1.599)     | (2.114)     | (.644)    |
| Suburban     | 1.791       | 1.547       | −.008     |
|              | (1.347)     | (1.782)     | (.543)    |
| Constant     | 15.805      | .373        | 12.495    |
|              | (8.189)     | (10.832)    | (3.301)   |
| Adjusted R²  | .10         | .08         | .14       |

*Note:* Unstandardized coefficients; standard errors in parentheses.

a   Omitted categories: mother only; respondent married; respondent not employed; city residence.

b   Coefficient differs significantly from coefficient for female R's.

*    p < .05.        ** p < .01.        *** p < .001.

**TABLE C.3.13**

Alternative Measures of Sibling Structure and Interactions of Sibling Structure with Gender: Regression Coefficients Predicting Visits, Phone Calls, and Help from Respondents to Noncoresiding Biological Parents (N = 404)

| | Visit/month | | Phone/month | | Help/week | |
|---|---|---|---|---|---|---|
| | Direct effects | Inter-action | Direct effects | Inter-action | Direct effects | Inter-action |
| Gender | 1.581 | 4.205** | 3.903*** | 4.052* | .396 | 1.554* |
| # siblings | −.433* | .248 | −.747** | −.708 | −.093 | .207 |
| Gender* siblings | | −1.046* | | −.059 | | −.462* |
| | | | | | | |
| Gender | 1.597 | 4.158** | 3.934*** | 3.992* | .390 | 1.583* |
| # sisters | −.236 | .401 | −.361 | −.479 | −.201 | .059 |
| # brothers | −.611* | .080 | −1.100** | −.950 | .012 | .372 |
| Gender* sisters | | −1.036 | | .223 | | −.414 |
| Gender* brothers | | −1.007 | | −.255 | | −.534 |
| | | | | | | |
| Gender | 1.437 | 2.769 | 3.862*** | 4.393 | .308 | .166 |
| Only child | 3.685* | −2.023 | 1.228 | −2.211 | 2.576* | −.228 |
| One brother only[a] | 1.891 | 2.190 | −1.450 | 2.789 | 1.542* | .245 |
| Two or more siblings | −.121 | 1.467 | −2.713 | −2.611 | .736 | 1.074 |
| Gender* only child | | 8.252* | | 5.119 | | 4.161* |
| Gender* one brother | | −.805 | | −6.747 | | 1.958 |
| Gender* 2 + siblings | | −2.962 | | −.289 | | −.666 |

Note: All equations include control variables as in Table C.3.2.

a   Omitted category: respondents with one sister only.

*   p < .05.        ** p < .01.        *** p < .001.

**TABLE C.5.1**

Percentage of Women and Men with Combinations of "Active Roles," by Age

|  | 40–44 | 45–49 | 50–54 | 55–59 | 60–64 |
|---|---|---|---|---|---|
| **Women** | | | | | |
| None | 6% | 10% | 13% | 19% | 31% |
| Job only | 14 | 15 | 13 | 9 | 12 |
| Child only | 22 | 21 | 23 | 34 | 29 |
| Parent only | 1 | 0 | 3 | 5 | 5 |
| Job and child | 32 | 33 | 37 | 22 | 11 |
| Job and parent | 7 | 6 | 3 | 4 | 0 |
| Child and parent | 10 | 7 | 5 | 6 | 7 |
| All three roles | 8 | 8 | 3 | 0 | 4 |
| N | 125 | 86 | 93 | 77 | 102 |
| **Men** | | | | | |
| None | 5% | 3% | 11% | 12% | 31% |
| Job only | 26 | 18 | 24 | 36 | 9 |
| Child only | 2 | 7 | 7 | 10 | 20 |
| Parent only | 1 | 2 |  | 2 | 4 |
| Job and child | 47 | 51 | 45 | 28 | 22 |
| Job and parent | 0 | 2 | 4 | 4 | 5 |
| Child and parent | 2 | 2 |  | 2 | 9 |
| All three roles | 16 | 16 | 9 | 6 | 0 |
| N | 93 | 61 | 55 | 50 | 55 |

*Note:* "Job" means outside employment of 35 or more hours per week. "Child" means help to adult children of three or more hours per week or coresiding with a child of any age. "Parent" means help to parents and in-laws of three or more hours per week or coresiding with any parent or in-law.

**TABLE C.5.2**

Means and Standard Deviations for Variables Used in Analyses of Burden, Stress, and Life Satisfaction

| | Women | | Men | |
|---|---|---|---|---|
| | Mean | s.d. | Mean | s.d. |
| Age | 51.30 | 7.62 | 50.30 | 7.75 |
| Health | 4.06 | .86 | 4.16 | .80 |
| Black | .07 | .25 | .07 | .26 |
| Income | $35,458 | $19,520 | $42,518 | $19,866 |
| Income missing | .10 | .30 | .03 | .17 |
| Married | .61 | .49 | .76 | .43 |
| Full-time work | .50 | .50 | .77 | .42 |
| Have living parent/in-laws | .91 | .29 | .86 | .35 |
| Have living children | .68 | .47 | .78 | .42 |
| Children: help or coreside | .54 | .50 | .55 | .50 |
| Parents: help or coreside | .20 | .40 | .17 | .38 |
| Burden | 2.36 | .79 | 2.02 | .59 |
| Stress | 2.92 | 2.58 | 2.41 | 2.30 |
| Life satisfaction | 5.62 | 1.29 | 5.57 | 1.15 |
| N | 463 | | 304 | |

**TABLE C.5.3**
The Effects of Role Incumbencies on Well-Being, for Women and Men

|  | Women | | | Men | | |
|---|---|---|---|---|---|---|
|  | Burden | Distress | Satis. | Burden | Distress | Satis. |
| **Control variables** | | | | | | |
| Age | −.038*** | −.027 | .025** | −.006 | −.032 | .022** |
| Health | −.076 | −1.291*** | .291*** | −.063 | −1.126*** | .370*** |
| Black | −.109 | −.079 | .616** | .097 | .602 | −.483* |
| Income ($1,000s) | −.004* | −.018** | .007* | −.001 | −.016** | .004 |
| Income missing | .001 | .764* | −.174 | −.234 | −.396 | −.368 |
| **Role incumbencies** | | | | | | |
| Married | .266*** | −.093 | .442*** | .158 | −.110 | .655*** |
| Full-time work | .008 | .428 | −.049 | .090 | −.017 | −.052 |
| Have living parents/in-laws | −.081 | −.195 | .240 | −.033 | −.057 | −.112 |
| Have living children | .493*** | .819* | .145 | .054 | .883* | −.211 |
| Constant | 4.266*** | 9.397*** | 2.276*** | 2.424*** | 8.814*** | 2.575*** |
| $R^2$ | .171 | .248 | .132 | .031 | .234 | .208 |
| N | | 463 | | | 304 | |

*   p < .05.       ** p < .01.       *** p < .001.

**TABLE C.5.4**

Effects of Active Roles on Well-Being, for Women and Men

| | Women | | | Men | | |
|---|---|---|---|---|---|---|
| | Burden | Distress | Satis. | Burden | Distress | Satis. |
| **Control variables** | | | | | | |
| Age | −.028*** | −.008 | .020** | −.003 | −.018 | .023** |
| Health | −.073 | −1.287*** | .295*** | −.069 | −1.130*** | .359*** |
| Black | −.088 | −.048 | .640** | .107 | .706 | −.487* |
| Income ($1,000s) | −.004* | −.018** | .007* | −.001 | −.015** | .004 |
| Income missing | .028 | .692* | −.152 | −.219 | −.198 | −.417 |
| **Active roles** | | | | | | |
| Married | .314*** | −.015 | .483*** | .124 | .002 | .535*** |
| Full-time work | .007 | .432 | −.055 | .079 | −.024 | −.098 |
| Children: help or coreside | .210* | .309 | .055 | .087 | .315 | .064 |
| Parents: help or coreside | .165* | .503 | −.128 | −.005 | .208 | −.158 |
| Constant | 3.954*** | 8.687*** | 2.802*** | 2.311*** | 8.479*** | 2.388*** |
| $R^2$ | .157 | .247 | .127 | .034 | .225 | .207 |
| N | | 463 | | | 304 | |

\* $p < .05$.　　\*\* $p < .01$.　　\*\*\* $p < .001$.

**TABLE C.5.5**

Effects of Active Roles and Role Combinations on Well-Being, for
Women and Men

|  | Women | | | Men | | |
|---|---|---|---|---|---|---|
|  | Burden | Distress | Satis. | Burden | Distress | Satis. |
| **Control variables** | | | | | | |
| Age | − .028*** | − .013 | .020** | − .003 | − .021 | .023** |
| Health | − .070 | − 1.195*** | .286*** | − .072 | − 1.107*** | .356*** |
| Black | − .064 | − .097 | .681** | .140 | .812 | − .511* |
| Income ($1,000s) | − .004* | − .018** | .007* | − .001 | − .015** | .004 |
| Income missing | .036 | .670* | − .142 | − .271 | − .482 | − .327 |
| **Active roles** | | | | | | |
| Married | .310* | − .376 | .585** | .196 | − .378 | .511 |
| Full-time work | − .101 | − .438 | .058 | .107 | − .513 | .014 |
| Children: help or coreside | .040 | 1.069** | .064 | − .159 | .361 | .162 |
| Parents: help or coreside | .204 | .821 | − .454 | .395 | 1.510 | − .524 |
| **Role interactions** | | | | | | |
| Married + work | − .100 | 1.622*** | − .323 | − .097 | .678 | − .070 |
| Married + children | .107 | − .938* | .043 | .045 | − .412 | .206 |
| Married + parents | .053 | − .303 | .377 | − .198 | − .127 | .253 |
| Work + children | .280* | − .364 | .017 | .282 | .530 | − .316 |
| Work + parents | .055 | .036 | .404 | − .398 | − .920 | .421 |
| Children + parents | − .170 | − .213 | − .204 | .072 | − .829 | − .228 |
| Constant | 4.019*** | 8.865*** | 2.779*** | 2.251*** | 8.741*** | 2.386*** |
| $R^2$ | .167 | .273 | .137 | .053 | .243 | .215 |
| N |  | 463 |  |  | 304 |  |

* p < .05.    ** p < .01.    *** p < .001.

**TABLE C.6.1**

Means and Standard Deviations of Variables Used in Analyses of Neighboring and Formal Assistance (N = 1,187)

|  | *Mean* | *s.d.* |
|---|---|---|
| Age | 58.13 | 12.54 |
| Health | 3.96 | .86 |
| Income | $29,143 | $22,518 |
| Income missing | .11 | .31 |
| Part-time employment | .10 | .30 |
| Full-time employment | .41 | .49 |
| Black | .05 | .23 |
| Female | .63 | .48 |
| Married | .57 | .50 |
| Number children at home | .46 | .91 |
| Live with others | .51 | .50 |
| Years in neighborhood | 4.92 | 1.40 |
| Homeowner | .81 | .40 |
| Suburban | .22 | .41 |
| Rural | .12 | .32 |
| Perceived safety | 3.35 | .78 |
| Median income | $33,579 | $12,808 |
| Residential stability | .58 | .15 |
| Neighborhood children | .49 | .13 |
| Black/Hispanic proportion | .09 | .15 |
| N of neighbors known (ln) | 2.05 | 1.01 |
| Family neighbors | .30 | .70 |
| Phoning in neighborhood | 7.17 | 12.19 |
| Visiting in neighborhood | 7.27 | 12.19 |
| Outside help | .34 | .47 |
| Help from parents or children | .21 | .40 |
| Help from relatives | .06 | .25 |
| Help from neighbors | .04 | .20 |
| Help from friends | .06 | .24 |

**TABLE C.6.2**
Predicting the Number of Neighbors Known by Respondents (Natural Log) and
the Number of Family Neighbors (N = 1,187)

|  | Neighbors known (ln) | | Family neighbors | |
|---|---|---|---|---|
|  | b | SE (b) | b | SE (b) |
| **Constraints** | | | | |
| Age | −.004 | (.003) | −.004* | (.002) |
| Health | .082* | (.035) | −.025 | (.026) |
| Income ($1,000s) | .004** | (.002) | −.003* | (.001) |
| Income missing | .031 | (.100) | −.067 | (.073) |
| Part-time employment | .033 | (.100) | −.082 | (.073) |
| Full-time employment | −.101 | (.079) | .061 | (.058) |
| Black | −.355** | (.142) | .335*** | (.104) |
| Female | −.065 | (.061) | .047 | (.045) |
| **Investments** | | | | |
| Years in neighborhood | .236*** | (.022) | .046** | (.016) |
| Homeowner | .151 | (.081) | −.040 | (.059) |
| Children at home | .062 | (.035) | .006 | (.025) |
| Married | .025 | (.065) | .080 | (.048) |
| **Neighborhood context** | | | | |
| Suburban | .038 | (.074) | .058 | (.054) |
| Rural | .396*** | (.090) | .309*** | (.066) |
| Perceived safety | .064 | (.037) | −.025 | (.027) |
| Median income ($1,000s) | .002 | (.003) | −.002 | (.002) |
| Residential stability | .007** | (.002) | −.002 | (.002) |
| Neighborhood children | −.007*** | (.002) | .001 | (.002) |
| Racial composition | .0004 | (.002) | .006** | (.001) |
| Constant | .235 | (.336) | .559* | (.247) |
| Adjusted $R^2$ | .164 | | .066 | |

*   $p < .05$.     ** $p < .01$.     *** $p < .001$.

**TABLE C.6.3**

Predicting Social Interaction in the Neighborhood: Phoning, Visiting, and Helping (N = 1,187)

| | Phone | | Visit | | Help received (ln) | |
|---|---|---|---|---|---|---|
| **Local network** | | | | | | |
| Family neighbors | 9.717*** | (.423) | 9.535*** | (.430) | .967*** | (.057) |
| Other neighbors (ln) | 1.673*** | (.311) | 1.237*** | (.316) | .020 | (.042) |
| **Constraints** | | | | | | |
| Age | .018 | (.034) | −.023 | (.035) | .009* | (.004) |
| Health | −.459 | (.378) | −.100 | (.385) | −.087 | (.051) |
| Income ($1,000s) | .003 | (.018) | −.035 | (.019) | .001 | (.003) |
| Income missing | .746 | (1.057) | .105 | (1.075) | −.009 | (.143) |
| Part-time employment | −.209 | (1.059) | −.962 | (1.076) | −.210 | (.143) |
| Full-time employment | −1.176 | (.836) | −.820 | (.849) | −.075 | (.113) |
| Black | 1.193 | (1.515) | −2.877 | (1.539) | −.229 | (.204) |
| Female | 1.224* | (.649) | .247 | (.660) | .100 | (.087) |
| **Investments** | | | | | | |
| Years in neighborhood | .272 | (.250) | .488* | (.254) | .009 | (.033) |
| Homeowner | −.706 | (.860) | −1.920* | (.874) | .145 | (.116) |
| Children at home | .118 | (.371) | −.270 | (.377) | .091 | (.050) |
| Married | −.454 | (.690) | .074 | (.702) | −.269** | (.093) |
| **Neighborhood context** | | | | | | |
| Suburban | 1.593* | (.786) | 1.223 | (.799) | .099 | (.106) |
| Rural | 2.656** | (.973) | 1.279 | (.989) | .072 | (.131) |
| Perceived safety | .548 | (.400) | .724 | (.407) | −.035 | (.054) |
| Median income ($1,000s) | −.018 | (.028) | −.004 | (.029) | −.001 | (.004) |
| Residential stability | .005 | (.024) | .013 | (.025) | .002 | (.003) |
| Neighborhood children | −.036 | (.026) | −.086** | (.026) | −.002 | (.003) |
| Racial composition | −.004 | (.028) | .041 | (.029) | −.003 | (.003) |
| Constant | .118 | (3.565) | 4.651 | (3.623) | .075 | (.481) |
| Adjusted R² | .358 | | .336 | | .215 | |

*Note:* Unstandardized coefficients with standard errors in parentheses.

\*  p < .10.       \*\* p < .05.       \*\*\* p < .01.

**TABLE C.6.4**
Logistic Regression Analysis of the Usage of Paid or Organizational Services
(N = 1,188)

|                              | b          | SE (b)  |
|------------------------------|------------|---------|
| **Informal network**         |            |         |
| Married                      | −1.485***  | (.164)  |
| Live with others             | −.833***   | (.151)  |
| Help from parents or children| −.455**    | (.178)  |
| Help from relatives          | −.673**    | (.273)  |
| Help from neighbors          | .109       | (.318)  |
| Help from friends            | .428       | (.280)  |
| **Needs**                    |            |         |
| Age                          | .014       | (.008)  |
| Health                       | −.225**    | (.086)  |
| Income                       | .020***    | (.004)  |
| Income missing               | .242       | (.237)  |
| Black                        | .160       | (.295)  |
| Full-time employment         | .044       | (.200)  |
| Part-time employment         | .138       | (.248)  |
| **Predisposition**           |            |         |
| Gender                       | .478***    | (.154)  |
| **Enabling factors**         |            |         |
| Rural                        | −.638**    | (.231)  |
| Suburban                     | −.815***   | (.185)  |
| Intercept                    | −.102      | (.637)  |
| Model chi-square (16 df)     | 233.84     |         |

\*   $p < .05$, two-tailed test.      \*\* $p < .01$, two-tailed test.      \*\*\* $p < .001$, two-tailed test.

**TABLE C.6.5**

Means and Standard Deviations of Variables Used to Predict Service Use by
Older Respondents (N = 554)

| | Mean | s.d. |
|---|---|---|
| **Informal network** | | |
| Married | .47 | .50 |
| Live with others | .15 | .36 |
| Receive help from children | .29 | .45 |
| Receive help from relatives | .10 | .30 |
| Receive help from neighbors | .08 | .26 |
| Receive help from friends | .07 | .26 |
| Receive paid help | .40 | .49 |
| **Needs** | | |
| Age | 69.80 | 7.40 |
| Health | 3.18 | .41 |
| Income | $19,870 | $19,390 |
| Income missing | .16 | .37 |
| Proportion black | .04 | .20 |
| Proportion employed full-time | .19 | .39 |
| **Predisposition** | | |
| Sociability: number of memberships | 1.40 | 1.60 |
| Proportion female | .68 | .47 |
| Adopt older age identity | .34 | .47 |
| Belief in senior entitlement | 1.83 | .45 |
| **Enabling factors** | | |
| Availability: home-delivered meals | 3.10 | 1.40 |
| Availability: congregrate meals | 1.00 | .60 |
| Availability: day activities | 2.10 | .90 |
| Proportion suburban | .19 | .39 |
| Proportion rural | .10 | .30 |
| Mobility: number of trips | 6.30 | 6.70 |

**TABLE C.6.6**
Logistic Regression Analysis of the Usage of Senior Services by Persons Aged 60 or Older (N = 512)

| | Home-based services | | Senior center/ meals | | Other community-based services | |
|---|---|---|---|---|---|---|
| **Informal network** | | | | | | |
| Married | −.810# | (.440) | .037 | (.308) | −.865# | (.499) |
| Live with others | .765* | (.378) | −.536# | (.305) | −.472 | (.466) |
| Help from children | .068 | (.341) | −.772** | (.289) | −.816# | (.478) |
| Help from relatives | −.390 | (.514) | −.390 | (.404) | −.728 | (.692) |
| Help from neighbors | .495 | (.491) | .386 | (.424) | −.505 | (.806) |
| Help from friends | .575 | (.493) | .420 | (.436) | 1.094* | (.540) |
| Paid help | .527 | (.371) | −.022 | (.285) | −.039 | (.443) |
| **Needs** | | | | | | |
| Age | .064** | (.024) | .035# | (.020) | −.052 | (.033) |
| Health | −.202 | (.193) | −.433** | (.157) | −.323 | (.224) |
| Income | −.018 | (.016) | −.049*** | (.013) | −.012 | (.015) |
| Income missing | .072 | (.470) | −.510 | (.381) | −.218 | (.613) |
| Black | .548 | (.784) | −.016 | (.681) | 1.671** | (.692) |
| Full-time employment | −1.227 | (1.075) | −.163 | (.509) | −.335 | (.750) |
| Part-time employment | −.434 | (.677) | −.480 | (.492) | 1.131* | (.507) |
| **Predisposition** | | | | | | |
| Sociability | .103 | (.112) | .423*** | (.083) | .145 | (.128) |
| Gender | −.313 | (.398) | .615* | (.311) | .204 | (.459) |
| Older age identity | .776* | (.336) | .128 | (.271) | .512 | (.411) |
| Senior entitlement | .310 | (.387) | .159 | (.272) | .731# | (.440) |
| **Enabling factors** | | | | | | |
| **Availability** | | | | | | |
| Home-delivered meals | .245# | (.142) | — | — | — | — |
| Congregate meals | — | — | −.195 | (.270) | — | — |
| Day activities | — | — | .160 | (.246) | — | — |
| **Accessibility** | | | | | | |
| Rural | .440 | (.569) | .351 | (.534) | −1.395 | (1.061) |
| Suburban | .342 | (.452) | .268 | (.385) | .143 | (.521) |
| Mobility | .011 | (.020) | .001 | (.021) | .031 | (.020) |
| Intercept | −6.508** | (2.124) | −2.406 | (1.662) | .835 | (2.599) |
| Model chi-square (22 df) | 68.77 | | 88.38 | | 47.49 | |

\# $p < .05$, one-tailed test.    *$p < .05$, two-tailed test.    **$p < .01$, two-tailed test.
***$p < .001$, two-tailed test.

# References

Abel, Emily K. 1990a. "Family Care of the Frail Elderly." Pp. 65–91 in *Circles of Care*, eds. Emily K. Abel and Margaret K. Nelson. Albany: SUNY Press.

———. 1990b. "Informal Care for the Disabled Elderly: A Critique of Recent Literature." *Research on Aging* 12: 139–57.

———. 1991. *Who Cares for the Elderly: Public Policy and the Experiences of Adult Daughters.* Philadelphia: Temple University Press.

Ahrons, C. R., and M. E. Bowman. 1982. "Changes in Family Relationships Following Divorce of Adult Child: Grandmothers' Perceptions." *Journal of Divorce* 5:49–68.

Alba, Richard. 1987. "Interpreting the Parameters of Log-Linear Models." *Sociological Methods and Research* 16: 45–77.

Aldous, Joan. 1987. "New Views on the Family Life of the Elderly and the Near-Elderly." *Journal of Marriage and the Family* 49: 227–34.

———. 1995. "New Views of Grandparents in Intergenerational Context." *Journal of Family Issues* 16: 104–22.

Aldous, Joan, and David Klein. 1991. "Sentiment and Services: Models of Intergenerational Relationships in Mid-Life." *Journal of Marriage and the Family* 53 (August): 595–608.

Amato, Paul R. 1993. "Children's Adjustment to Divorce: Theories, Hypotheses, and Empirical Support." *Journal of Marriage and the Family* 55: 23–38.

Andersen, Ronald. 1968. *A Behavioral Model of Families' Use of Health Services.* Chicago: Chicago Center for Health Administration Studies, University of Chicago.

Anderson, Elijah. 1990. *Streetwise: Race, Class, and Change in an Urban Community.* Chicago: University of Chicago Press.

Anspach, D. F. 1976. "Kinship and Divorce." *Journal of Marriage and the Family* 38: 323–30.

Aquilino, William S. 1990. "The Likelihood of Parent-Child Coresidence: Effects of Family Structure and Parental Characteristics." *Journal of Marriage and the Family* 52: 405–19.

———. 1991. "Predicting Parents' Experiences with Coresident Adult Children." *Journal of Family Issues* 12: 323–42.

———. 1994. "Later-Life Parental Divorce and Widowhood: Impact on Young

Adults' Assessment of Parent-Child Relations." *Journal of Marriage and the Family* 56: 908–22.

Aquilino, William S., and Khalil R. Supple. 1991. "Parent-Child Relations and Parent's Satisfaction with Living Arrangements when Adult Children Live at Home." *Journal of Marriage and the Family* 53: 13-27.

Barber, Clifton. 1989. "Transition to the Empty Nest." In *Aging and the Family*, eds. Stephen Bahr and Evan Peterson. Lexington, MA: Lexington Books.

Barer, Barbara M., and Colleen L. Johnson. 1990. "A Critique of the Caregiving Literature." *The Gerontologist* 30:26–29.

Barnett, Rosalind C., Nazli Kibria, Grace K. Baruch, and Joseph H. Pleck. 1991. "Adult Daughter-Parent Relationships and Their Associations with Daughters' Subjective Well-Being and Psychological Distress." *Journal of Marriage and the Family* 53: 29–42.

Barnett, Rosalind C., Nancy L. Marshall, and Judith D. Singer. 1992. "Job Experiences over Time, Multiple Roles, and Women's Mental Health: A Longitudinal Study." *Journal of Personality and Social Psychology* 62: 634–44.

Becker, G. S. 1981. *A Treatise on the Family*. Cambridge, MA: Harvard University Press.

Bell, I. P. 1970. "The Double Standard of Aging." *Trans-Action* 6: 75–80.

Bengtson, Vern, Robert A. Harootyan, and Contributors. 1994. *Intergenerational Linkages: Hidden Connections in American Society*. New York: Springer Publishing Company.

Bengtson, Vern, and J. A. Kuypers, 1971. "Generational Difference and the 'Developmental Stake.' " *Aging and Human Development* 2: 249–60.

Bengtson, Vern, and L. Tonya M. Murray. 1993. " 'Justice' across Generations (and Cohorts): Sociological Perspectives on the Life Course and Reciprocities over Time." Pp. 111–38 in *Justice across Generations: What Does It Mean?*, ed. L. Cohen. Washington, DC: American Association of Retired Persons.

Bengtson, Vern, and Robert E. L. Roberts. 1991. "Intergenerational Solidarity in Aging Families: An Example of Formal Theory Construction." *Journal of Marriage and the Family* 53: 856–70.

Bengtson, Vern, Carolyn Rosenthal, and Linda Burton. 1990. "Families and Aging: Diversity and Heterogeneity." Pp. 263–87 in *Handbook of Aging and the Social Sciences*, 3rd Edition, eds. Robert H. Binstock and Linda K. George. New York: Academic Press.

Berk, Sarah Fenstermaker. 1985. *The Gender Factory*. New York: Plenum.

Bernard, Jessie, 1972. *The Future of Marriage*. New York: Bantam.

Binstock, R. H. 1972. "Interest-Group Liberalism and the Politics of Aging." *The Gerontologist* 12: 265–80.

Block, Jeanne, Jack Block, and Per Gjerde. 1986. "The Personality of Children Prior to Divorce." *Child Development* 57: 827-40.

Blum, Terry, and Paul W. Kingston. 1984. "Homeownership and Social Attachment." *Sociological Perspectives* 27: 159–180.

Brody, Elaine M. 1979. "Women's Changing Roles and Care of the Aging Family." Pp. 11–16 in *Aging: Agenda for the Eighties*. Washington, DC: Government Research Corporation.

———. 1981. " 'Women in the Middle' and Family Help to Older People." *The Gerontologist* 21: 471–79.

———. 1985. "Parent Care as a Normative Family Stress." *The Gerontologist* 25: 19–29.

Brody, Elaine M., Pauline T. Johnson, and Marc C. Fulcomer. 1984. "What Should Adult Children Do for Elderly Parents? Opinions and Preferences of Three Generations of Women." *Journal of Gerontology* 39: 736–46.

Brody, Elaine M., Pauline T. Johnsen, Marc C. Fulcomer, and A. Lang. 1983. "Women's Changing Roles and Help to Elderly Parents: Attitudes of Three Generations of Women." *Journal of Gerontology* 38: 597–607.

Brody, Elaine M., Sandra J. Litvin, Steven M. Albert, and Christine J. Hoffman. 1994. "Marital Status of Daughters and Patterns of Parent Care." *Journals of Gerontology: Social Sciences* 49: S95-103.

Brody, Elaine M., Sandra J. Litvin, Christine J. Hoffman, and Morton H. Kleban. 1992. "Differential Effects of Daughters' Marital Status on Their Parent Care Experiences." *The Gerontologist* 32: 58–67.

Brody, Elaine M., and Claire B. Schoonover. 1986. "Patterns of Parent Care When Adult Daughters Work and When They Do Not." *The Gerontologist* 26: 372–81.

Bross, C., S. Danziger, and E. Smolenski. 1987. "Interpreting Changes in the Economic Status of the Elderly, 1949–1979." *Contemporary Policy Issues* 5: 98–112.

Brubaker, Timothy H. 1991. "Families in Later Life: A Burgeoning Research Area." In *Contemporary Families: Looking Forward, Looking Back*, ed. Alan Booth. Minneapolis, MN: National Council on Family Relations.

Brubaker, Timothy, and Edward Powers. 1976. "The Stereotype of Old: A Review and Alternative Approach." *Journal of Gerontology* 31: 441–47.

Bulcroft, Kris A., and Richard A. Bulcroft. 1991. "The Timing of Divorce: Effects on Parent-Child Relationships in Later Life." *Research on Aging* 13: 226–43.

Bultena, Gordon, and Edward Powers. 1978. "Denial of Aging: Age Identification and Reference Group Orientations." *Journal of Gerontology* 33: 748–54.

Bumpass, Larry L. 1990. "What's Happening to the Family? Interactions between Demographic and Institutional Change." *Demography* 27: 483–98.

Burke, Peter, and Judy Tully. 1977. "The Measurement of Role Identity." *Social Forces* 55: 881–97.

Callahan, Daniel. 1987. *Setting Limits: Medical Goals in an Aging Society*. New York: Simon and Schuster.

Campbell, Karen, and Barrett Lee. 1990. "Gender Differences in Urban Neighboring" *Sociological Quarterly* 31: 495–512.

———. 1992. "Sources of Personal Neighbor Networks: Social Integration, Need, or Time?" *Social Forces* 70: 1077–100.

Cantor, Marjorie H. 1979. "Neighbors and Friends: An Overlooked Resource in the Informal Support System." *Research on Aging* 1: 434–63.

———. 1991. "Family and Community: Changing Roles in an Aging Society." *The Gerontologist* 31: 337–46.

Carp, Frances, and Abraham Carp. 1981. "Age, Deprivation, and Personal Competence: Effects on Satisfaction." *Research on Aging* 3: 279–98.

Carp, Frances. 1976. "Housing and Living Environments of Older People." Pp. 244–71 in *Handbook of Aging and the Social Sciences*, eds. Robert H. Binstock and Ethel Shanas. New York: Van Nostrand Reinhold Co.

Chappell, Neena. 1987. "The Interface among Three Systems of Care: Self, Informal, and Formal." In *Health and Aging: Sociological Issues and Policy Directions*, eds. Russell Ward and Sheldon Tobin. New York: Springer.

Cherlin, Andrew, and Frank Furstenberg Jr. 1986. *The New American Grandparent: A Place in the Family, A Life Apart*. New York: Basic Books.

Cicirelli, V. G. 1981. *Helping Elderly Parents: The Role of Adult Children*. Boston, MA: Auburn House.

———. 1983a. Adult Children and Their Elderly Parents. Pp. 31–46 in *Family Relationships in Later Life*, ed. T. H. Brubaker. Beverly Hills, CA: Sage.

———. 1983b. Adult Children's Attachment and Helping Behavior to Elderly Parents: A Path Model. *Journal of Marriage and the Family* 45: 815–25.

———. 1983c. A Comparison of Helping Behavior to Elderly Parents of Adult Children with Intact and Disrupted Marriages. *The Gerontologist* 23: 619–25.

Coe, Rodney M., Fredric D. Wolinsky, Douglas K. Miller, and John M. Prendergast. 1984. "Complementary and Compensatory Functions in Social Network Relationships among the Elderly." *The Gerontologist* 24: 396–400.

Coleman, Marilyn, and Lawrence H. Ganong. 1991. "Remarriage and Stepfamily Research in the 1980s." Pp. 192–207 in *Contemporary Families: Looking Forward, Looking Back*, ed. Alan Booth. Minneapolis: National Council on Family Relations.

Cooney, Teresa, 1989. "Co-Residence with Adult Children: A Comparison of Divorced and Widowed Women." *The Gerontologist* 29: 779–84.

———. 1994. "Young Adults' Relations with Parents: The Influence of Recent Parental Divorce." *Journal of Marriage and the Family* 56: 45–56.

Cooney, Teresa, and Peter Uhlenberg. 1990. "The Role of Divorce in Men's Relations with Their Adult Children after Mid-Life." *Journal of Marriage and the Family* 52: 677–88.

———. 1992. "Support from Parents over the Life Course: The Adult Child's Perspective." *Social Forces* 71: 63–84.

Coontz, Stephanie. 1992. *The Way We Never Were: American Families and the Nostalgia Trap.* New York: Basic Books.

Coser, Rose Laub. 1975. "The Complexity of Roles as a Seedbed of Individual Autonomy." In *The Idea of Social Structure*, ed. Lewis A. Coser. New York: Harcourt Brace Jovanovich.

Coverman, Shelley. 1989. "Role Overload, Role Conflict, and Stress: Addressing Consequences of Multiple Role Demands." *Social Forces* 67: 965–82.

Coverman, Shelley, and Joseph F. Sheley. 1986. "Change in Men's Housework and Child-Care Time, 1965–1975." *Journal of Marriage and the Family* 48: 413–22.

Coward, Raymond T., and Stephen J. Cutler. 1991. "The Composition of Multigenerational Households that Include Elders." *Research on Aging* 13 (March): 55–73.

Coward, Raymond T., and Jeffrey W. Dwyer, 1990. "The Association of Gender, Sibling Network Composition, and Patterns of Parent Care by Adult Children." *Research on Aging* 12: 158–81.

Crimmins, Eileen, and Dominique Ingegneri. 1990. "Interaction and Living Arrangements of Older Parents and Their Children." *Research on Aging* 12: 3–35.

Cutler, N. E., and J. R. Schmidhauser. 1975. "Age and Political Behavior." Pp. 374–406 in *Aging: Scientific Perspectives and Social Issues*, eds. D. Woodruff and J. Birren. New York: Van Nostrand Company.

DaVanzo, Julie, and Frances Goldscheider, 1990. "Coming Home Again: Returns to the Nest in Young Adulthood." *Population Studies* 44: 241–55.

Day, Alice T. 1985. "Who Cares? Demographic Trends Challenge Family Care for the Elderly." *Population Trends and Public Policy #9.* Washington, DC: Population Reference Bureau.

Demo, D. H., and A. C. Acock. 1991. "The Impact of Divorce on Children. Pp. 162–91 in *Contemporary Families*, ed. A. Booth. Minneapolis: National Council on Family Relations.

DeWit, David J., Andrew V. Wister, and Thomas K. Burch. 1988. "Physical Distance and Social Contact between Elders and Their Adult Children." *Research on Aging* 1:56–80.

diLeonardo, Micaela. 1987. "The Female World of Cards and Holidays: Women, Families, and the Work of Kinship." *Signs* 12: 440–53.

Dono, John E., Cecilia M. Falbe, Barbara C. Kail, Eugene Litwak, Roger H. Sherman, and David Siegel. 1979. "Primary Groups in Old Age: Structure and Function." *Research on Aging* 1: 404–33.

Duffy, Michael. 1982. "Divorce and the Dynamics of the Family Kinship System." *Journal of Divorce* 5: 3–18.

Dwyer, Jeffrey W., and Raymond T. Coward. 1991. "A Multivariate Comparison of the Involvement of Adult Sons Versus Daughters in the Care of Impaired Parents." *Journals of Gerontology: Social Sciences* 46: S259–69.

———. 1992. "Gender, Family, and Long-Term Care of the Elderly." In *Gender, Families and Elder Care*, eds. Jeffrey W. Dwyer and Raymond T. Coward. Newbury Park: Sage Publications.

Dwyer, Jeffrey W., John C. Henretta, Raymond T. Coward, and Amy J. Barton. 1992. "Changes in the Helping Behaviors of Adult Children as Caregivers." *Research on Aging* 14: 351–75.

Edwards, John N. 1987. "Changing Family Structure and Youthful Well-Being." *Journal of Family Issues* 8: 355–72.

Eggebeen, David J. 1989. "Changes in Sibling Configurations for American Preschool Children: 1940–1980." Paper presented at the Population Association of America meetings, Baltimore.

———. 1991. "Patterns of Giving and Receiving in the Later Life Course." Paper presented at the Population Association of America meetings, Washington.

———. 1992. "Family Structure and Intergenerational Exchanges." *Research on Aging* 14 (Dec.): 427–447.

Eggebeen, David J., and Dennis P. Hogan. 1990. "Giving Between Generations in American Families." *Human Nature* 1: 211–32.

Elder, Glen H., Jr. 1985. *Life Course Dynamics: Trajectories and Transitions, 1968–1980*. Ithaca: Cornell University Press.

Enright, Robert B., Jr., and Lynn Friss. 1987. "Impact of Caregiving on Employment." Paper presented at the Gerontological Society of American meetings, Washington, DC, November 18–22.

Farber, Bernard. 1987. "The future of the American Family: A Dialectical Account." *Journal of Family Issues* 8: 431–33.

Ferree, Myra Marx. 1991. "Feminism and Family Research." In *Contemporary Families*, ed. Alan Booth. Minneapolis: National Council on Family Relations.

Finley, Nancy J. 1989. "Theories of Family Labor as Applied to Gender Differences in Caregiving for Elderly Parents." *Journal of Marriage and the Family* 51: 79–86.

Finley, Nancy J., M. Diane Roberts, and Benjamin F. Banahan. 1988. "Motivators and Inhibitors of Attitudes of Filial Obligation toward Aging Parents." *The Gerontologist* 28: 73–78.

Fischer, Claude. 1982. *To Dwell among Friends*. Berkeley: University of California Press.

———. 1992. *America Calling: A Social History of the Telephone to 1940.* Berkeley: University of California Press.

Foner, Anne. 1974. "Age Stratification and Age Conflict in Political Life." *American Sociological Review* 39: 187–96.

Forrest, Ray, and Murie Alan. 1991. "Transformation through Tenure? The Early Purchasers of Council Houses, 1968–1973." *Journal of Social Policy* 20: 1–25.

Furstenberg, Frank, Jr., J. Brooks-Gunn, and S. P. Morgan. 1987. *Adolescent Mothers and Their Children in Later Life.* Cambridge: Cambridge University Press.

Furstenberg, Frank, Jr. and Andrew Cherlin. 1991. *Divided Families.* Cambridge, MA: Harvard University Press.

Furstenberg, Frank, S. P. Morgan, and Paul Allison. 1986. "Paternal Participation and Children's Well-Being after Marital Disruption." *American Sociological Review* 52: 695–701.

Furstenberg, Frank, Jr., Christine Nord, James Peterson, and Nicholas Zill. 1983. "The Life Course of Children of Divorce: Marital Disruption and Parental Contact." *American Sociological Review* 48: 656–68.

Furstenberg, Frank F., Jr., and Graham B. Spanier. 1984. *Recycling the Family.* Beverly Hills: Sage Publications.

George, Linda. 1987. "Easing Caregiver Burden: The Role of Informal and Formal Supports." In *Health and Aging: Sociological Issues and Policy Direction,* eds. Russell Ward and Sheldon Tobin. New York: Springer.

———. 1990. "Social Structure, Social Processes, and Social-Psychological States." Pp. 186–204 in *Handbook of Aging and the Social Sciences,* 3rd edition, eds. Robert Binstock and Linda K. George. New York: Van Nostrand Reinhold Co.

George, Linda, Elizabeth Mutran, and Margaret Pennybacker. 1980. "The Meaning and Measurement of Age Identity." *Experimental Aging Research* 6: 283–98.

Giarrusso, Roseann, Michael Stallings, and Vern L. Bengtson. 1995. "The 'Intergenerational Stake' Hypothesis Revisited: Parent-Child Differences in Perceptions of Relationships Twenty Years Later." In *Adult Intergenerational Relations,* eds. Vern L. Bengtson, K. Warner Schaie, Linda M. Burton. New York: Springer Publishing Co.

Gibeau, Janice L., and Jeane W. Anastas. 1987. "Breadwinners and Caregivers: Interviews with Working Women." Paper presented at the Gerontological Society of American meetings, Washington, DC, November 18–22.

Gilder, George. 1981. *Wealth and Poverty.* New York: Basic Books.

Glenn, Norval. 1987. "Continuity Versus Change, Sanguineness Versus Concern: Views of the American Family in the Late 1980s." *Journal of Family Issues* 8: 348–54.

———. 1993. "A Plea for Objective Assessment of the Notion of Family Decline." *Journal of Marriage and the Family* 55: 542–44.

Glick, Paul, and Sung-Ling Lin. 1986. "More Young Adults Are Living with Their Parents: Who Are They?" *Journal of Marriage and the Family* 48: 107–12.

Golant, Stephen M., Graham Rowles, and Judith W. Meyer. 1989. "Aging and the Aged." In *Geography in America*, eds. Gary Gaile and Cort Willmott. Columbus, OH: Merrill Publishing Co.

Golant, Stephen M., Philip Taietz, and Robert Atchley. 1981. *Review of Reported Differences between Rural and Urban Elderly*. Bethesda, MD: Ecosometrics.

Goldscheider, Frances K. 1990. "The Aging of the Gender Revolution: What Do We Know and What Do We Need to Know?" *Research on Aging* 12 (December): 531–45.

Goldscheider, Frances, and Linda Waite. 1991. *New Families, No Families? The Transformation of the American Home*. Berkeley: University of California Press.

Goode, William J. 1960. "A Theory of Role Strain." *American Sociological Review* 25: 483–96.

Gordon, Linda. 1988. *Heroes of Their Own Lives: The Politics and History of Family Violence*. New York: Viking.

Gorey, Kevin M., Robert W. Rice, and Gary C. Brice. 1992. "The Prevalence of Elder Care Responsibilities among the Work Force Population: Response Bias among a Group of Cross-Sectional Surveys." *Research on Aging* 14: 376–98.

Gove, Walter R., and Michael R. Geerken. 1977. "The Effect of Children and Employment on the Mental Health of Married Men and Women." *Social Forces* 56:66–76.

Gove, Walter R., Suzanne Ortega, and Carolyn Style. 1989. "The Maturational and Role Perspectives on Aging and Self through the Adult Years: An Empirical Evaluation." *American Journal of Sociology* 94: 1117–45.

Goyder, John. 1985. "Face-to-Face Interviews and Mailed Questionnaires: The Net Difference in Response Rate." *Public Opinion Quarterly* 49: 234–52.

Gross, Andrea. 1989. "The Good Daughters." *Ladies Home Journal*, November.

Hamon, R. R. 1988. "Filial Responsibility among Adult Child–Older Parent Pairs." Presented at the annual meetings of the Gerontological Society of America.

Herzog, Elizabeth, and Cecilia Sudia. 1973. "Children in Fatherless Families" Pp. 142–232 in *Review of Child Development Research*, volume 3, eds. B. Caldwell and H.N. Ricciuti. Chicago: University of Chicago Press.

Hess, Beth B., and Joan M. Waring. 1978. "Parent and Child in Later Life: Rethinking the Relationships." Pp. 241–73 in *Child Influences on Marital and*

*Family Interaction: A Life-Span Perspective*, eds. R. M. Lerner and G. B. Spanier. New York: Academic Press.

Hochschild, Arlie, with Anne Machung. 1989. *The Second Shift: Working Parents and the Revolution at Home.* New York: Viking.

Hofferth, Sandra. 1984. "Kin Networks, Race, and Family Structure." *Journal of Marriage and the Family* 46: 791–806.

Hoffman, Lois Wladis. 1987. "The Effects on Children of Maternal and Paternal Employment." Pp. 362–95 in *Families and Work*, eds. Naomi Gerstel and Harriet Gross. Philadelphia: Temple University Press.

Hogan, Dennis P., and David J. Eggebeen. 1995. "Sources of Emergency Help and Routine Assistance in Old Age." *Social Forces* 73: 917–38.

Hogan, Dennis P., Ling-Xin Hao, and William Paris. 1990. "Race, Kin Networks, and Assistance to Mother-Headed Families." *Social Forces* 68: 797–812.

Holden, Karen. 1988. "Poverty and Living Arrangements among Older Women: Are Changes in Economic Well-Being Underestimated?" *Journal of Gerontology* 43: S22–27.

Horowitz, Amy. 1985. "Sons and Daughters as Caregivers to Older Parents: Differences in Role Performance and Consequences." *The Gerontologist* 25: 612–17.

———. 1992. "Methodological Issues in the Study of Gender within Family Caregiving Relationships." In *Gender, Families, and Elder Care*, eds. Jeffrey W. Dwyer and Raymond T. Coward. Newbury Park: Sage Publications.

Houser, Betsy B., Sherry L. Berkman, and Phil Bardsley. 1985. "Sex and Birth Order Differences in Filial Behavior." *Sex Roles* 13: 641–51.

Hoyert, D. L. 1991. "Financial and Household Exchanges between Generations." *Research on Aging* 13: 205–25.

Hudson, Robert B. 1978. "The 'Graying' of the Federal Budget and Its Consequences for Old-Age Policy." *The Gerontologist* 18: 428–40.

Hunt, Janet G., and Larry L. Hunt. 1987. "Here to Play: From Families to Life-Styles." *Journal of Family Issues* 8: 440–43.

Hurlbert, Jeanne, and Alan Acock. 1990. "The Effects of Marital Status on the Form and Composition of Social Networks." *Social Science Quarterly* 71: 163–74.

Ishii-Kuntz, Masako, and Karen Seccombe. 1989. "The Impact of Children upon Social Support Networks Throughout the Life Course." *Journal of Marriage and the Family* 51: 777–90.

Johnson, C. L. 1983. "A Cultural Analysis of the Grandmother." *Research on Aging* 5: 547–67.

———. 1988a. "Active and Latent Functions of Grandparenting During the Divorce Process." *The Gerontologist* 28: 185–91.

———. 1988b. "Postdivorce Reorganization of Relationships between Divorcing Children and Their Parents." *Journal of Marriage and the Family* 50: 221–31.

———. 1989. "Divorce-Related Changes in Relationships: Parents, Their Adult Children, and Children-in-Law." In *Aging Parents and Adult Children*, ed. J. A. Mancini. Lexington, MA: D. C. Heath.

Johnson, Elizabeth S. 1981–82. "Role Expectations and Role Realities of Older Italian Mothers and Their Daughters." *International Journal of Aging and Human Development* 14: 271–76.

Johnson, E. S., and B. H. Vinick. 1982. "Support of the Parent when an Adult Son or Daughter Divorces." *Journal of Divorce* 5: 69–77.

Kandel, Denise B., Mark Davies, and Victoria H. Raveis. 1985. "The Stressfulness of Daily Social Roles for Women: Marital, Occupational and Household Roles." *Journal of Health and Social Behavior* 26: 64–78.

Karp, David. 1988. "A Decade of Reminders: Changing Age Consciousness between Fifty and Sixty Years Old." *The Gerontologist* 28: 727–38.

Kasarda, John, and Morris Janowitz. 1974. "Community Attachment in Mass Society." *American Journal of Sociology* 39: 328–39.

Kingson, E. R. 1988. "Generational Equity: An Unexpected Opportunity to Broaden the Politics of Aging." *The Gerontologist* 28: 765–72.

Kitson, Gay C., and Leslie A. Morgan. 1991. "The Multiple Consequences of Divorce." Pp. 150–61 in *Contemporary Families: Looking Forward, Looking Back*, ed. Alan Booth. Minneapolis: National Council on Family Relations.

Klemmack, David L., and Lucinda Lee Roff. 1980. "Public Support for Age as an Eligibility Criterion for Programs for Older Persons." *The Gerontologist* 20: 148–53.

Kotlikoff, Laurence, and John Morris. 1990. "Why Don't the Elderly Live with Their Children? A New Look." In *Issues in the Economics of the Aging*, ed. David Wise. Chicago: University of Chicago Press.

Kulis, Stephen S. 1992. "Social Class and the Locus of Reciprocity in Relationships with Adult Children." *Journal of Family Issues* 13 (December): 482–504.

Lang, Abigail M., and Elaine M. Brody. 1983. "Characteristics of Middle-Aged Daughters and Help to Their Elderly Mothers." *Journal of Marriage and the Family* 45: 193–202.

Lasch, Christopher. 1977. *Haven in a Heartless World: The Family Besieged*. New York: Basic Books.

Lawton, Leora, and Merril Silverstein. 1992. "The Effect of Divorce on the Geographic Distance between Parents and Adult Children." Annual meeting of the Gerontological Society of America, Washington, DC.

Lawton, Leora, Merril Silverstein, and Vern L. Bengtson. 1994. "Solidarity between Generations in Families." Pp. 19–42 in *Intergenerational Linkages: Hidden Connections in American Society*, eds. Vern L. Bengtson and Robert A. Harootyan. New York: Springer Publishing Company.

Lawton, M. P., and B. L. Simon. 1968. "The Ecology of Social Relationships in Housing for the Elderly." *The Gerontologist* 8: 108–15.

Lee, Gary R. 1987. "Aging and Intergenerational Relations." *Journal of Family Issues* 8: 448–50.

———. 1992. "Gender Differences in Family Caregiving: A Fact in Search of a Theory." In *Gender, Families and Elder Care*, eds. Jeffrey W. Dwyer and Raymond T. Coward. Newbury Park: Sage Publications.

Lee, Gary R., Jeffrey W. Dwyer, and Raymond T. Coward. 1993. "Gender Differences in Parent Care: Demographic Factors and Same-Gender Preferences." *Journals of Gerontology* 48: S9–16.

Lee, Gary R., and E. L. Ellithorpe. 1982. "Intergenerational Exchange and Subjective Well-Being among the Elderly. *Journal of Marriage and the Family* 44: 217–24.

Leslie, Leigh A., and Katherine Grady. 1985. "Changes in Mothers' Social Networks and Social Support Following Divorce." *Journal of Marriage and the Family* 47: 663–73.

Litwak, Eugene. 1960. "Geographic Mobility and Extended Family Cohesion." *American Sociological Review* 25: 385–94.

———. 1985. *Helping the Elderly: The Complementary Roles of Informal Networks and Formal Systems.* New York: The Guilford Press.

Litwak, Eugene, and Charles F. Longino Jr. 1987. "Migration Patterns among the Elderly: A Development Perspective." *The Gerontologist* 27: 266–72.

Logan, John R., and Harvey Molotch. 1987. *Urban Fortunes: The Political Economy of Place.* Berkeley: University of California Press.

Logan, John R., and Glenna Spitze. 1988a. "Informal and Formal Assistance in Aging." National Institute on Aging Grant #AG06831-01A1.

———. 1988b. "Suburbanization and Public Services for the Aging." *The Gerontologist* 28: 644–47.

———. 1994. "Family Neighbors." *American Journal of Sociology* 100 (September): 453–76.

Logan, John R., Russell Ward, and Glenna Spitze. 1992. "As Old As You Feel: Age Identity in Middle and Later Life." *Social Forces* 71: 451–67.

Longino, Charles F., Jr. and Aaron Lipman. 1981. "Married and Spouseless Men and Women in Planned Retirement Communities: Support Network Differentials." *Journal of Marriage and the Family* 43: 169–77.

Loomis, Laura Spencer, and Alan Booth. 1995. "Multigenerational Caregiving and Well-Being: The Myth of the Beleaguered Sandwich Generation." *Journal of Family Issues* 16: 131–48.

Lye, Diana N., and Anjanette Nelson. 1993. "Childhood Living Arrangements and Attitudes toward Intergenerational Support." Presented at the annual meetings of the Population Association of America, Cincinnati.

Madigan, Timothy, and Dennis Hogan. 1990. "Kin Access and Residential Mobility among Young Mothers." Paper presented at annual meetings of the Population Association of America, Toronto.

Marini, Margaret. 1984. "Age and Sequencing Norms in the Transition to Adulthood." *Social Forces* 63: 229–44.

Marks, Stephen. 1977. "Multiple Roles and Role Strain: Some Notes on Human Energy, Time and Commitment." *American Sociological Review* 42: 921–36.

Martin, T. C., and L. L. Bumpass. 1989. "Recent Trends in Marital Disruption." *Demography* 26: 37–51.

Matthews, Sarah H. 1987a. "Perceptions of Fairness in the Development of Responsibility for Old Parents." *Social Justice Research* 1: 425–37.

———. 1987b. "Provision of Care to Old Parents." *Research on Aging* 9: 45–60.

———. 1988. "The Burdens of Parent Care: A Critical Evaluation of Recent Findings." *Journal of Aging Studies* 2: 157–65.

———. 1995. "Gender and the Division of Filial Responsibility between Lone Sisters and Their Brothers." *Journals of Gerontology: Social Sciences* 50B: S312–S320.

Matthews, Sarah H., and Tena Tarler Rosner. 1988. "Shared Filial Responsibility: The Family as the Primary Caregiver." *Journal of Marriage and the Family* 50: 185–96.

Matthews, Sarah H., and Janet E. Werkner. 1985. "Employed and Nonemployed Sisters' Relative Contributions of Help to Their Elderly Parents." Paper presented at the Gerontological Society of America meetings, New Orleans, November 22–26.

McLanahan, Sara, and Julia Adams. 1987. "Parenthood and Psychological Well-being." In *Annual Review of Sociology* 13, eds. W. Richard Scott and James F. Short Jr. Palo Alto, CA: Annual Reviews.

———. 1989. "The Effects of Children on Adults' Psychological Well-Being: 1957–1976." *Social Forces* 68: 124–46.

McLanahan, Sara, and Karen Booth. 1989. "Mother-Only Families: Problems, Prospects, and Politics." *Journal of Marriage and the Family* 51: 557–80.

McLanahan, Sara, and Gary Sandefur. 1994. *Growing Up with a Single Parent: What Hurts, What Helps.* Cambridge, MA: Harvard University Press.

Mederer, Helen J. 1993. "Division of Labor in Two-Earner Homes: Task Accomplishment Versus Household Management as Critical Variables in Perceptions about Family Work." *Journal of Marriage and the Family* 55: 133–45.

Mellins, Claude A., Sandra L. Boyd, and Margaret Gatz. 1988. "Caregiving as a Family Network Event." Paper presented at the Geronthological Society of American meetings, San Francisco.

Menaghan, Elizabeth. 1989. "Role Changes and Psychological Well-Being: Variations in Effects by Gender and Role Repertoire." *Social Forces* 67: 693–714.

Menaghan, Elizabeth G., and Tony L. Parcel. 1991. "Parental Employment and Family Life." Pp. 361–80 in *Contemporary Families: Looking Forward, Looking Back,* ed. Alan Booth. Minneapolis: National Council on Family Relations.

Menken, Jane, 1985. "Age and Fertility: How Late Can You Wait?" *Demography* 22: 469–83.

Merton, Robert K. 1957. "The Role-Set: Problems in Sociological Theory." *British Journal of Sociology* 8: 106–20.

Milardo, R. M. 1987. "Changes in Social Networks of Women and Men Following Divorce: A Review." *Journal of Family Issues* 8: 78–96.

Miller, Baila. 1989. "Adult Children's Perceptions of Caregiver Stress and Satisfaction." *The Journal of Applied Gerontology* 3: 275–93.

Miller, Baila, and Andrew Montgomery. 1990. "Family Caregivers and Limitations in Social Activities." *Research on Aging* 12: 72–93.

Miner, Sonia. 1995. "Racial Differences in Family Support and Formal Service Utilization among Older Persons: A Nonrecursive Model." *Journals of Gerontology: Social Sciences* 50B: S143–53.

Moen, Elizabeth. 1978. "The Reluctance of the Elderly to Accept Help." *Social Problems* 25: 293–303.

Moen, Phyllis, Donna I. Dempster-McClain, and Robin M. Williams Jr. 1989. "Social Integration and Longevity: An Event History Analysis of Women's Roles and Resilience." *American Sociological Review* 54: 635–47.

———. 1992. "Successful Aging: A Life-Course Perspective on Women's Multiple Roles and Health." *American Journal of Sociology* 97: 1612–38.

Moen, Phyllis, Julie Robison, and Vivian Fields. 1994. "Women's Work and Caregiving Roles: A Life Course Approach." *Journals of Gerontology: Social Sciences* 49: S176–S186.

Montgomery, Rhonda J. V. 1992. "Gender Differences in Patterns of Child-Parent Caregiving Relationships." In *Gender, Families and Elder Care,* eds. Jeffrey W. Dwyer and Raymond T. Coward. Newbury Park: Sage Publications.

Montgomery, Rhonda J. V., and Barbara A. Hirshorn. 1991. "Current and Future Family Help with Long-Term Care Needs of the Elderly." *Research on Aging* 13 (June): 171–204.

Montgomery, Rhonda J. V., and Yoshinori Kamo. 1989. "Parent Care by Sons and Daughters." Pp. 213–30 in *Aging Parents and Adult Children,* ed. Jay A. Mancini. Lexington, MA: Lexington Books.

Moore, Kristin, Daphne Spain, and Suzanne Bianchi. 1984. "The Working Wife and Mother." *Marriage and Family Review* 7: 77–98.

Moss, Miriam, Sidney Moss, and Elizabeth Moles. 1985. "The Quality of Relationships between Elderly Parents and Their Out-of-Town Children." *The Gerontologist* 25: 134–40.

Moynihan, Daniel P. 1965. *The Negro Family: The Case for National Action.* Washington, DC: Office of Policy Planning and Research, U.S. Department of Labor.

Murray, Charles. 1984. *Losing Ground: American Social Policy, 1950–1980.* New York: Basic Books.

Mutchler, Jan E. 1990. "Household Composition among the nonmarried Elderly: A Comparison of Black and White Women." *Research on Aging* 12 (December): 487–506.

Mutran, Elizabeth, and Peter Burke. 1979. "Personalism as a Component of Age Identities." *Research on Aging* 1: 37–63.

Mutran, Elizabeth, and Linda George. 1982. "Alternate Methods of Measuring Role/Identity: A Research Note." *Social Forces* 60: 866–75.

Mutran, Elizabeth, and Donald Reitzes. 1981. "Retirement, Identity and Well-Being: Realignment of Role Relationships." *Journal of Gerontology* 36: 733–40.

Neal, Margaret B., et al. 1987. "Work and Elder Care: A Survey of Employees." Paper presented at the Gerontological Society of America meetings, Washington, DC, November 18–22.

Norton, A. J., and J. E. Moorman. 1987. "Current Trends in Marriage and Divorce among Amerian Women." *Journal of Marriage and the Family* 49: 3–14.

Older Women's League. 1989. *Failing America's Caregivers: A Status Report on Women Who Care.* Washington, DC.

Pampel, F. C., and J. B. Williamson. 1989. *Age, Class, Politics, and the Welfare State.* New York: Cambridge University Press.

Popenoe, David. 1988. *Disturbing the Nest: Family Change and Decline in Modern Societies.* New York: Aldine de Gruyter.

———. 1993. "American Family Decline, 1960–1990: A Review and Appraisal." *Journal of Marriage and the Family* 55: 527–55.

Presser, H. B. 1989. "Some Economic Complexities of Child Care Provided by Grandmothers." *Journal of Marriage and the Family* 51: 581–91.

Preston, S. H. 1984. "Children and the Elderly: Divergent Paths for America's Dependents." *Demography* 21: 435–57.

Pruchno, Rachel A. 1990. "The Effects of Help Patterns on the Mental Health of Spouse Caregivers." *Research on Aging* 12: 57–71.

Riley, Matilda White. 1983. "The Family in an Aging Society: A Matrix of Latent Relationships." *Journal of Family Issues* 4: 439–54.

Riley, Matilda White, and John W. Riley Jr. 1993. "Connections: Kin and Cohort." Pp. 169–89 in *The Changing Contract across Generations,* eds. Vern Bengston and W. Andrew Achenbaum. New York: Aldine de Gruyter.

Robinson, Betsy, and Majda Thurnher. 1979. "Taking Care of Aged Parents: A Family Cycle Transition." *The Gerontologist* 19: 586–93.

Rose, Arnold. 1965. "The Subculture of Aging: A Framework for Research in

Social Gerontology." Pp. 3–16 in *Older People and Their Social World*, eds. Arnold Rose and Warren Peterson. Philadelphia: F. A. Davis Co.

Rosenthal, Carolyn J. 1985. "Kinkeeping in the Familial Division of Labor." *Journal of Marriage and the Family* 47: 965–74.

Rosenthal, Carolyn J., Sarah H. Matthews, and Victor W. Marshall, 1989. "Is Parent Care Normative? The Experiences of a Sample of Middle-Aged Women." *Research on Aging* 11: 244–60.

Rossi, Alice S., and Peter H. Rossi. 1990. *Of Human Bonding: Parent-Child Relations Across the Life Course*. New York: Aldine de Gruyter.

Rowles, Graham A. 1978. *Prisoners of Space? Exploring the Geographical Experience of Older People*. Boulder: Westview Press.

Sampson, Robert. 1991. "Linking the Micro- and Macrolevel Dimensions of Community Social Organization." *Social Forces* 70: 43–64.

Seccombe, Karen, and Masako Ishii-Kuntz. 1991. "Perceptions of Problems Associated with Aging: Comparisons among Four Older Age Cohorts." *The Gerontologist* 31: 527–33.

Seelbach, W. C. 1977. "Gender Differences in Expectations for Filial Responsibility." *The Gerontologist* 17: 421–25.

Seltzer, Judith, and Suzanne Bianchi, 1988. "Children's Contact with Absent Parents." *Journal of Marriage and the Family* 50: 663–77.

Shanas, Ethel. 1960. "Family Responsibility and the Health of Older People." *Journal of Gerontology* 15: 408–11.

———. 1979. "Social Myth as Hypothesis; The Case of the Family Relations of Old People." *The Gerontologist* 19: 3–9.

Sherman, Susan, Russell Ward, and Mark LaGory. 1988. "Women as Caregivers of the Elderly: Instrumental and Expressive Support." *Social Work* 33: 164–67.

Sieber, Sam. 1974. "Toward a Theory of Role Accumulation." *American Sociological Review* 39: 567–78.

Skolnick, Arlene. 1991. *Embattled Paradise: The American Family in an Age of Uncertainty*. New York: Basic Books.

Smith, J. P., and O. B. Martinson. 1984. "Socio-Political Bases of Senior Citizen Mobilization: Salient Issues Beyond Health Policy." *Research on Aging* 6: 213–24.

Smyer, Michael, and Brian Hofland. 1982. "Divorce and Family Support in Later Life." *Journal of Family Issues* 3: 61–77.

Sontag, Susan. 1972. "The Double Standard of Aging." *Saturday Review* 55: 29–38.

South, Scott, and Glenna Spitze. 1994. "Housework in Marital and Nonmarital Households." *American Sociological Review* 59 (June): 327–47.

Spanier, Graham B., and Sandra Hanson. 1982. "The Role of Extended Kin in the Adjustment to Marital Separation." *Journal of Divorce* 5: 33–48.

Spanier, Graham B., and Linda Thompson. 1984. *Parting.* Beverly Hills, CA: Sage.

Speare, Alden, Jr., and Roger Avery. 1993. "Who Helps Whom in Older Parent-Child Families." *Journals of Gerontology: Social Sciences* 48: S64–S73.

Speare, Alden, Jr., Roger Avery, and Leora Lawton. 1991. "Disability, Residential Mobility, and Changes in Living Arrangements." *Journals of Gerontology: Social Sciences* 46: S133–142.

Spicer, J. W., and G. D. Hampe. 1975. "Kinship Interaction after Divorce." *Journal of Marriage and the Family* 37: 133–19.

Spitze, Glenna. 1986. "The Division of Task Responsibility in U.S. Households: Longitudinal Adjustments to Change." *Social Forces* 64 (March): 689–701.

———. 1988. "Women's Employment and Family Relations: A Review." *Journal of Marriage and the Family* 50: 595–18.

Spitze, Glenna, and John R. Logan. 1989. "Gender Differences in Family Support: Is There a Payoff?" *The Gerontologist* 29: 108–13.

———. 1990a. "More Evidence on Women (and Men) in the Middle." *Research on Aging* 12: 182–98.

———. 1990b. "Sons, Daughters, and Intergenerational Social Support." *Journal of Marriage and the Family* 52: 420–30.

———. 1991a. "Employment and Filial Relations: Is There a Conflict?" *Sociological Forum* 6: 681–97.

———. 1991b. "Sibling Structure and Intergenerational Relations." *Journal of Marriage and the Family* 53: 871–84.

———. 1992. "Helping as a Component of Parent–Adult Child Relations." *Research on Aging* 14: 291–312.

Spitze, Glenna, John Logan, Glenn Deane, and Suzanne Zerger. 1994. "Adult Children's Divorce and Intergenerational Relationships." *Journal of Marriage and the Family* 56 (May): 279–93.

Spitze, Glenna, John R. Logan, Genevieve Joseph, and Eunju Lee. 1994. "Middle Generation Roles and the Well-Being of Men and Women." *Journal of Gerontology* 49 (May): S107–S116.

Spitze, Glenna, and Russell Ward. 1995 "Housework in Intergenerational Households." *Journal of Marriage and the Family* 57 (May): 355–61.

Spreitzer, Elmer, Eldon E. Snyder, and David L. Larson, 1979. "Multiple Roles and Psychological Well-Being." *Sociological Focus* 12: 141–47.

Stacey, Judith. 1991. *Brave New Families: Stories of Domestic Upheaval in Late Twentieth Century America.* New York: Basic Books.

Stack, Carol. 1974. *All Our Kin: Strategies for Survival in a Black Community.* New York: Harper and Row.

Steuve, Ann, and Lydia O'Donnell. 1989. "Interactions between Women and Their Elderly Parents: Constraints of Daughters' Employment." *Research on Aging* 11: 331–53.

Stoller, Eleanor Palo. 1983. "Parental Caregiving by Adult Children." *Journal of Marriage and the Family* 45: 851–58.

Stoller, Eleanor Palo, and Lorna L. Earl. 1983. "Help with Activities of Everyday Life: Sources of Support of the Noninstitutionalized Elderly." *The Gerontologist* 23: 64–70.

Stoller, Eleanor Palo, and Karen L. Pugliesi. 1989. "Other Roles of Caregivers: Competing Responsibilities or Supportive Resources?" *Journals of Gerontology: Social Sciences* 44: S231–S238.

Stone, Robyn, Gail Cafferata, and Judith Sangl. 1987. "Caregivers of the Frail Elderly: A National Profile." *The Gerontologist* 27: 616–26.

Stull, Donald E., Karen Bowman, and Virginia Smerglia. 1994. "Women in the Middle: A Myth in the Making?" *Family Relations* 43: 319–24.

Suitor, J. Jill, and Karl Pillemer. 1988. "Explaining Generational Conflict when Adult Children and Elderly Parents Live Together." *Journal of Marriage and the Family* 50: 1037–47.

Sussman, Marvin. 1976. "The Family Life of Old People." In *Handbook of Aging and the Social Sciences*, eds. Robert Binstock and Ethel Shanas. New York: Van Nostrand Reinhold Company.

Taylor, Robert Joseph, Linda M. Chatters, and James S. Jackson. 1993. "A Profile of Familial Relations among Three-Generation Black Families." *Family Relations* 42: 332–41.

Thoits, Peggy A. 1983. "Multiple Identities and Psychological Well-Being: A Reformulation and Test of the Social Isolation Hypothesis." *American Sociological Review* 48: 174–87.

———. 1986. "Multiple Identities: Examining Gender and Marital Status Differences in Distress." *American Sociological Review* 51: 259–72.

Townsend, Peter. 1968. "The Structure of the Family." Pp. 132–76 in *Old People in Three Industrial Societies*, eds. E. Shanas, P. Townsend, D. Wederburn, P. Hilhof, and J. Stenhouwer. New York: Atherton Press.

Treas, Judith. 1977. "Family Support Systems for the Aged: Some Social and Demographic Considerations." *The Gerontologist* 17: 486–91.

Treas, Judith, and Vern Bengtson. 1987. "The Family in Later Years." In *Handbook of Marriage and the Family*, eds. Marvin Sussman and Suzanne Steinmetz. New York: Plenum Press.

Trela, James E. 1971. "Some Political Consequences of Senior Center and other Old Age Group Membership." *The Gerontologist* 22: 118–23.

Troll, Lillian E., Sheila J. Miller, and Robert C. Atchley. 1979. *Families in Later Life.* Belmont, CA: Wadsworth.

Turner, Ralph H. 1975. "Role-Taking: Process Versus Conformity." Pp. 109–22 in *Life as Theater: A Dramaturgical Sourcebook*, eds. Dennis Brissett and Charles Edgley. Chicago: Aldine.

Uhlenberg, Peter, and Mary Anne P. Myers. 1981. "Divorce and the Elderly." *The Gerontologist* 21: 276–82.

Umberson, Debra. 1989a. "Parenting and Well-Being: The Importance of Context." *Journal of Family Issues* 10: 427–39.

———. 1989b. "Relationships with Children: Explaining Parents' Psychological Well-Being." *Journal of Marriage and the Family* 51: 999–1012.

———. 1992. "Relationships between Adult Children and Their Parents: Psychological Consequences for Both Generations." *Journal of Marriage and the Family* 54: 664–85.

Umberson, Debra, and Walter R. Gove. 1989. "Parenthood and Psychological Well-Being: Theory, Measurement and Stage in the Family Life Course." *Journal of Family Issues* 4: 440–62.

Voydanoff, Patricia, and Brenda Donnelly. 1990. *Adolescent Sexuality and Pregnancy*. Newbury Park, CA: Sage.

Waehrer, Keith and Stephen Crystal, 1995. "The Impact of Coresidence on Economic Well-Being of Elderly Widows." *Journals of Gerontology: Social Sciences* 50B: S250–58.

Wagner, Donna, and Frederick Keast. 1981. "Informal Groups and the Elderly: A Preliminary Examination of the Mediation Function." *Research on Aging* 3: 325–32.

Walker, Alexis J. 1992. "Conceptual Perspectives on Gender and Family Caregiving." In *Gender, Families and Elder Care*, eds. Jeffrey W. Dwyer and Raymond T. Coward. Newbury Park: Sage Publications.

Walker, Alexis J., Sally Martin, and Laura L. Jones. 1992. "The Benefits and Costs of Caregiving and Care Receiving for Daughters and Mothers." *Journals of Gerontology* 47: S130–139.

Walker, Alexis J., Clara C. Pratt, Hwa-Yong Shin, and Laura L. Jones. 1989. Pp. 199–212 in *Aging Parents and Adult Children*, ed. Jay A. Mancini. Lexington, MA: Lexington Books.

Wan, Thomas, and Barbara Gill Odell. 1981. "Factors Affecting the Use of Social and Health Services among the Elderly." *Aging and Society* 1: 95–115.

Ward, Russell A. 1977. "The Impact of Subjective Age and Stigma on Older Persons." *Journal of Gerontology* 32: 227–32.

———. "The Marginality and Salience of Being Old: When Is Age Relevant?" *The Gerontologist* 24: 227–32.

Ward, Russell A., Mark LaGory, and Susan Sherman. 1988. *The Environment for Aging: Interpersonal, Social, and Spatial Contexts*. Tuscaloosa, AL: University of Alabama Press.

Ward, Russell A., John R. Logan, and Glenna Spitze. 1992. "The Influence of Parent and Child Needs on Coresidence in Middle and Later Life." *Journal of Marriage and the Family* 54: 209–21.

Ward, Russell A., Susan Sherman, and Mark LaGory. 1984. "Informal Networks and Knowledge of Services for Older Persons." *Journal of Gerontology* 39: 216–23.

Ward, Russell A., and Glenna Spitze. 1992. "Consequences of Parent-Adult Child Coresidence: A Review and Research Agenda." *Journal of Family Issues* 13: 553–72.

Watkins, Susan Cott, Jane A. Menken, John Bongaarts. 1987. "Demographic Foundations of Family Change." *American Sociological Review* 52: 346–58.

Weaver, Jerry. 1976. "The Elderly as a Political Community: The Case of National Health Policy." *Western Political Quarterly* 29: 610–19.

Weinstein, Grace W. 1989. "Help Wanted—The Crisis of Elder Care." *Ms. Magazine* (October).

Weiss, Robert S. 1987. "On the Current State of the American Family." *Journal of Family Issues* 8: 464–67.

Wellman, Barry. 1979. "The Community Question: The Intimate Networks of East Yorkers." *American Journal of Sociology* 84: 1201–31.

———. 1990. "The Place of Kinfolk in Personal Community Networks." *Marriage and Family Review* 15: 195–228.

Wheaton, Blair. 1990. "Life Transitions, Role Histories, and Mental Health." *American Sociological Review* 55: 209–23.

White, Lynn K., and Alan Booth. 1985. "The Quality and Stability of Remarriages: The Role of Stepchildren." *American Sociological Review* 50: 689–98.

White, Lynn K., and David B. Brinkerhoff. 1981. "The Sexual Division of Labor: Evidence from Childhood." *Social Forces* 60: 170–81.

White, Lynn K., and John N. Edwards. 1990. "Emptying the Next and Parental Well-Being: An Analysis of National Panel Data." *American Sociological Review* 55: 235–42.

Williamson, John, Linda Evans, Lawrence Powell, and Sharlene Hesse-Biber. 1982. *The Politics of Aging: Power and Policy.* Springfield, IL: Charles C. Thomas.

Wilson, William J. 1987. *The Truly Disadvantaged.* Chicago: University of Chicago Press.

Wirth, Louis. 1938. "Urbanism as a Way of Life." *American Journal of Sociology* 44: 3–24.

Wolf, Douglas, Vicki Freedman, Beth Soldo, and Elizabeth Stephen. 1991. "Making Room for Mom: Coresidence of Married Couples and Elderly Mothers." Paper presented at annual meeting of Population Association of America, Washington, DC.

Wolf, Douglas, and Beth Soldo. 1988. "Household Composition Choices of Older Unmarried Women." *Demography* 25: 387–403.

Wolf, Jacquelyn, Naomi Breslau, Amasa Ford, Henry Ziegler, and Anna Ward.

1983. "Distance and Contacts: Interactions of Black Urban Elderly Adults with Family and Friends." *Journal of Gerontology* 38: 465–71.

Wolinsky, Fredric, Rodney Coe, Douglas Miller, John Prendergast, M. Creel, and M. Chavez. 1983. "Health Services Utilization among the Noninstitutionalized Elderly." *Journal of Health and Social Behavior* 24: 325–37.

Young, Michael, and Peter Willmott. 1957. *Family and Kinship in East London.* Glencoe: Free Press.

# Author Index

# Subject Index